Publishers of Architecture, Art, and Design
Gordon Goff: Publisher
Published by ORO Editions
www.oroeditions.com
info@oroeditions.com

Cover Design: Caleb White and Leon Yi-Liang Ko. Bingkun Deng, Ming Jiang, Yang Yang (Cover Image)
Book Design: Leon Yi-Liang Ko and Yang Yang

ORO Project Coordinator: Kirby Anderson
Color Separations and Printing: ORO Group Ltd.
Printed in China.

ORO Editions makes a continuous effort to minimize the overall carbon footprint of its publications. As part of this goal, ORO Editions, in association with Global ReLeaf, arranges to plant trees to replace those used in the manufacturing of the paper produced for its books. Global ReLeaf is an international campaign run by American Forests, one of the world's oldest nonprofit conservation organizations. Global ReLeaf is American Forests' education and action program that helps individuals, organizations, agencies, and corporations improve the local and global environment by planting and caring for trees.

10 9 8 7 6 5 4 3 2 1 First Edition
Library of Congress data available upon request. World Rights: Available
ISBN: 978-1-954081-58-1

International Distribution: www.oroeditions.com/distribution

FUTURE OFFICES EDITED BY ALI RAHIM

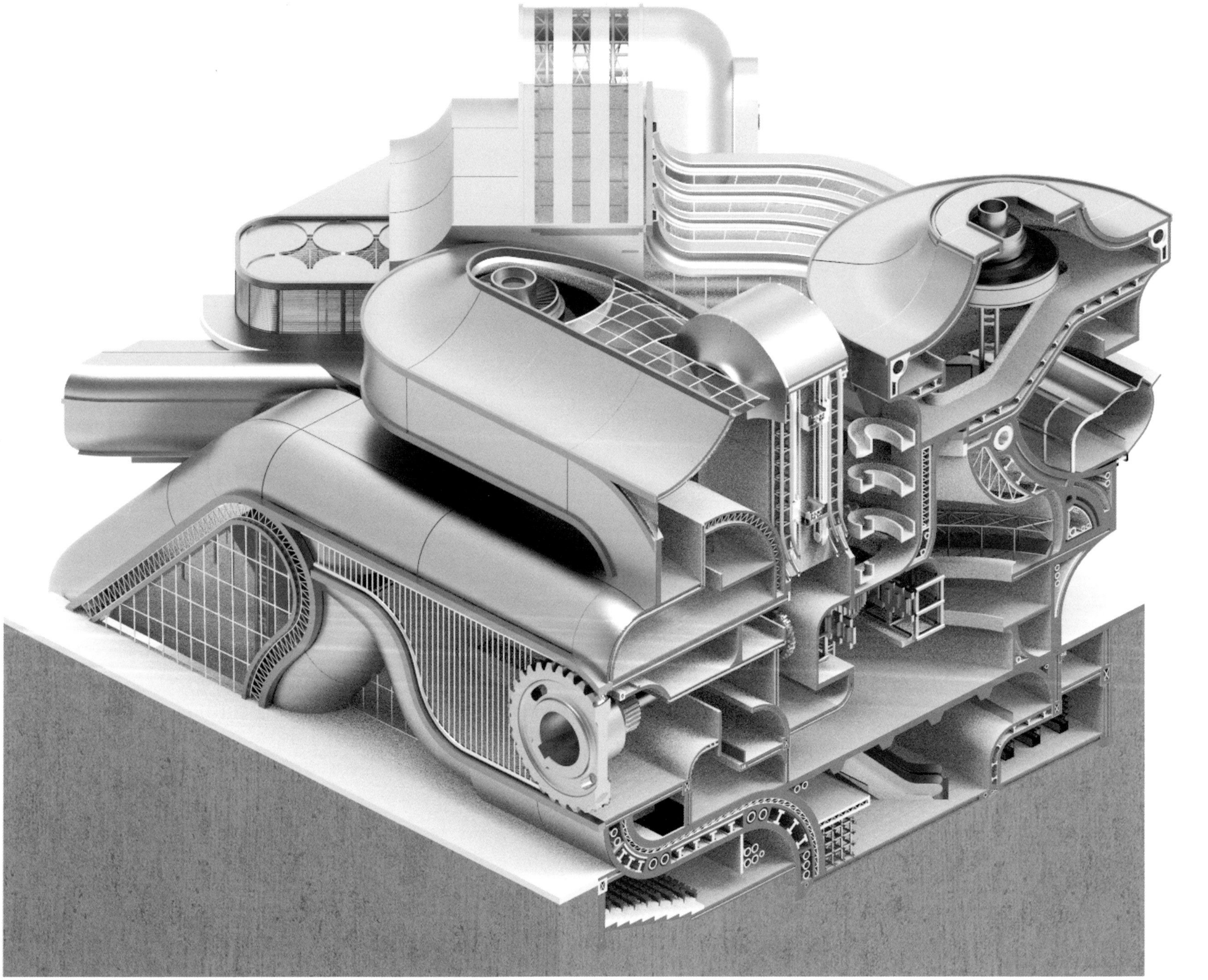

CONTENTS

Section Model Rendering. Project by Yuyan Huang and Qiao Wang

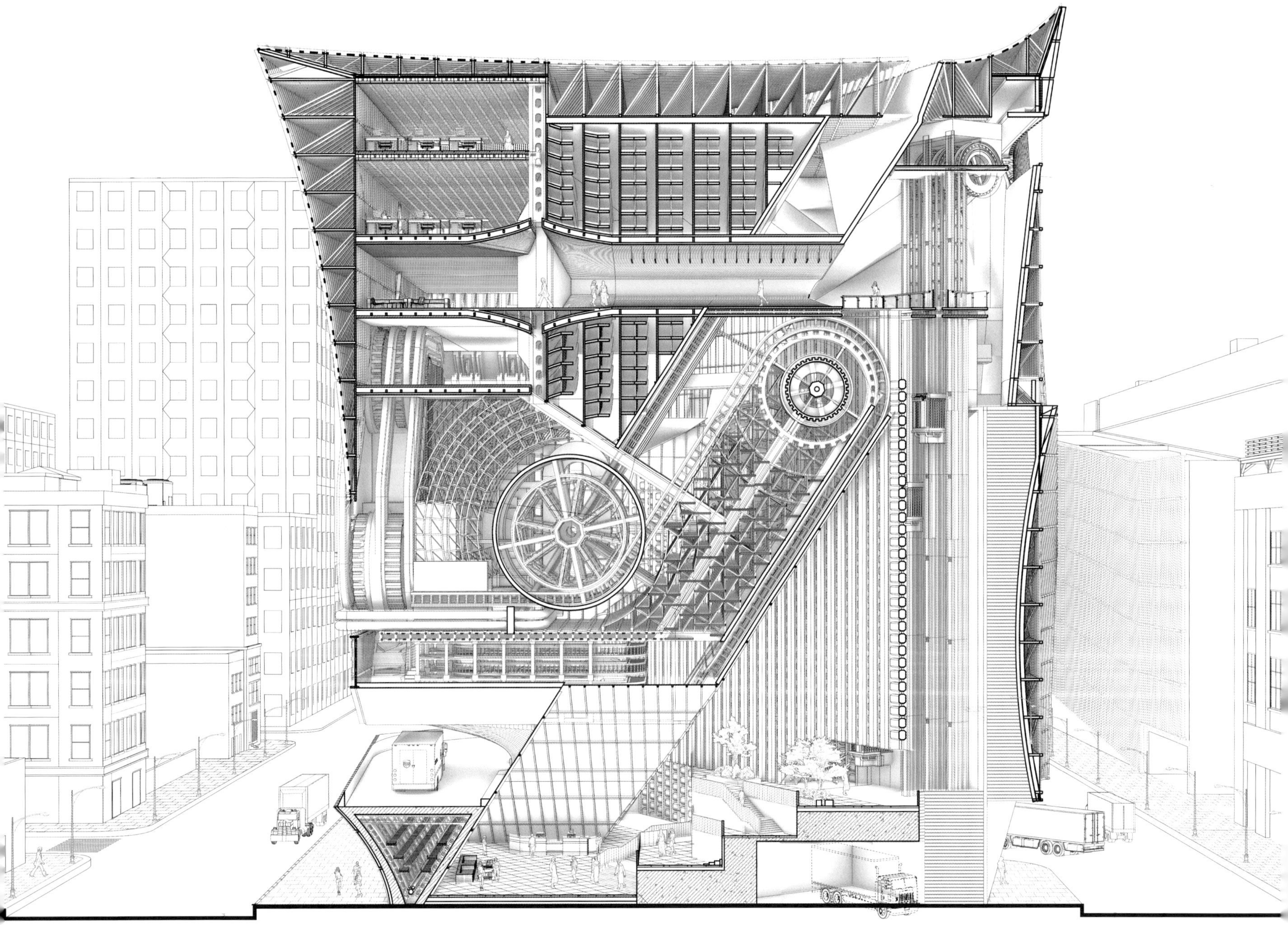

PROJECTS

Cross Section. Project by Chengzhe Zhu, Qi Che, and Zhihui Li

Student Work was produced at The University of Pennsylvania
Stuart Weitzman School of Design
Masters of Science in Design: Advanced Architectural Design [MSD-AAD]

00 INTRODUCTION

Ali Rahim

Rapid changes in culture, technology, and society have inaugurated paradigm shifts in labor and logistics in the U.S. and around the world. While companies and capital have become increasingly consolidated, contemporary workplaces have become increasingly decentralized. Multinational corporations have increased their dominance over specific industries by buying out smaller, more agile companies. The size and scope of mergers since 2010 have been the largest and most frequent in the history of finance, generating in 2015 alone for instance 4.7 trillion dollars.[1] Facebook acquired WhatsApp and Instagram among dozens of other tech and social media firms; AT&T and Time Warner merged in 2018 to form the largest telecommunications company ever; Disney bought 21st Century Fox in 2017 to consolidate its hold over entertainment and distribution; Kraft and Heinz merged to become the third largest food company globally; Dow Chemical and Dupont joined in 2015 to create the largest chemical company in the world; and CVS Pharmacies acquired the health insurance company Aetna in one of the biggest deals in health insurance history. At the same time, decentralization has been underway across a wide array of social and economic activities from transportation, hospitality, and real estate vis-à-vis the “sharing” or “gig” economy, to dispersed energy production via renewable sources and smart grids, highly localized “just in time” logistics and outsourcing, cryptocurrency’s challenge to centralized banking authorities, and the metaverse’s challenge to social relations altogether. Office decentralization has been underway with larger companies becoming more flexible in their organization and hierarchical structure, blurred boundaries between management layers, new management layers, and increased reliance on independent contractors—all of which have contributed to increased flexibility in terms of the location of employees. The COVID-19 pandemic accelerated implementations of remote work and further catalyzed labor decentralization, the results of which are here to stay and will be further exploited.

This tug of war between consolidation and decentralization has generated rifts between spatial and economic organization at multiple scales, from the places where people work, to urban/suburban organization, to global networks of connectivity. These include vacant office towers in major cities, turnover of sprawling corporate campuses, and struggling or obsolete transportation hubs and ports, among others. *Future Offices* centers architectural design to explore these rifts through a series of essays and design research projects from across the discipline focused on contemporary and future workplaces, shifting spatial economies, and the role/image of the headquarters building. This book’s authors posit that decentralization of labor poses a challenge to common conceptions of the office with typological implications for architecture.

Up until now, the primary concern of the office tower was to circulate and accommodate mass flows of workers and worker interactions from multiple departments as well as multiple businesses in a comprehensive and unified interior environment. The prototypical building occupant has by

01 Apparel Factory Layout around 1930s.
02 "Bürolandschaft" style office interior. Electrolux, Lilla Essingen, 1960s. Photography by Holger Ellgaard
03 The interior shows the idea of cubicle and "Action Office" invented by Robert Propst.
04 Facebook Headquarters shows the "Open Office" concept. Facebook Headquarters, Frank Gehry, Menlo Park, 2018. Photography by Christopher Michel

and large been conceived as the "average office worker" in a given context. As the office shifts from the primary site of daily worker operations, its value as a spatial asset should be reconsidered. To move beyond this conception of the office, some of the authors and projects included in this volume interrogate examples of architecture where presumed notions of the office's occupant, organization, and its societal functions are called into question. They speculate upon a future where offices acquire new facets as resources of space, knowledge, and production that participate in local and global economic and cultural contexts in new hybridized forms. At the heart of this is a recognition that the new ways in which companies integrate into and participate in society should be reflected in the building and its roles.

Together, the works collected here provide frameworks for understanding the complex and multifaceted nature of contemporary work, manufacturing, and commerce, and they aspire to influence new ways of conceiving architecture at multiple scales. Using New York City as a case study, *Future Offices* considers how cities can re-invent existing networks and adapt to shifts in global commerce. It speculates that a new architectural typology can fuse technological innovation with growth in the US economy and help sustain New York City's global financial leadership. The topic broadens and contributes to research on the future of work, logistics systems, and office typology.

The typology of the office has transformed a great deal since its 18th century introduction. Initially, offices were considered no different from factories and industrial manufacturing facilities, containing desks instead of machinery. This relationship was by and large practical, as different businesses could be swapped in and out of the same space, whether a grid of sewing machines, rows of conveyor belts, or the desks of telephone operators, typists, and architectural drafters (Fig. 01). In New York's flatiron district, one could move from floor to floor between all three. Such building layouts offered possibilities for symbiosis between businesses and contributed to the centralization of business districts and supply chains. The factory model of the office was re-evaluated in the 1950s with the introduction in Germany of "Bürolandschaft" or "office landscape," a concept which emerged during the shift between predominantly manufacturing-based pre-war economies to the service- and information-based post-war economies in Western nations (Fig. 02). The movement sought to diversify the office workspace and create a variety of semi-public spaces for work. In the U.S. context, the modular office offered a different model implementing the "cubicle" and other modular office furniture with the promise of greater layout flexibility and cheap reusable buildouts as well as increased worker privacy geared toward productivity and focus (Fig. 03). The monotony of the "cubicle farm," however, created an image of the office as isolated, sterile, and boring. To attract talent and promote innovative business models, many companies did away with the cubicle in favor of open office concepts. The "open office," which persists to this day, relies on the Modernist notion of the free plan (Fig. 04). Flexible, open, and adaptable, the open office has many qualities which make it economically desirable for businesses. Yet, it often suffers from being loud, chaotic, and contributing to a lack of productivity. It does not offer enough diversity of workspace to satisfy employees with different needs in terms of noise level, environmental comfort, and social interaction. Further, it does not present novel solutions regarding the multi-faceted nature of much contemporary work in terms of use of information and communication technologies, and the interplay between physical, virtual, and parasocial environments, instead, leaving such issues open to ad-hoc solutions.

In the wake of the COVID-19 pandemic, accelerated conversions to remote work, disruptions to supply chains, and the push towards direct consumer services have all upended common assumptions of the role of office typologies and even centralized urban business districts (Fig. 05). Between 2000 and 2010, the percentage of people working from home at least one day per week increased from 7.0 percent in to 9.5 percent of all workers.[2] In 2021, the number jumped to 45 percent, with no signs of significantly dropping.[3] While the recent explosion in remote work can be attributed to health policies and protocols put in place during the pandemic, the pandemic should be viewed as an accelerator of trends that were already in place and, indeed, will significantly increase, as many companies and workers find their new arrangements preferable in terms of both productivity and personal well-

05 The empty Times Square during Covid-19 pendamic, 2020. Photography by Steve Guttman NYC

06 Looking southwest across Houston and Washington Streets at St. John's Terminal.
Google Hudson Square, COOKFOX Architects, Manhattan, 2022. Photography by Jim Henderson

being.[4] The economic consequences of this shift are wide ranging and include impacts on transportation, gasoline and car sales, restaurants and retail in urban centers, office real estate, housing prices, urban and suburban populations, and various consumption patterns.[5] For instance, as numerous tech companies announced full-scale shifts to permanent remote work, median prices for one-bedroom apartments in San Francisco dropped by nearly 25 percent; at the same time, New York City has more apartment and office vacancies than ever recorded.[6] Such drastic changes invariably have ripple effects across intermediary industries and service providers. The question for cities is what productive spatial assets will maintain value in the face of these changes in ways that will support and grow their leadership into the future. Likewise, the question for architecture, given its longstanding perpetuation of the home/work separation, is how can it respond typologically?

In the history of the development of Manhattan, architecture became the expression of capital due to its augmentation of land value. Through the densification of building mass, architecture incorporated elements of the city to increase its value. In the 19th century, buildings incorporated and multiplied land vertically. In the beginning of the 20th century, land value was augmented by aesthetics, as buildings were designed to emblematize the companies that built them. Skyscrapers began to subsume whole city blocks, creating unprecedented interior urban environments. Speculating on the continuation of this logic in a contemporary context, to search for a new typology also means turning away from the building's functions related purely to human inhabitation and understanding architecture as a means of generating capital. As more and more companies embrace a "hybrid model" of work, where a mixture of in-office and remote work is incorporated into an employee's schedule, the role of the office is also shifting from a site of daily operations to a common resource with new potential for hybrid forms and spatial relations. This opens up new opportunities and inputs for architectural design focused on programmatic flexibility, social interactivity, and personal/collective dynamics, rather than maximizing productivity and rationalizing spatial allocation. Architecture can also consider new and forward-looking notions of hybridity that do not conform to past precedents of "mixed-use," post-modernist juxtaposition, or formalistic merging, but rather a deeper emphasis on the productive confluence of logistical complexities, and virtual and physical realities.

Parallel to the question of the 21st century office is the question of the 21st century headquarters. The headquarter building has traditionally served as a centralized location for coordinating the most important and sometimes all of the functions of an organization. The word's origins in military lingo allude to its relationship to centralized strategy, positioning, command, and symbolism, yet all of these are exploding out into digital platforms and global networks. Numerous tech companies have embraced 100% remote work and "virtual-first" policies, including Twitter, Spotify, Dropbox, and Facebook in the wake of the COVID-19 pandemic.[7] Some companies are even abandoning investments in centralized spatial strategies that now seem outmoded or even unfeasible in the face of critical changes to labor operations. For instance, REI, the retail outdoor recreation chain, immediately moved to sell its brand-new headquarters campus in Washington D.C. in 2020 upon completion of construction, opting instead for a series of smaller satellite campuses. The move served not only to shore up funds in the wake of the pandemic, but also as a recognition of the benefits of remote and distributed work strategies.[8] At the same time, other companies are doubling down on the enduring vitality of the headquarters building, signaling either its evolution or stubborn persistence. After a 2013 rezoning, the Hudson Square neighborhood, wedged between SoHo and Greenwich Village in lower Manhattan, has undergone major redevelopment, including the construction of Disney's 1.2-million-square-foot headquarters and Google's 2.1-billion-dollar purchase of St. John's Terminal for the proposed development of a 1.44-million-square-foot headquarters (Fig. 06). Whether such prominent examples will shift the future workings of the headquarters is uncertain; however, the future of work is certain to test their typological viability.

Elaborated through the projects featured in this book, the "logistics hub" is one typological proposal that addresses the relationship between the workplace and its urban context with a look toward the future of global commerce (Fig. 07). Price Waterhouse Coopers indicates that currently, 90-percent of global trade flows through 39 airports worldwide, which pales compared to 28,000 points of distribution for UPS alone along networks that can enhance efficiency nationally.[9] To promote a new versatile and robust manufacturing agenda, existing logistics networks and companies such as UPS, DHL, USPS, and FedEx can gain considerably by extending into facilities that aid in the development of quick prototypes, reducing costs and waste while increasing turnaround. Rapid prototyping and small-scale production using 3d-printing, robotic fabrication, and other CNC technology widely distributed across networks can provide counterpoints to the inflexibility of global supply chains.[10] The cities that become the most important along

07 Axon Model Rendering. Project by Chengzhe Zhu, Qi Che, and Zhihui Li

these networks will thrive. US manufacturing will benefit with an efficient hub accessible directly from New York City, establishing it as the leader of prototyping nationally. The new hub will increase the relevance of NYC as a leading place of business and logistics, making a stronger connection to global centers while strengthening development locally.

THE BOOK AND ITS CONTRIBUTORS

The following chapters identify critical issues at stake in the design of future workplaces. One of the central questions of this book's authors is what should the 21st century office look like and what will the implications of major social and technological shifts of its configuration be? Other authors are more specifically focused on the centrality of the office in work itself and headquarters building in particular as a type. Office buildings have always served as both functional sites for a range of company operations as well as symbols of company ideals and aspirations. As companies move into a decentralized, hybrid paradigm, this interpretation feels increasingly belabored and inconsistent. As such, the first section focuses on contemporary concerns and context at play in workplace design, projecting forward towards future shifts. Verda Alexander starts by probing the contemporary and future relevance of the workplace in Chapter 01, advocating for a socially and ecologically responsible role for workplace architecture in society. In Chapter 02, SOM provides a case study of their design for Disney's new global headquarters in the Hudson Square neighborhood of Lower Manhattan, outlining how an evolving set of needs and criteria among corporate leaders track with zoning policy and urban dynamics. In Chapter 03, Peter Cappelli and Ranya Nehmeh survey and analyze post-pandemic employer and employee perspectives to give greater depth and insight into decision making-factors and trends with an emphasis on their spatial implications.

The second section speculates on design imperatives, research strains, and strategies for the future workplace. The authors in this section examine the disciplinary history and legacy of office towers in particular and imagine new entanglements with technology, ecological systems, and urban culture. Patrick Monte first takes up the issue of office tower preservation

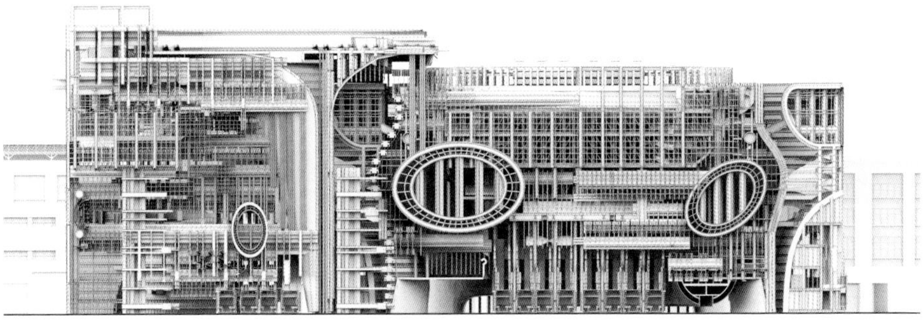

08 Hybrid Futures. Project by Dianqiu Zheng, Gordon Cheng, and Jing Yuan

09 Metabolic Futures. Project by Bingkun Deng, Ming Jiang, and Yang Yang

10 Decentered Futures. Project by Maoqiang Li, Bohao Sun, and Youyu Zhang

---

1 Leslie Picker, "A Standout Year for Deals, in Volume and Complexity," *The New York Times*, January 3, 2016, https://www.nytimes.com/2016/01/04/business/dealbook/a-standout-year-for-deals-in-volume-and-complexity.html.

2 US Census Bureau Public Information Office, "Census Bureau Report Shows Steady Increase in Home-Based Workers Since 1999," *U.S. Census Bureau*, October 4, 2012, https://www.census.gov/newsroom/releases/archives/employment_occupations/cb12-188.html.

3 Lydia Saad and Ben Wigert, "Remote Work Persisting and Trending Permanent," *Gallup.com*, October 13, 2021, https://news.gallup.com/poll/355907/remote-work-persisting-trending-permanent.aspx.

4 Ibid.

5 Susan Lund, Anu Madgavkar, James Manyika, and Sven Smit, "The Future of Remote Work: An Analysis of 2,000 Tasks, 800 Jobs, and 9 Countries | McKinsey," *McKinsey Global Institute*, October 23, 2020, https://www.mckinsey.com/featured-insights/future-of-work/whats-next-for-remote-work-an-analysis-of-2000-tasks-800-jobs-and-nine-countries.

and renovation in the context of New York City, arguing that shifts in the nature of work open up new opportunities to assert urban public culture in the reimagining of existing skyscrapers. Heeding a related concern, Ariane Harrison envisions the future office as "feral," "teeming with human, animal, and machinic species" that reposition architecture as an ecologically rehabilitative agent. Finally, Patrik Schumacher formulates a design research agenda for workplace metaverses and mixed reality architecture, where physical and virtual architectural spaces extend into and index one another in rich, multilayered, and amplificatory ways.

The two sections of texts are bookended by student projects developed at the University of Pennsylvania Stuart Weitzman School of Design in the Master of Science in Design Advanced Architectural Design degree program in studios led by Brian Deluna, Nate Hume, Na Wei, Mo Zheng and me. Each project is presented through images that serve to reflect upon and provoke the concepts presented across the book's chapters. They are grounded in the idea of a "logistics hub," a new hybrid architectural typology that acts as a node between industries, networks, and economies in the greater New York area and the globe. The site is a full block extending north from Spring Street to Houston Street between Washington and Greenwich Streets in Hudson Square of Manhattan. The existing site is uniquely positioned to speculate on the future of the network Hub due to its immediate proximity to major tech companies, its transport connections to major New York and New Jersey ports, and its access to the rest of the New York City and Tri-State area. Each project has three main programs: a distribution network that circulates and houses trucks, UPS headquarter offices, and a production space for rapid manufacturing of on-demand products. Taken together, they propose novel architectures that are unprecedented in linking local efficiency and production capacity with global demands.

As with the authored texts, the design projects have been grouped into sections: *Hybrid Futures* (Fig. 08), *Metabolic Futures* (Fig. 09), and *Decentered Futures* (Fig. 10). Each project section addresses a unique set of challenges concerning the larger scope and increased complexities of work, manufacturing, and logistics today. These categories are speculative and consider the expansion of direct-to-consumer (a.k.a business-to-consumer) production and on-demand manufacturing combined with advancements in communication and technology. *Hybrid Futures* considers the spatially productive tension between human- and machine-oriented spaces. *Urban Machines* looks at the networking potential between the urban environment, the internet of things, and distributed, localized production methods. Finally, *Decentered Systems* evokes the programmatic, spatial, and aesthetic implications of a radically decentered, anti-hierarchical workplace. Overall, the projects propose newfound productive capacities for architecture enabled by emerging or future technologies and empowered by localized distribution networks.

We hope that by providing both texts and projects, the book is both cohesive and flexible enough to allow the reader to find their own path for negotiating the content. The aim of this book is to investigate interactions with, and innovative responses from, its users. As a proxy for architecture's global integration with societal systems, *Future Offices* aims to push disciplinary bounds and provide frameworks for future architectures.

6 Ibid.

7 Gemma Church, "Revealed: The Tech Companies Abandoning Remote Work," *All Work*, July 15, 2021, https://allwork.space/?p=79192.

8 Tom Ryan, "REI Sells Its Headquarters. Others Should Take Notice.," *Forbes*, August 18, 2020, https://www.forbes.com/sites/retailwire/2020/08/18/rei-sells-its-headquarters-others-should-take-notice/.

9 PwC, "Transportation & Logistics 2030 Volume 4: Securing the supply chain." *PwC.com*, June 16, 2011, https://www.pwc.com/gx/en/transportation-logistics/pdf/tl2030_vol.4_web.pdf

10 Peter S. Goodman "What the Shipping Crisis Looks Like at a U.S. Port" The New York Times, October 10, 2021, https://www.nytimes.com/2021/10/11/business/supply-chain-crisis-savannah-port.html.

PROJECTS: HYBRID FUTURES

Workplace design has traditionally created spatial delineations along pragmatic lines. Utilities like manufacturing, storage, packing, shipping, and receiving are separated from the human and knowledge-based work of, for instance, product development, marketing, sales, and finance departments. Shifts in both the nature of manufacturing and of labor call into question the continuing relevance and vitality of workplace design rooted in such functional hierarchies. The projects in this section highlight productive frictions between logistics-oriented spaces, human-centered spaces, and building systems. Large swaths of each project represented here, as well as those that follow in the remaining sections, are devoted to mechanistic operations like loading/unloading, sorting, storage, and packing for goods ranging in scale from handheld boxes to shipping containers. These serve as transitional spaces for shifting scales in exchange, from freight to stock to delivery. They are positioned in close tension with offices and small-scale manufacturing spaces that work in conjunction to form assembly-line-like flows through the building, which are further calibrated with exterior distribution networks. Logistics mechanisms combine with, and nestle into, building circulation and ancillary spaces to form hybridized workplace architecture that defies traditional office and manufacturing typologies.

PROJECT 01

CAVERN

UPS Hub, West SOHO, New York

Sharvari Mhatre, Yichao Jin, Tianxiao Wang

Cavern combines functionality and flexibility to envision a new workplace typology. The project merges highly curated and nuanced spaces for a variety of workplace functions with a machine-like superstructure that can be adapted to a variety of logistical purposes. This superstructure acts as a backbone, providing structural support, housing mechanical systems, and taking on storage and distribution functions that interface with interior and exterior networks. The human-centered office spaces, on the other hand, are designed to cater to different types of work activities, with carefully crafted environments that enhance productivity and well-being. Its ability to adapt to changing needs challenges traditional notions of what a workplace can be and offers a glimpse into a more dynamic future.

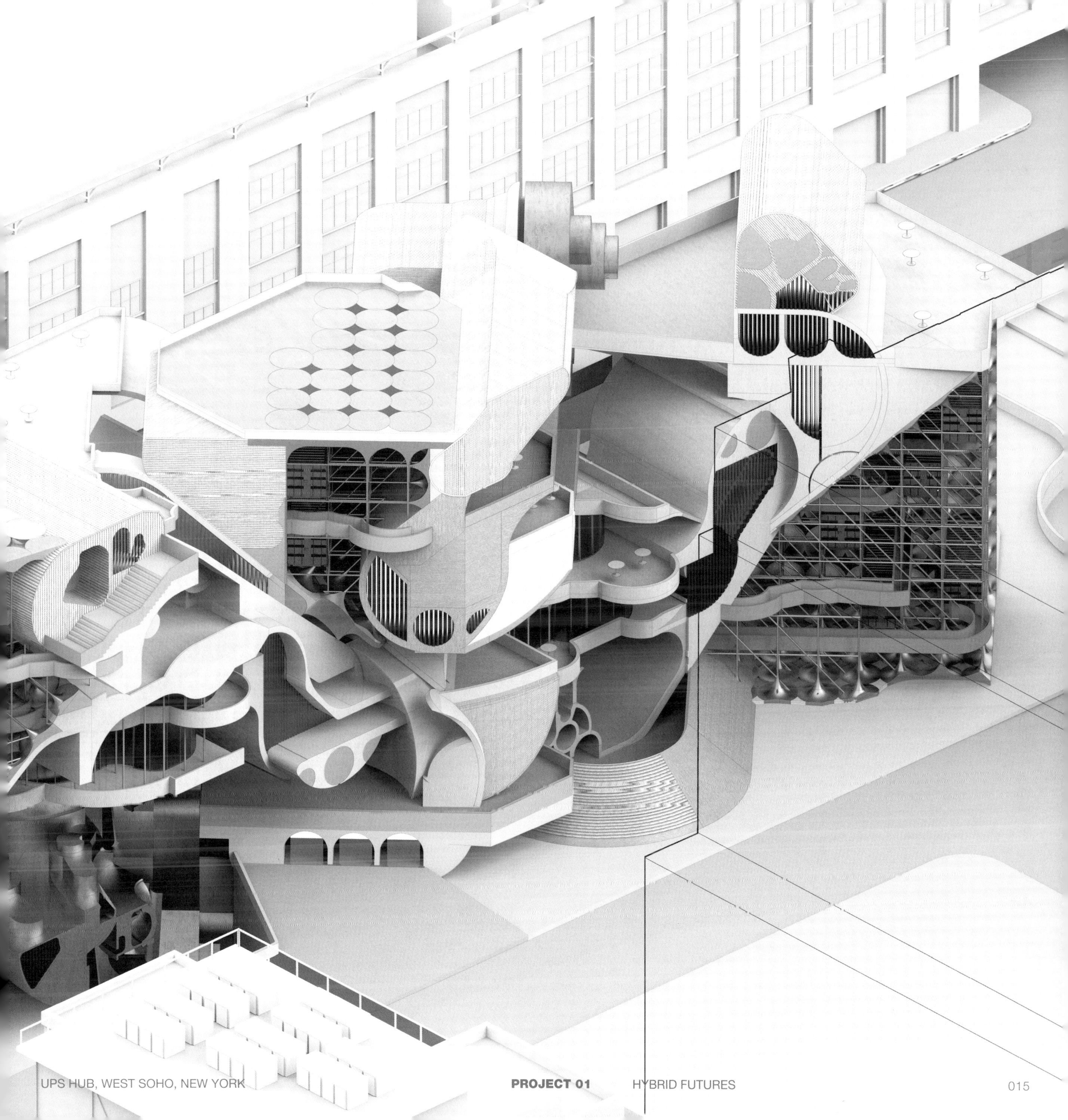

Top Right: Typical Floor Plan

Bottom: Long Building Section

01 Lobby
02 Bridge
03 Auditorium
04 Meeting Room
05 Training Center
06 Offices
07 Package Sorting System
08 Archive
09 Rest Area
10 Cargo Lift
11 Mechanical Room
12 Baggage Claim
13 Package Storage
14 WCargo Pick-up Area

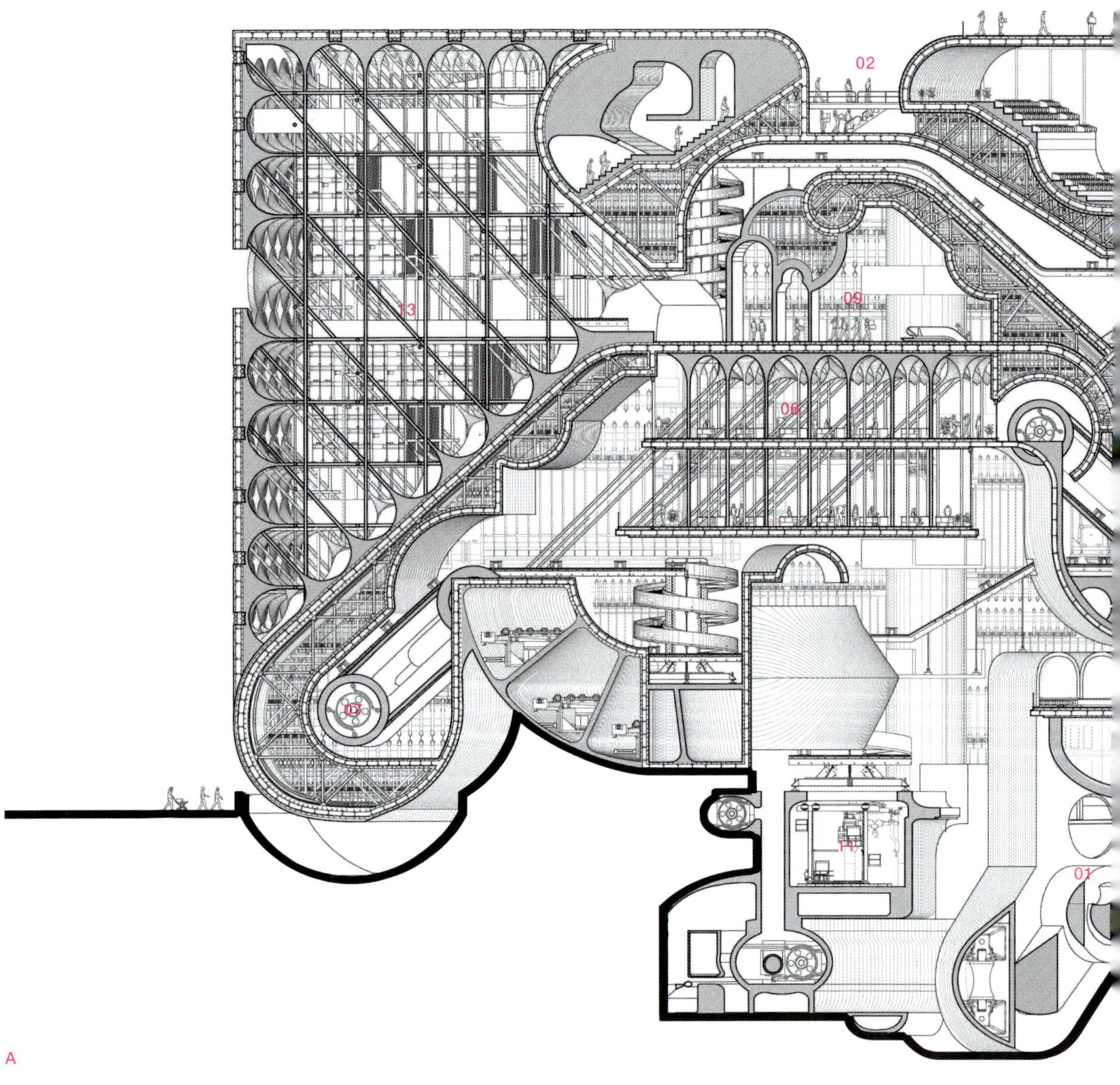

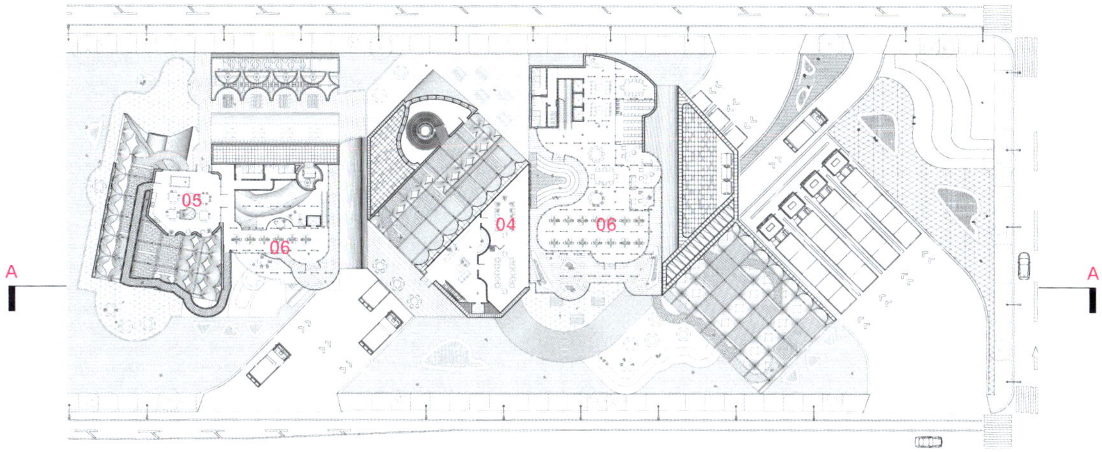
A
05
06
04
06
A

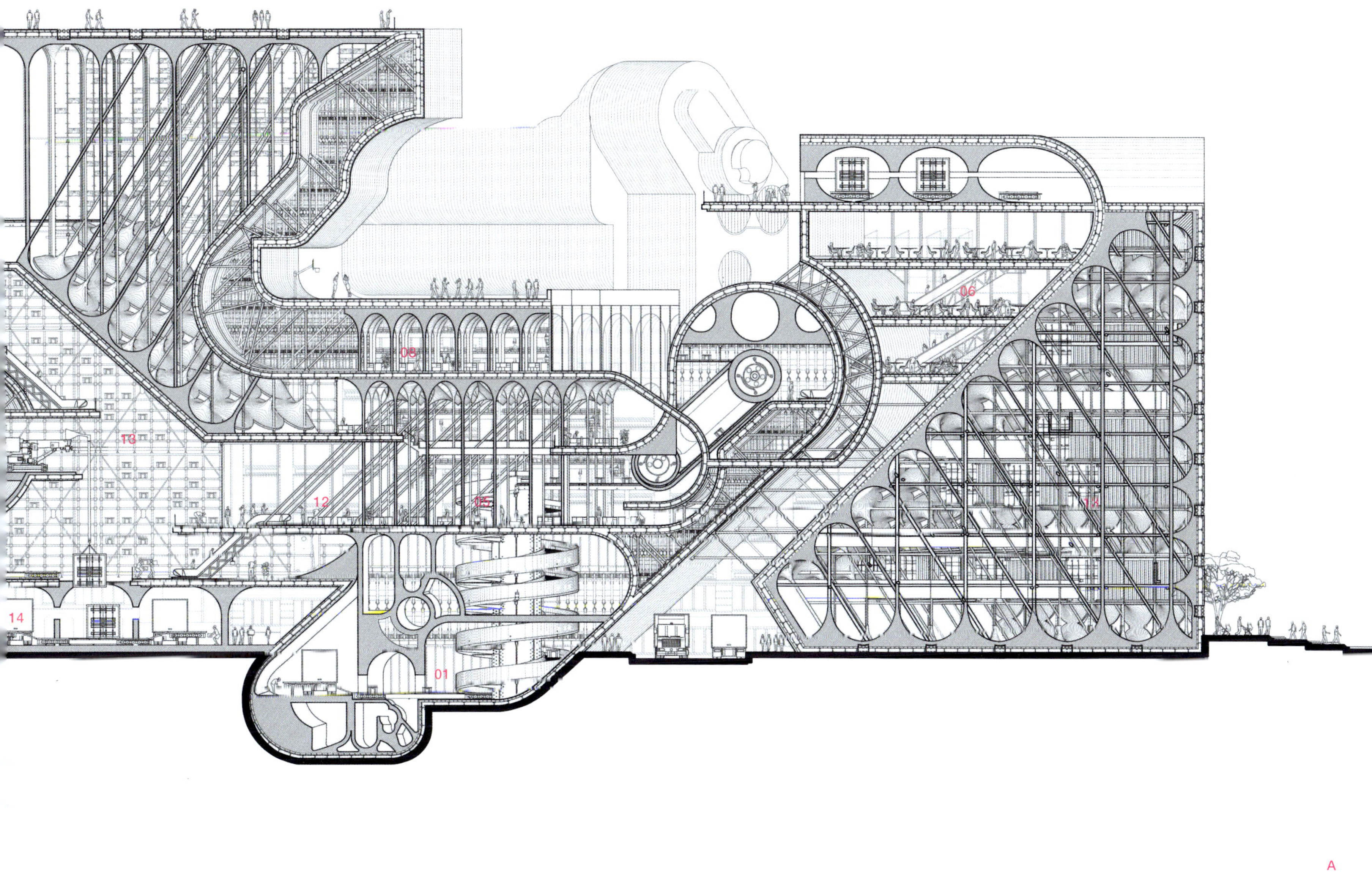
06
08
13
12
05
14
01
06
A

Elevation Rendering

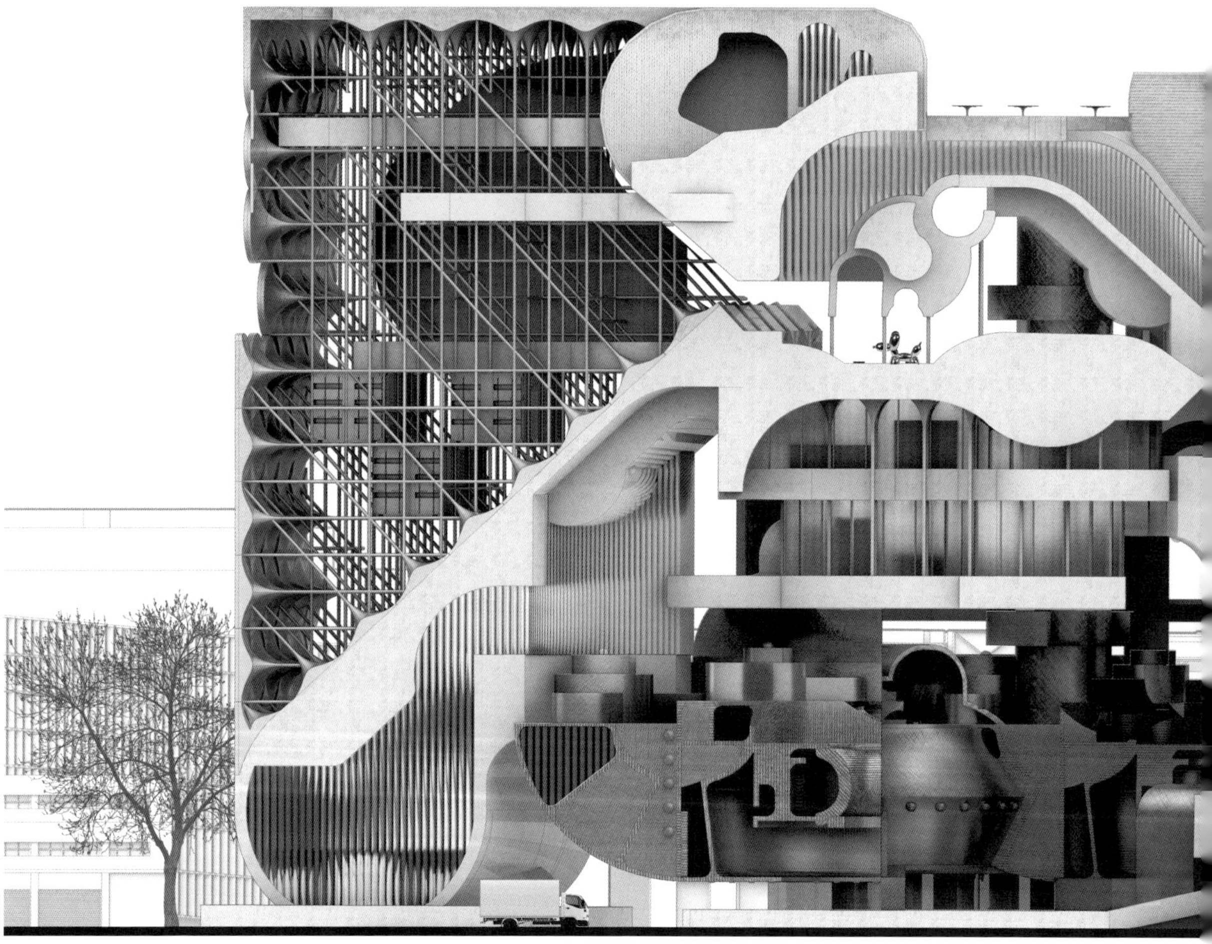

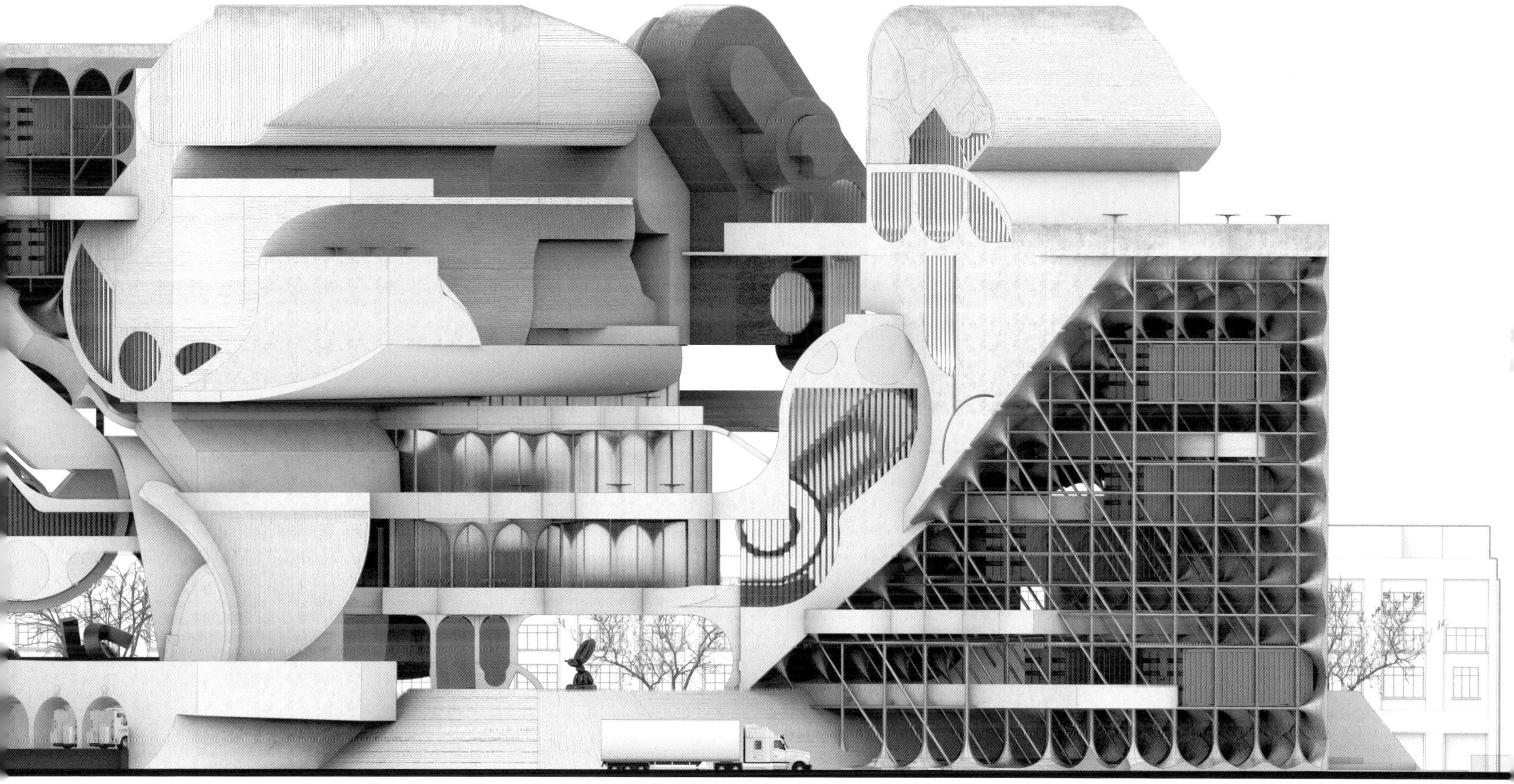

Right: Physical Section Model, 2'x2'x2', 3D Printed PLA

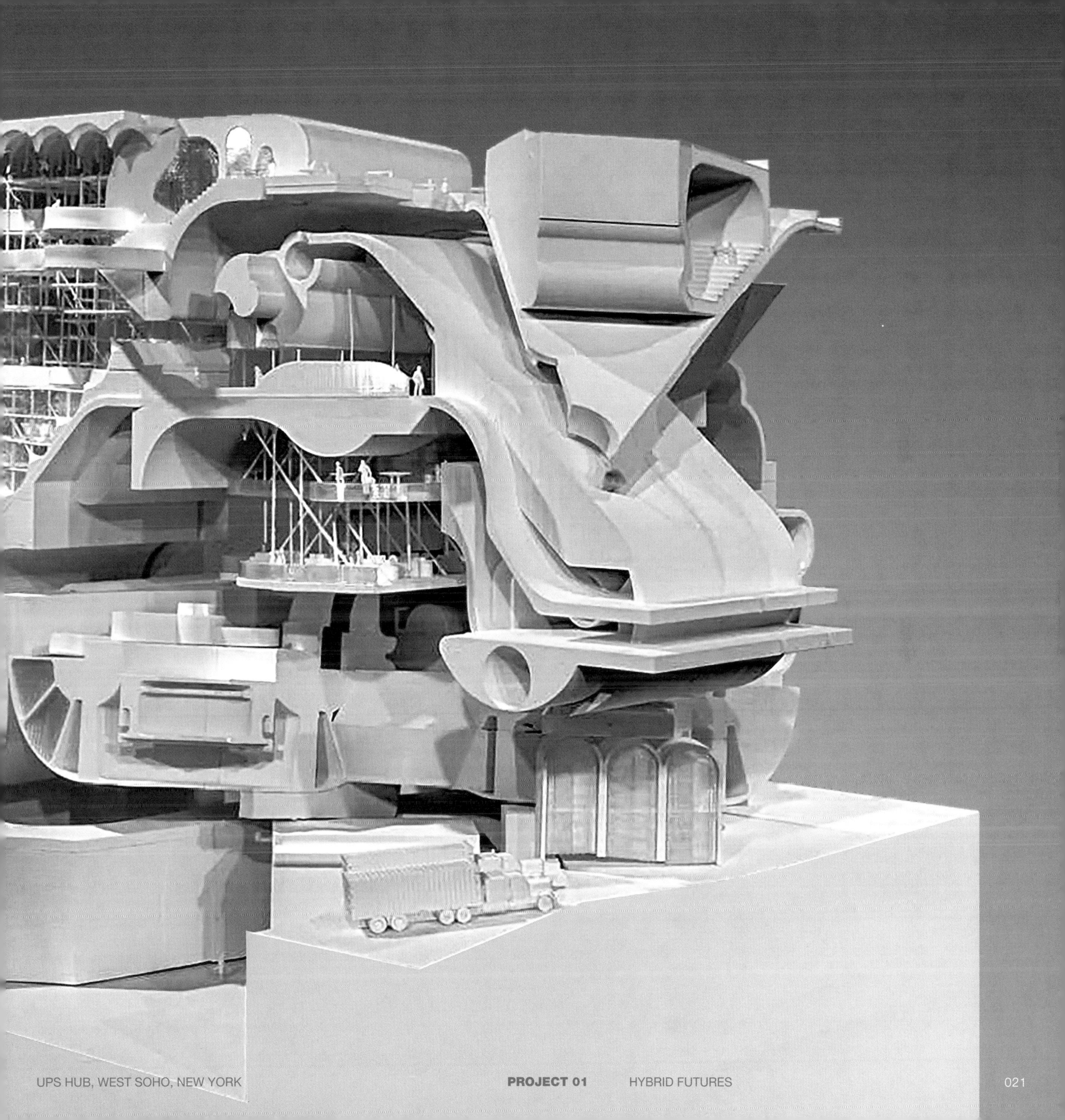

Right: Physical Section Model, 2'x2'x2', 3D Printed PLA

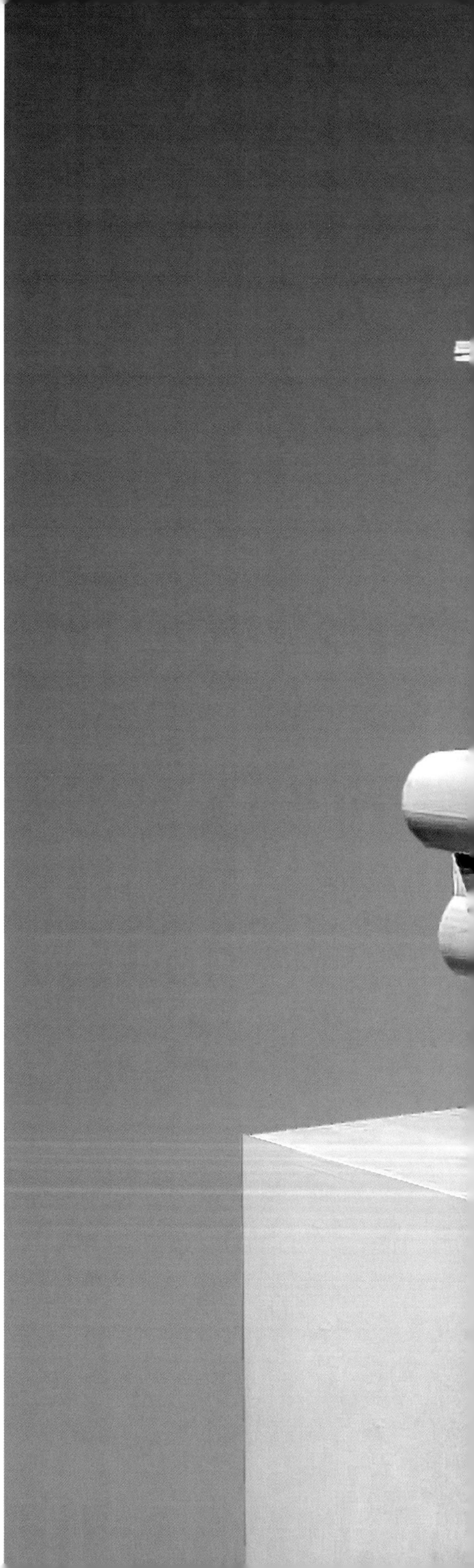

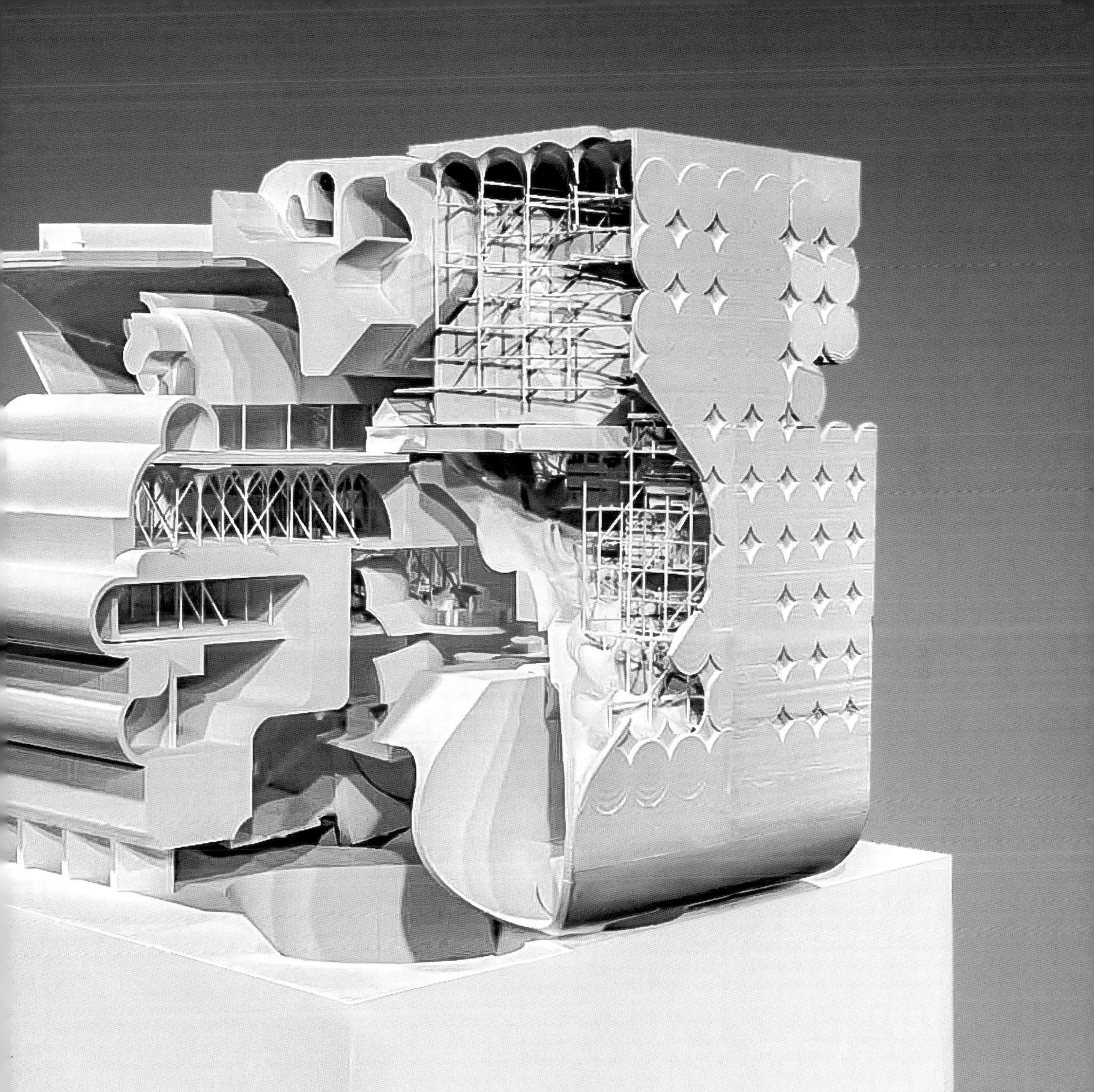

PROJECT 02

CONVEYOR

UPS Hub, West SOHO, New York

Chaoqiong Guo, Huajie Ma, Jingrong Ning

Conveyor, challenges the sterility and uniformity of corporate office towers by reintroducing the aesthetics of manufacturing and fabrication architecture. At the heart of the project are large conveyor belt structures that serve as key structural and functional elements, arranged in multiple directions to connect the building as a whole. These conveyors not only enable the processing and circulation of manufactured products but also work in conjunction with small-scale manufacturing workshops to emphasize productive output. The unique composition of parts creates a diversity of negative spaces that take on typical workplace programs while challenging conventional office configurations. By incorporating the language of manufacturing and fabrication, Conveyor offers an innovative and refreshing take on contemporary office design that is both functional and aesthetically striking.

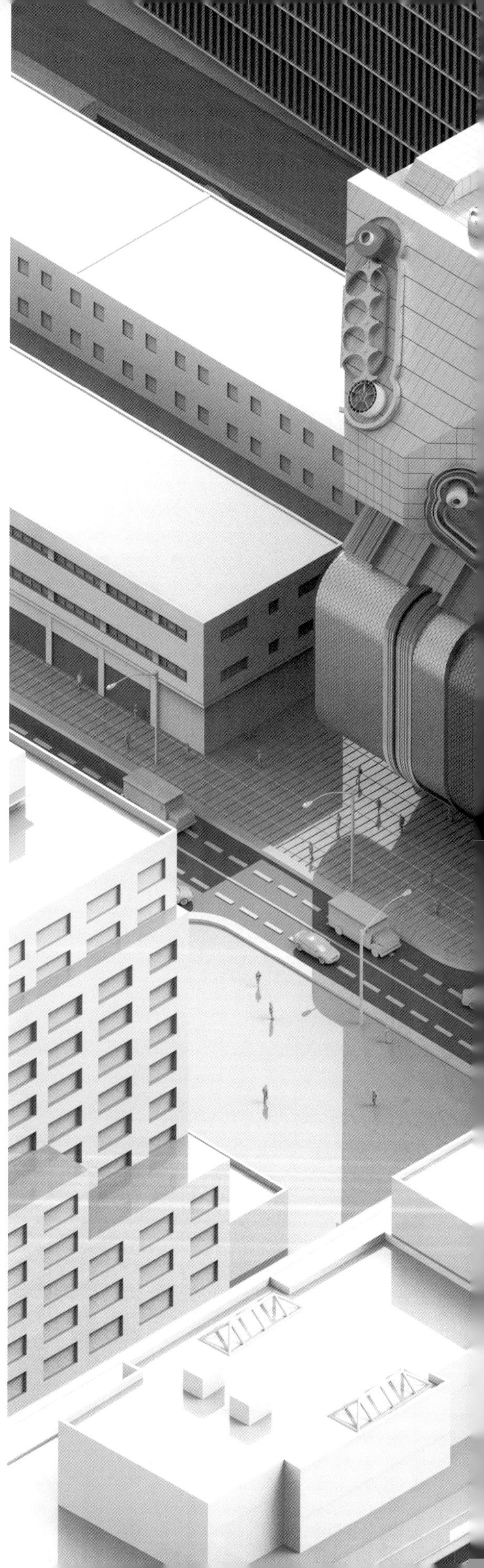

Right: Short Building Section

Left: Elevation Drawing

01 Package Distribution System
02 Package Drop-off Area
03 Visitor Drop-off Area
04 Offices
05 Meeting Room
06 Lounge
07 Cargo Pick-up and Drop-off
08 Main Hall
09 Cargo Transportation System
10 Package Storage

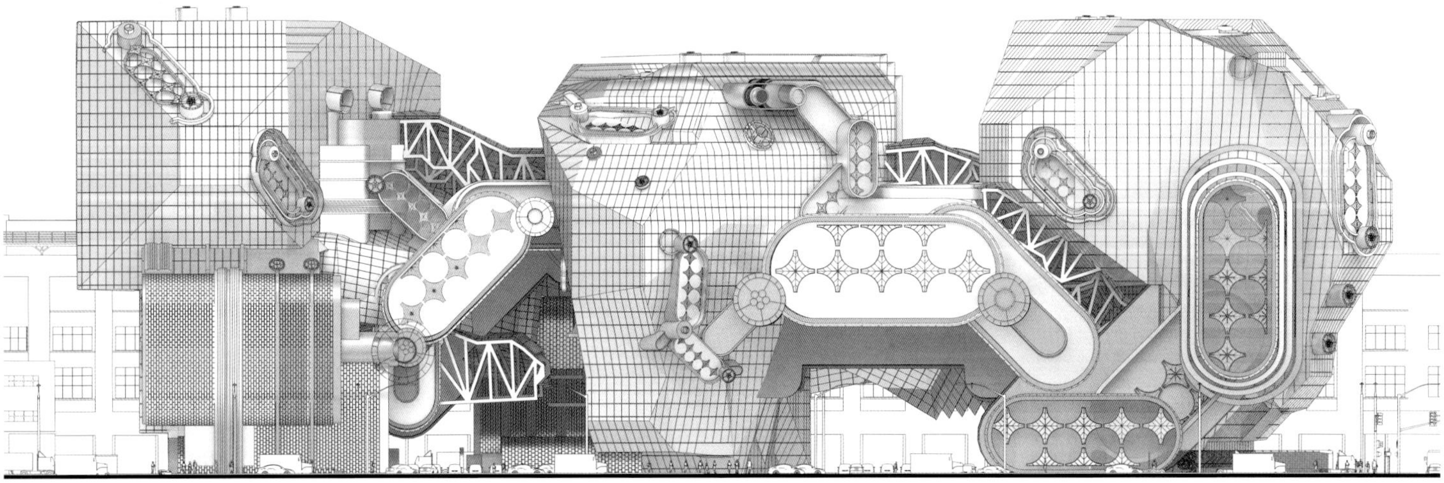

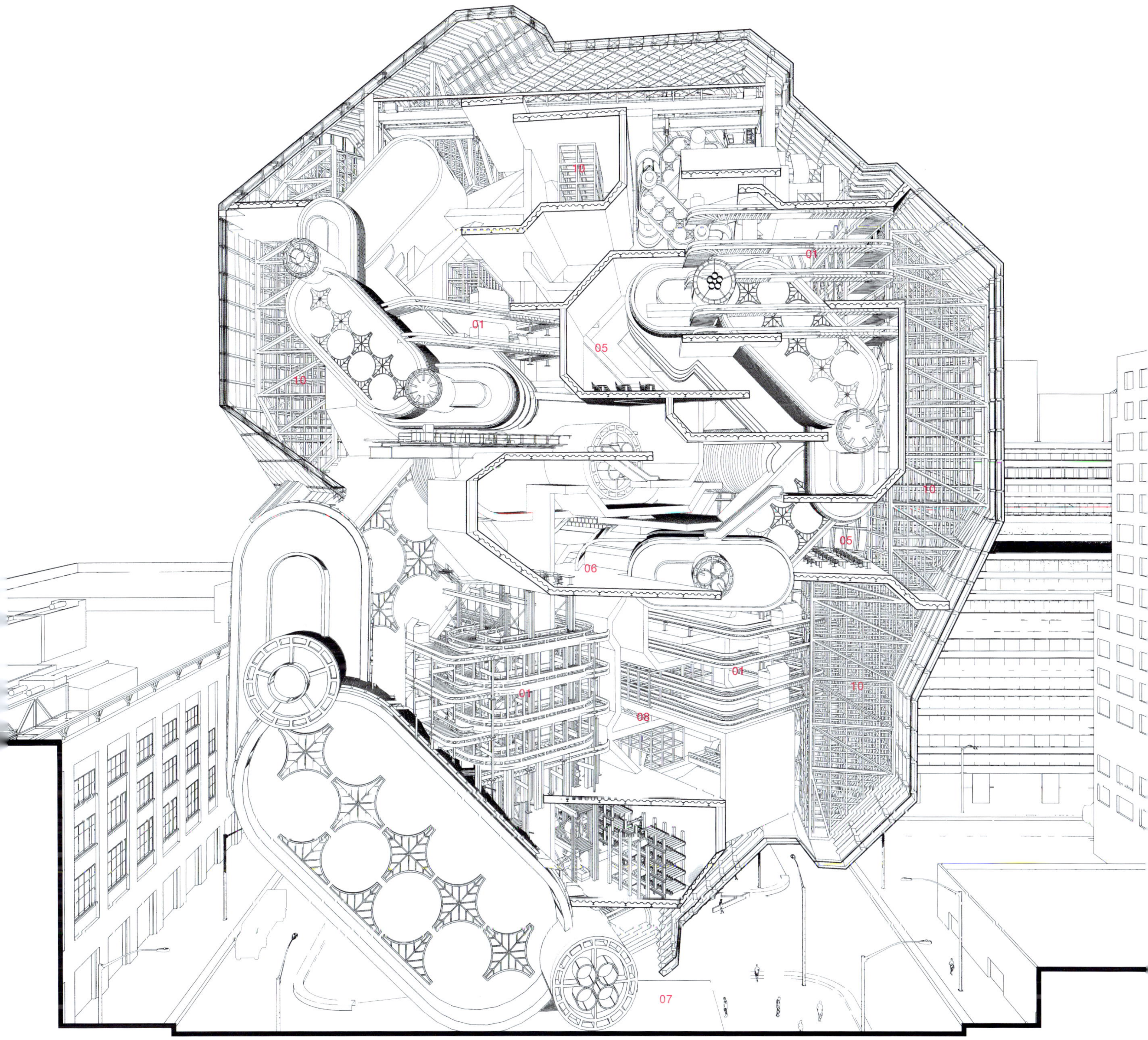
10
01
01
05
10
10
05
06
01
01
10
08
07

Long Building Section

01 Package Distribution System
02 Package Drop-off Area
03 Visitor Drop-off Area
04 Offices
05 Meeting Room
06 Lounge
07 Cargo Pick-up and Drop-off
08 Main Hall
09 Cargo Distribution System
10 Package Storage

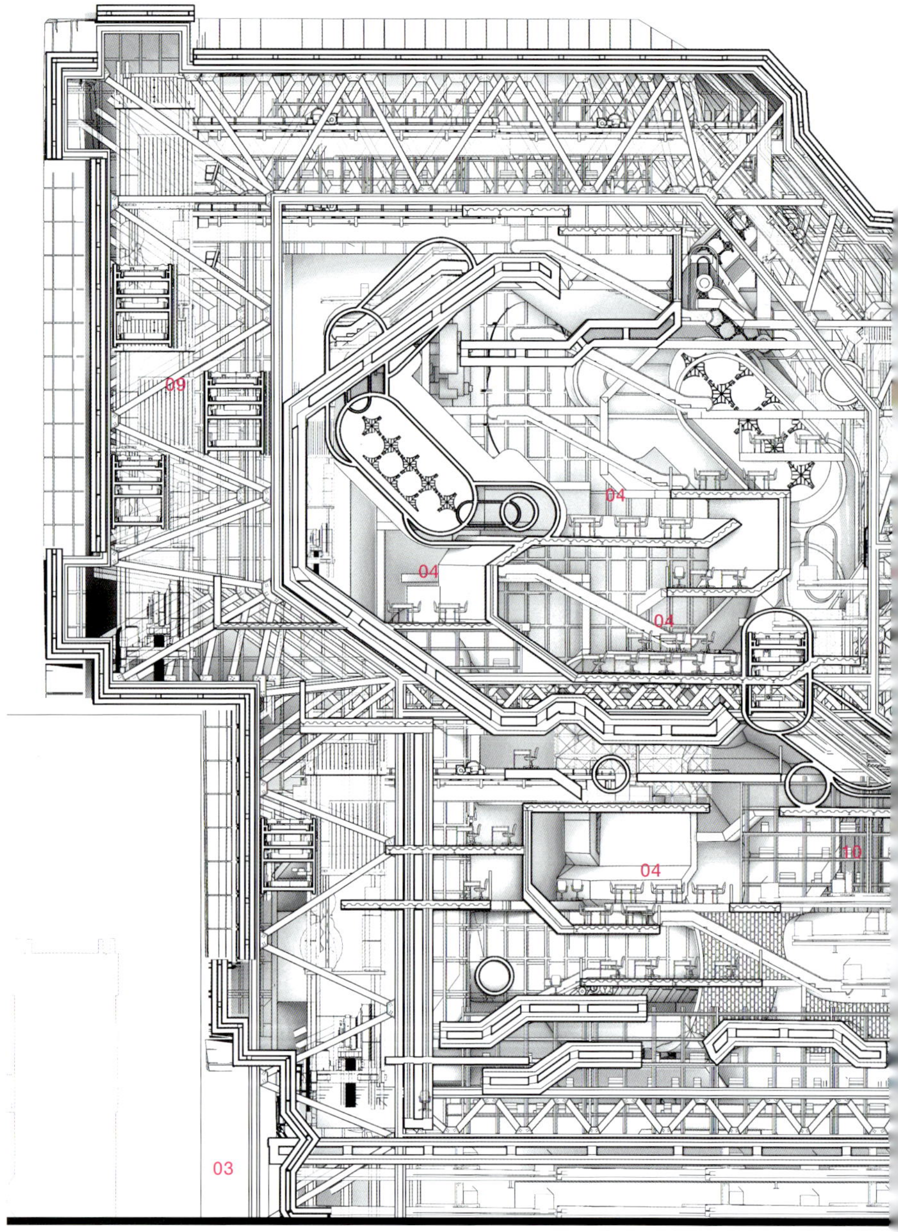

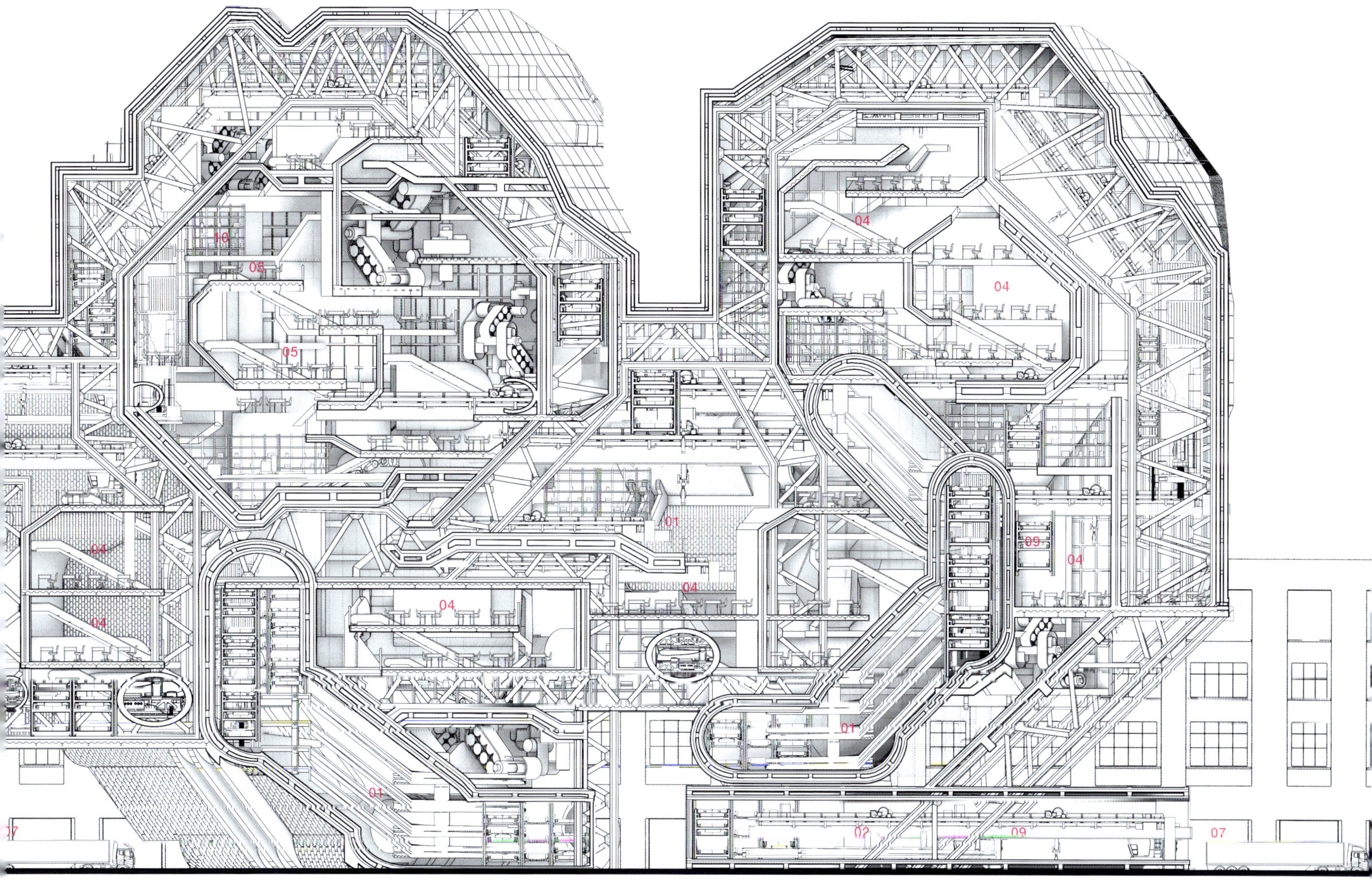
04
10
05
04
05
04
04
01
04
09
04
04
04
01
01
02
09
07

Right: Physical Section Model, 2'x2'x2', 3D Printed PLA

Left: Physical Section Model, 2'x2'x2', 3D Printed PLA

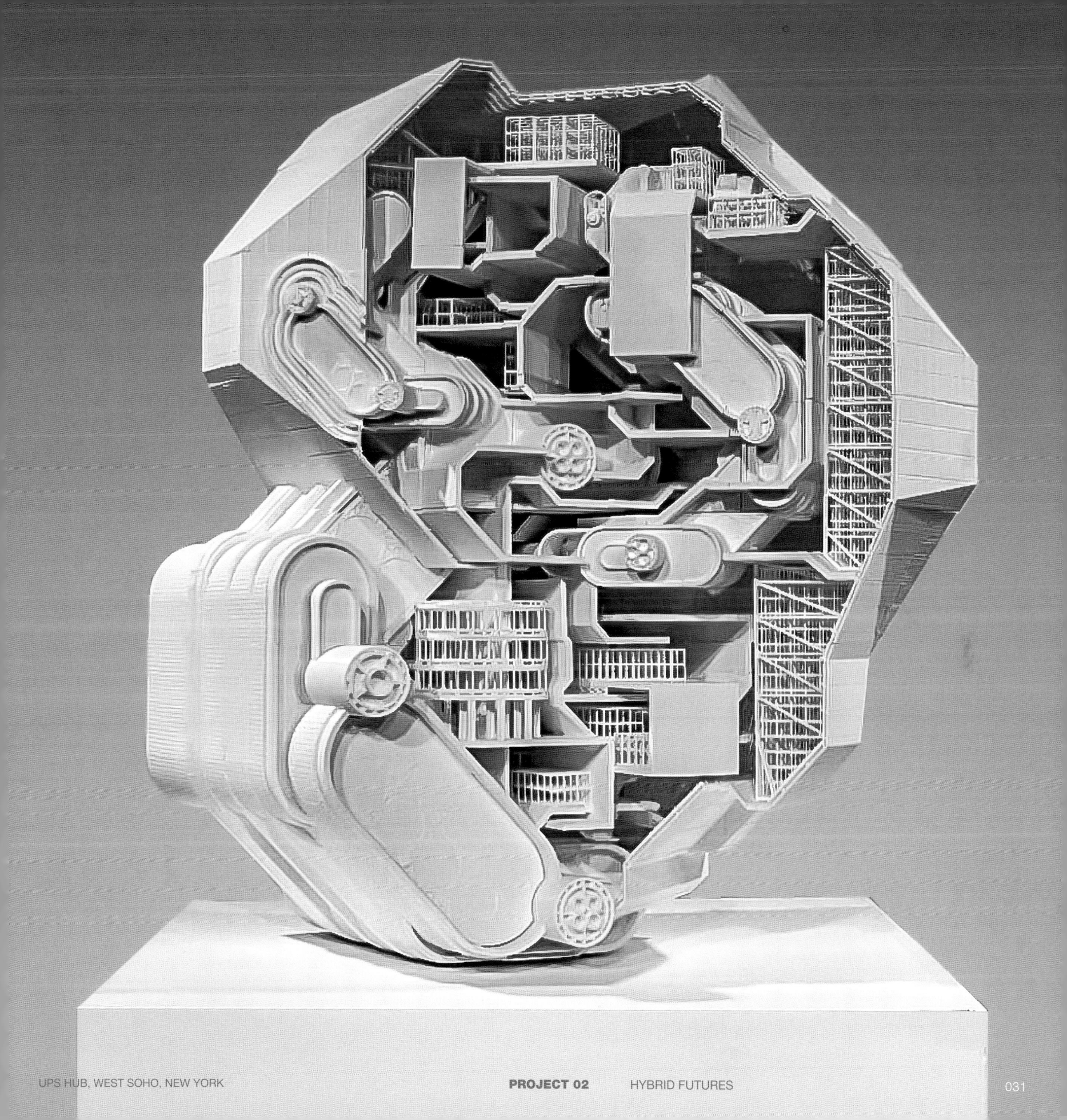

PROJECT 03

DISFIGURE

UPS Hub, West SOHO, New York

Zhe Zhong, Sijie Gao, Atharva Ranade

Disfigure is a bold break away from traditional workplace design spatial strategies. Through the techniques of bending, faceting, and stretching, the project decouples the office from its typical horizontal and vertical spatial strategies. Recognizing the increasing irrelevance of the repetitive individualized layouts to the contemporary digital workplace, the design favors exaggerations and expansions of programmatic spaces. These exaggerations create narrow and tight pockets of space that can fulfill logistical functions not tied to human activity. This hybrid of human and non-human spaces together create a varied aesthetic landscape within the building. By challenging conventional spatial strategies, Disfigure introduces a new approach to building performance, where the functionality of the space is not only defined by human use but also by its ability to accommodate logistical needs. This project is a testament to the power of architecture to adapt to the changing needs of the contemporary workplace and create spaces that are both functional and aesthetically inspiring.

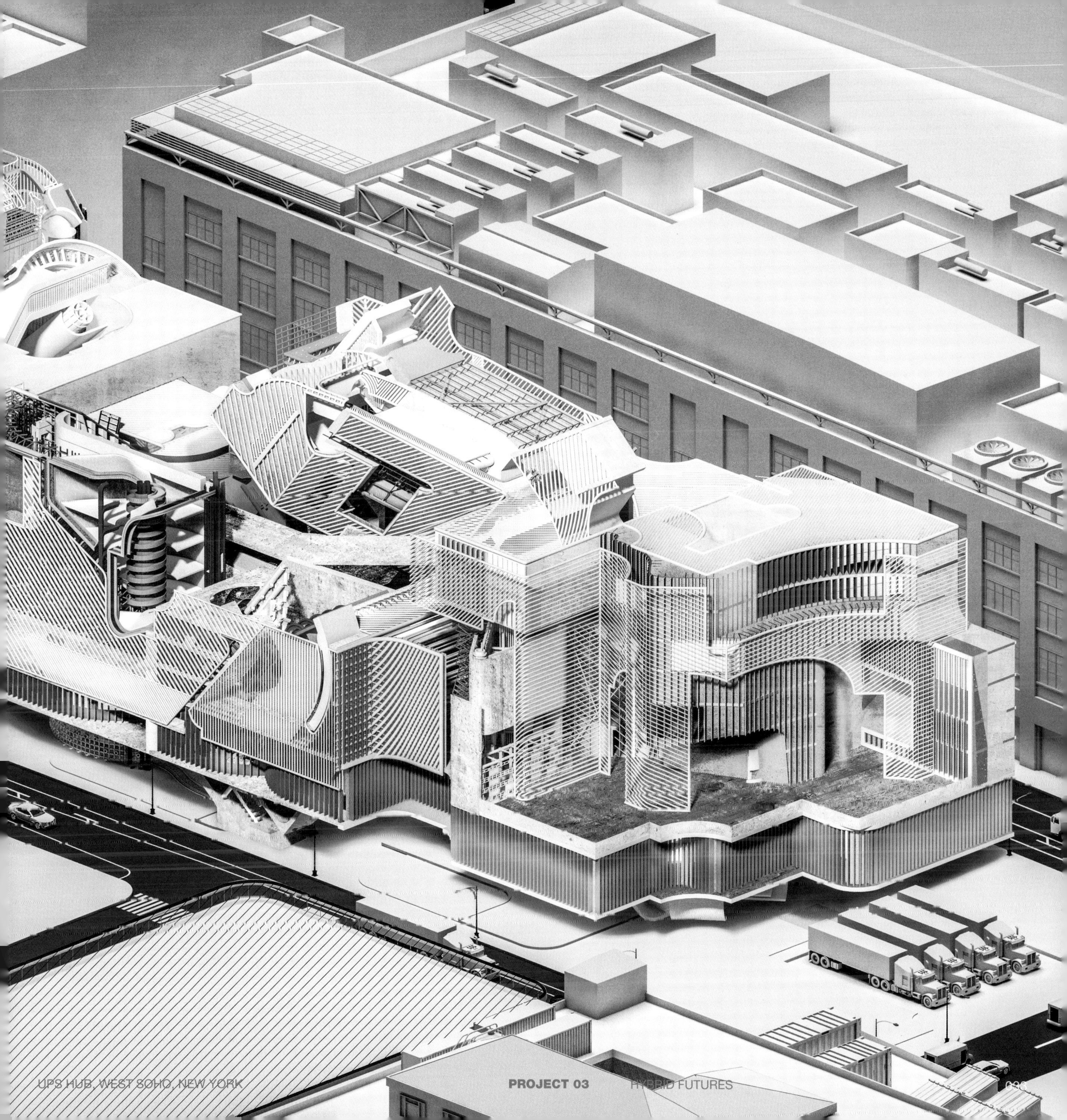

Top Right: Ground Floor Plan

Bottom: Long Building Section

01 Lounge
02 Conveyor Belt
03 Offices
04 Elevator
05 Package Storage
06 Cargo Drop-off Area
07 Meeting Room
08 Board Room
09 Lobby
10 Training Center
11 Truck Dock
12 Mechanical Room

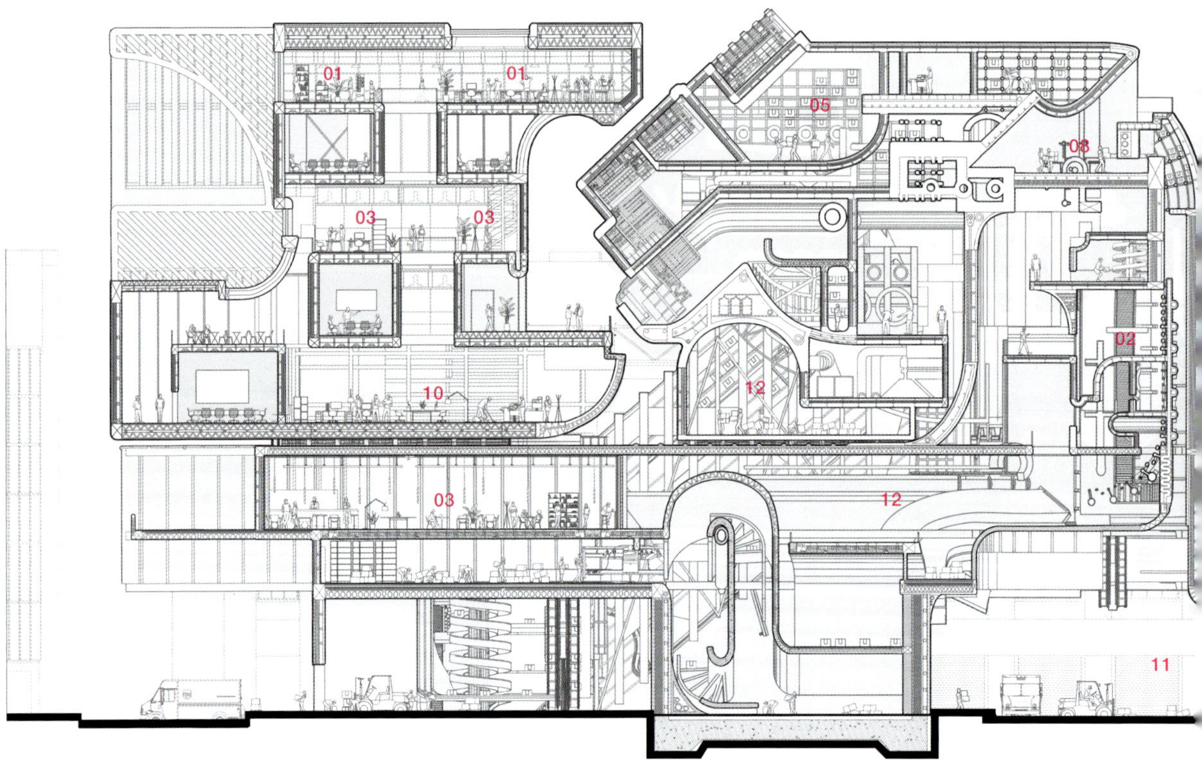

A

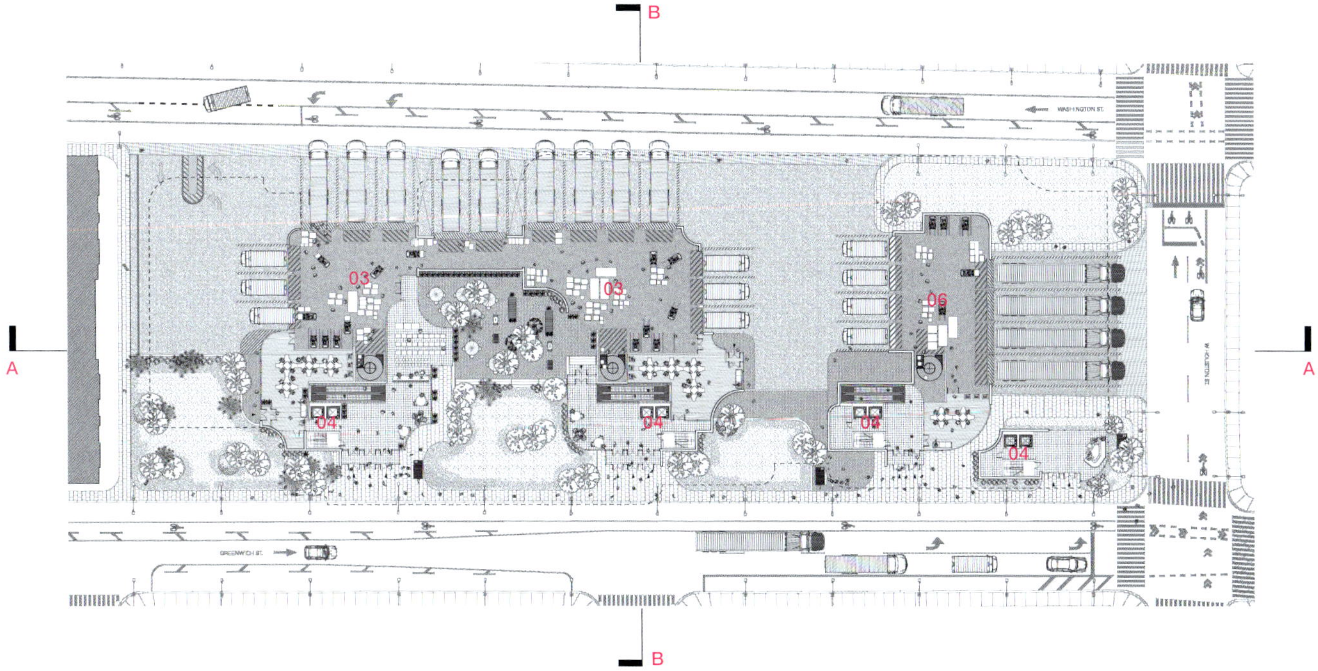
B
A
03
03
06
04
04
04
04
A
B

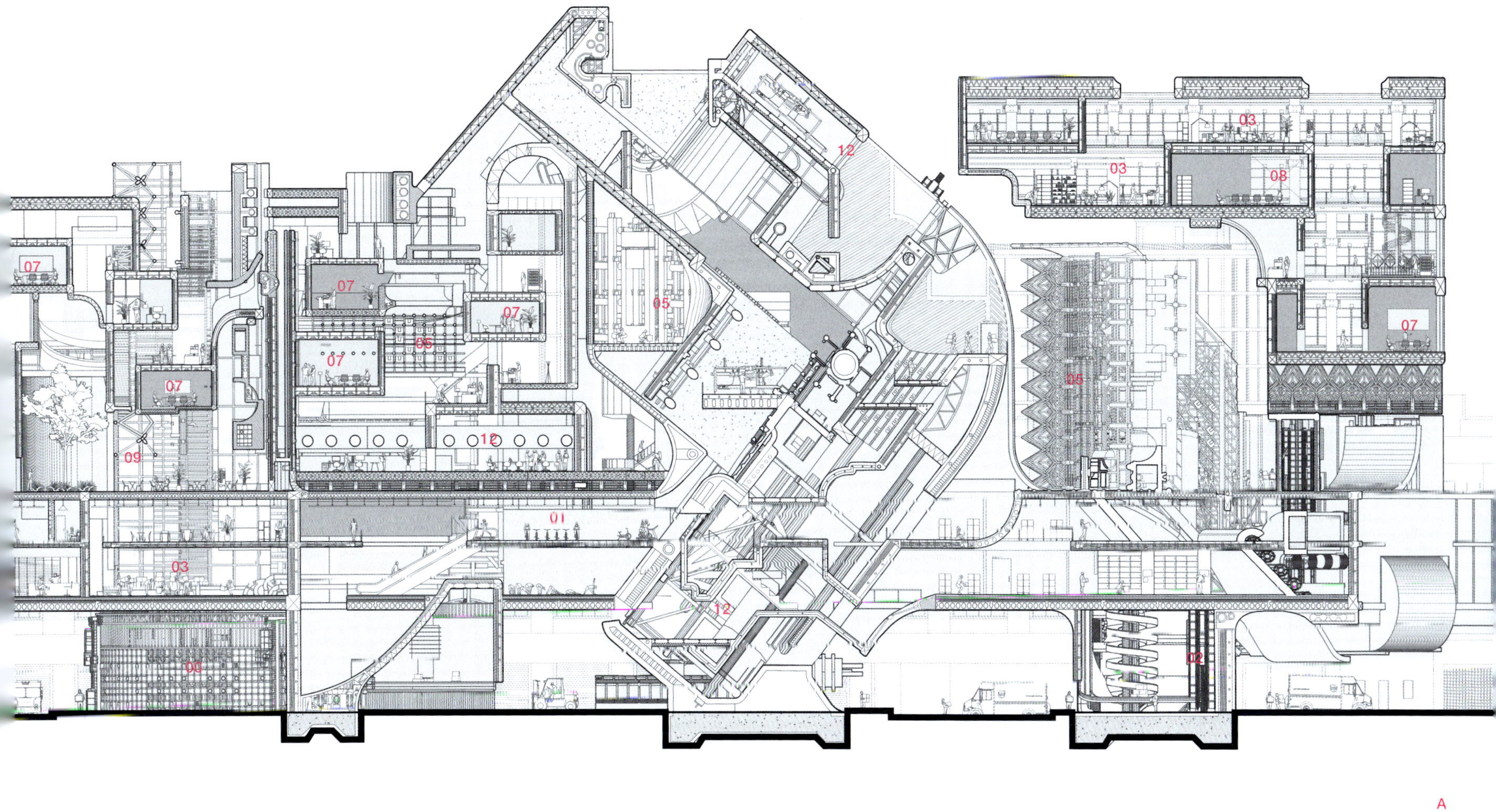
12
03
03
08
07
07
07
05
07
06
07
07
05
07
09
12
01
03
12
00
02
A

Elevation Rendering

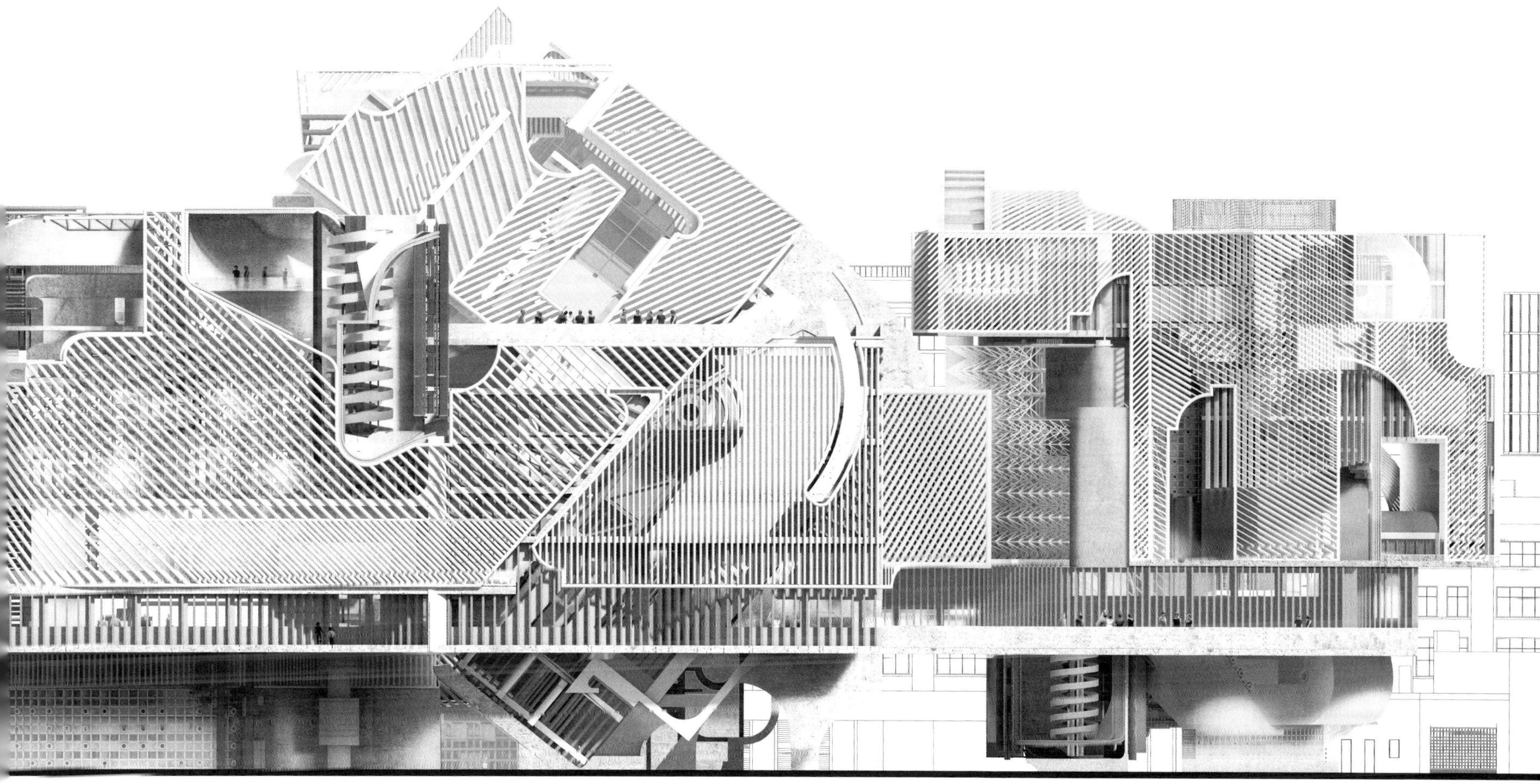

Right: Short Building Section

Left: Physical Section Model, 2'x2'x2', 3D Printed PLA

01 Lounge
02 Conveyor Belt
03 Offices
04 Elevator
05 Package Storage
06 Cargo Drop-off Area
07 Meeting Room
08 Board Room
09 Lobby
10 Training Center
11 Truck Dock
12 Mechanical Room

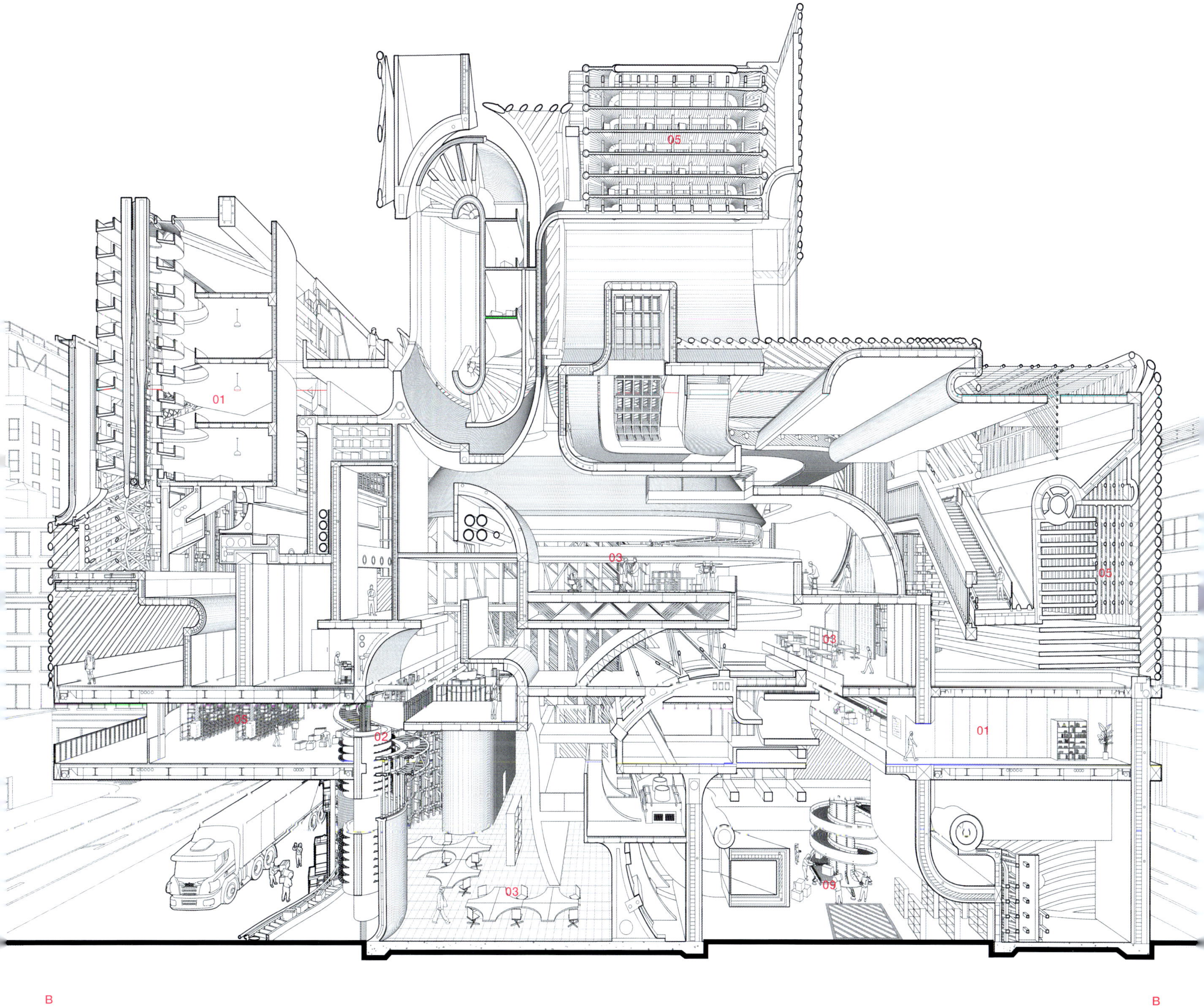
05
01
03
05
03
06
02
01
03
09
B
B

Physical Section Model, 2'x2'x2', 3D Printed PLA

PROJECT 04

CIRCUMVOLUTION

UPS Hub, West SOHO, New York

Dianqiu Zheng, Gordon Cheng, Jing Yuan

Circumvolution defies the conventional stacked floor plate strategy of traditional building design. Instead, large wave-like slabs flow both horizontally and vertically across the building site, interlocking at key junctures to create a dynamic and fluid structure that challenges traditional notions of spatial organization. These slabs not only serve as structural elements but also play a critical role in shaping the building's performance, influencing everything from light and access to circulation and spatial variety. The result is an incredibly versatile and flexible workspace that can adapt to a range of work activities and accommodate the changing needs of the contemporary office. By breaking away from the rigid, hierarchical structures of the past, Circumvolution advocates for a more holistic approach to architecture that places flexibility and versatility at the forefront

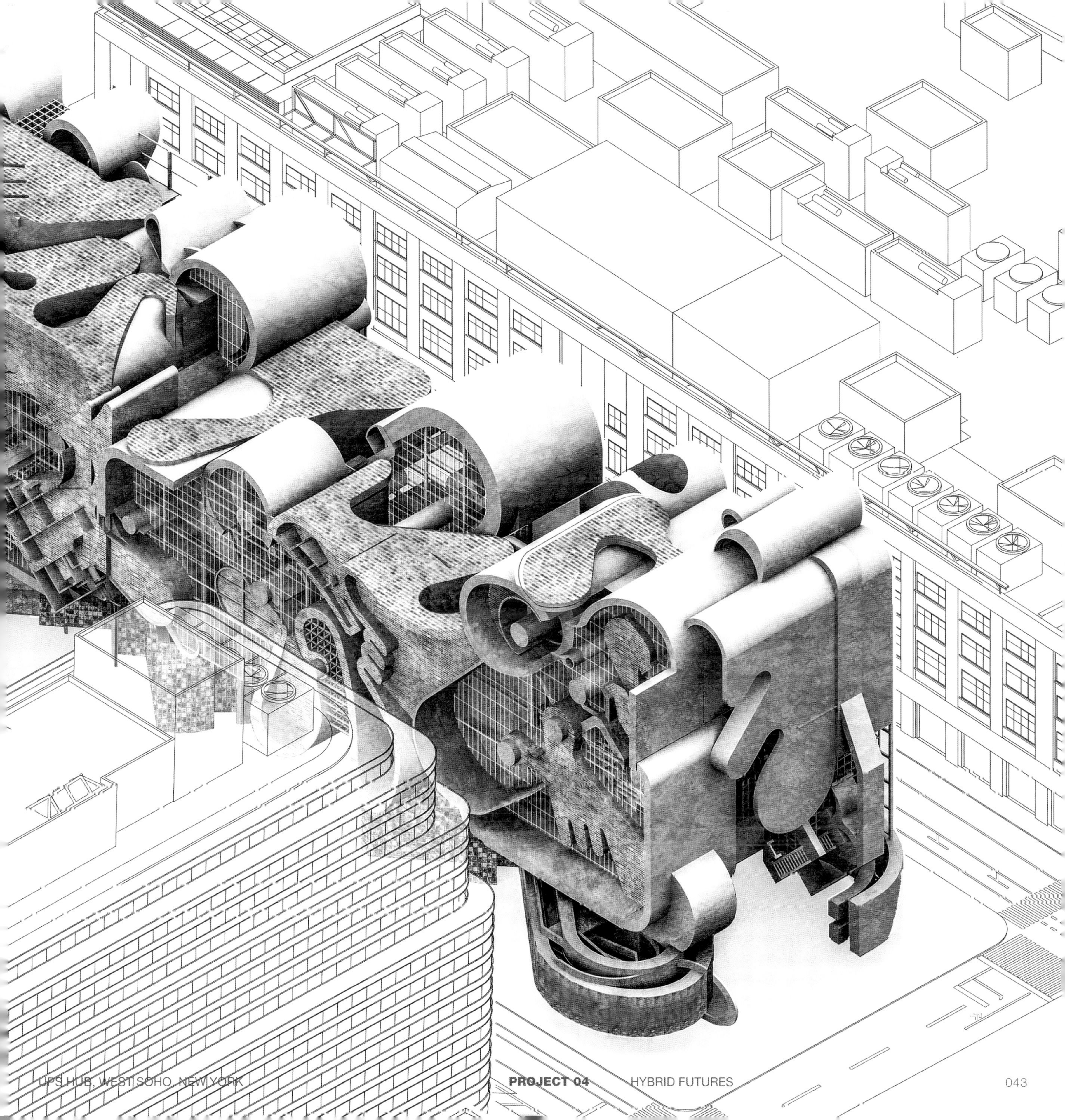

Elevation Rendering

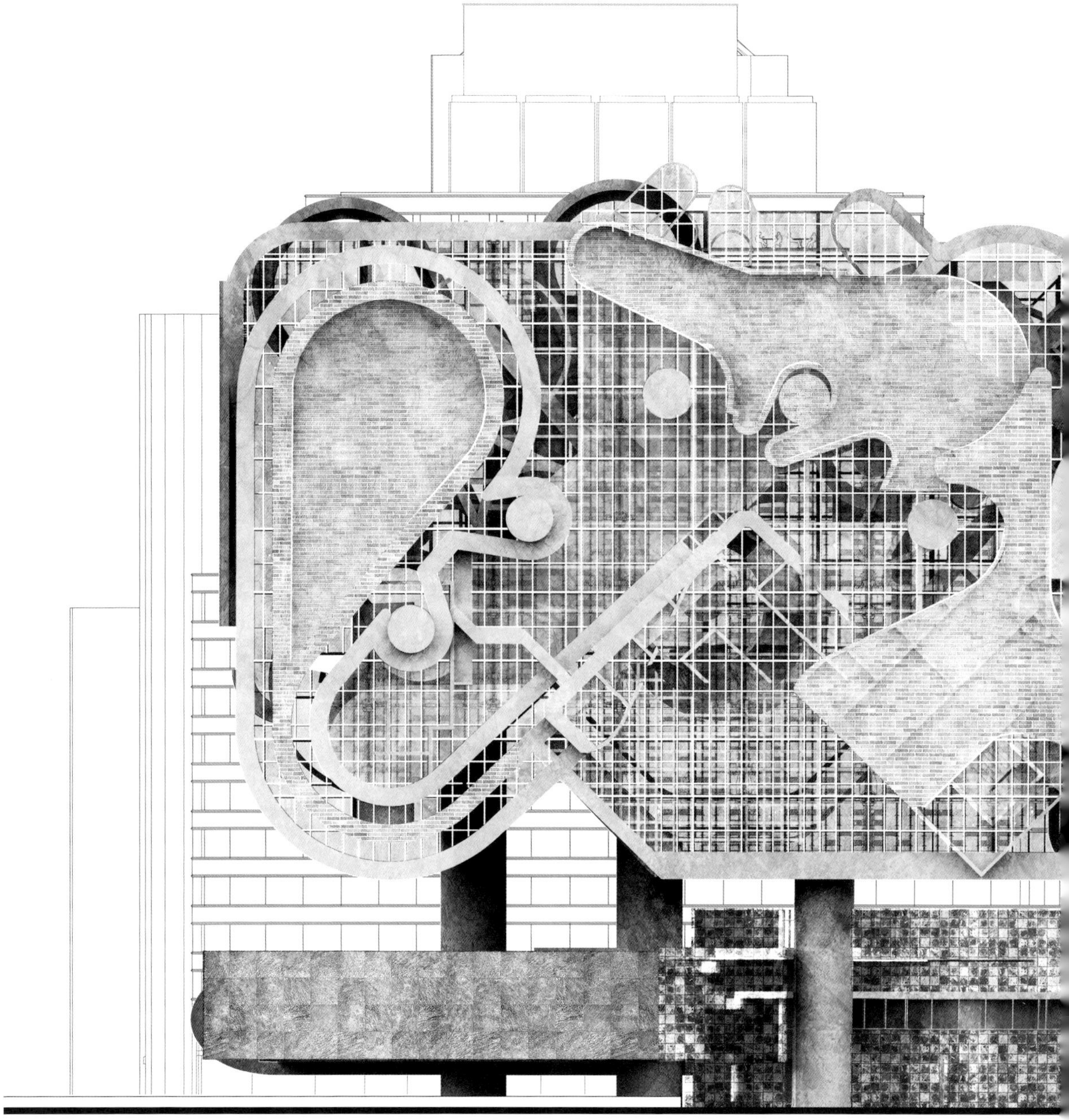

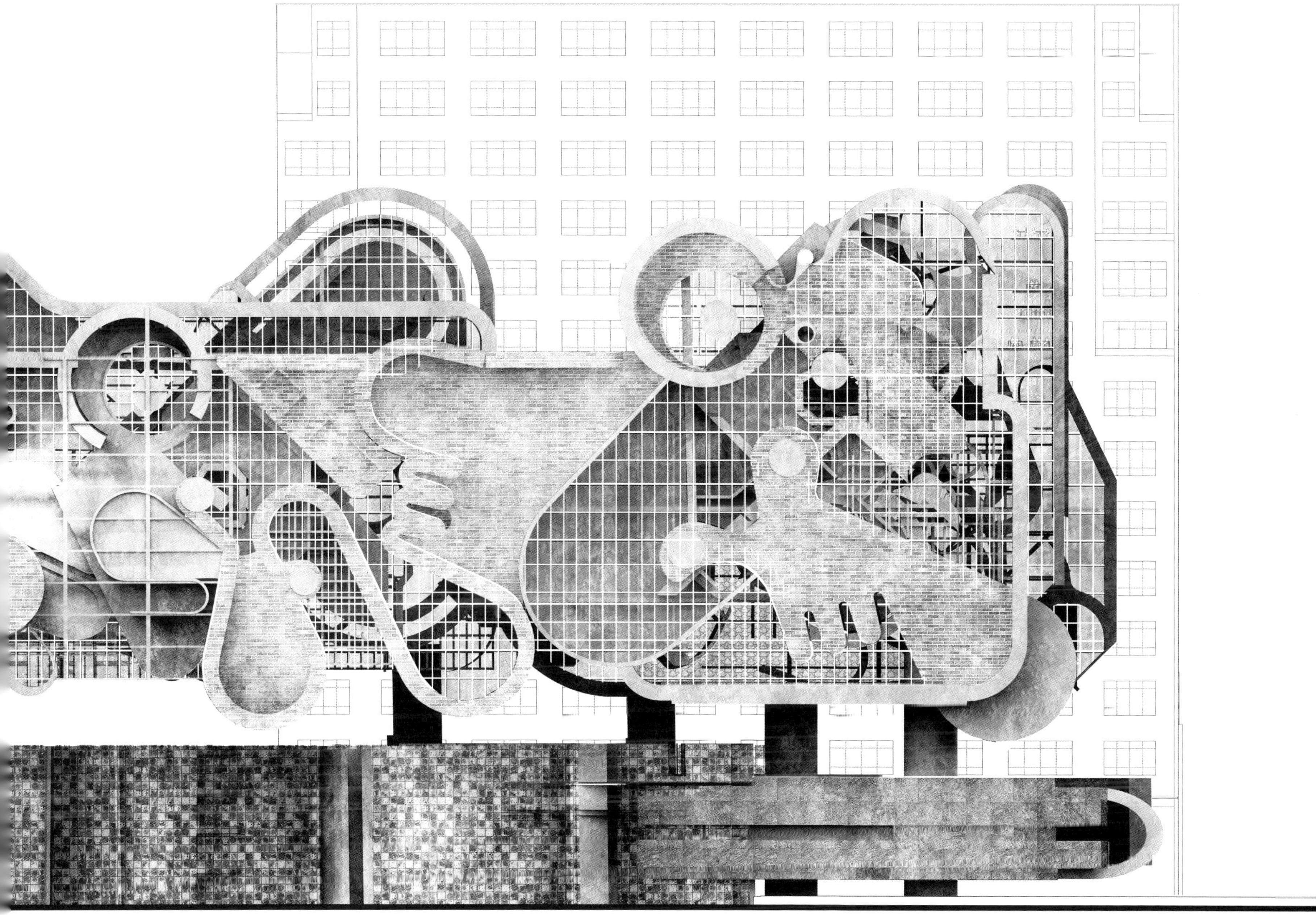

Right: Short Building Section

Left: Typical Floor Plan

01 Elevator
02 Meeting Area
03 Offices
04 Package Storage
05 Emergency Stairs
06 Lounge
07 Stair
08 Lobby

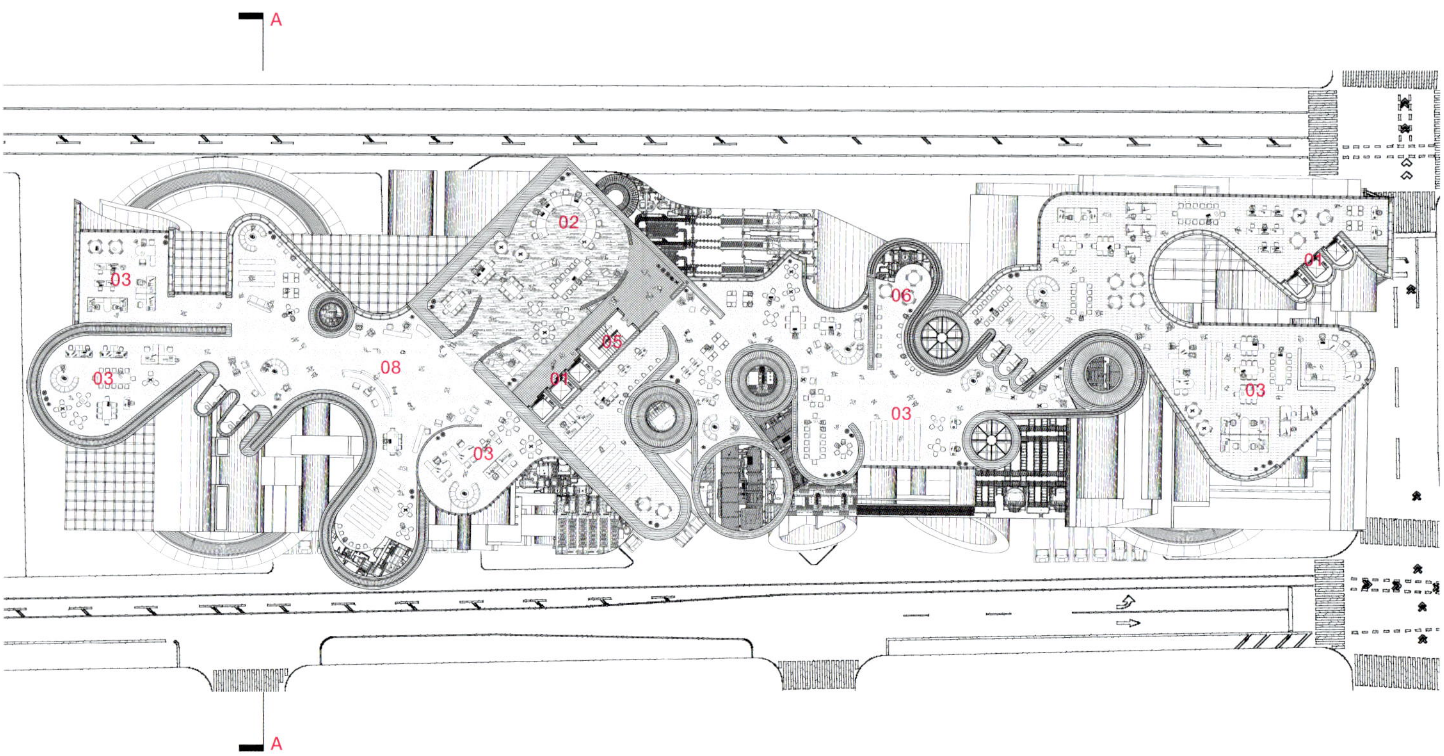

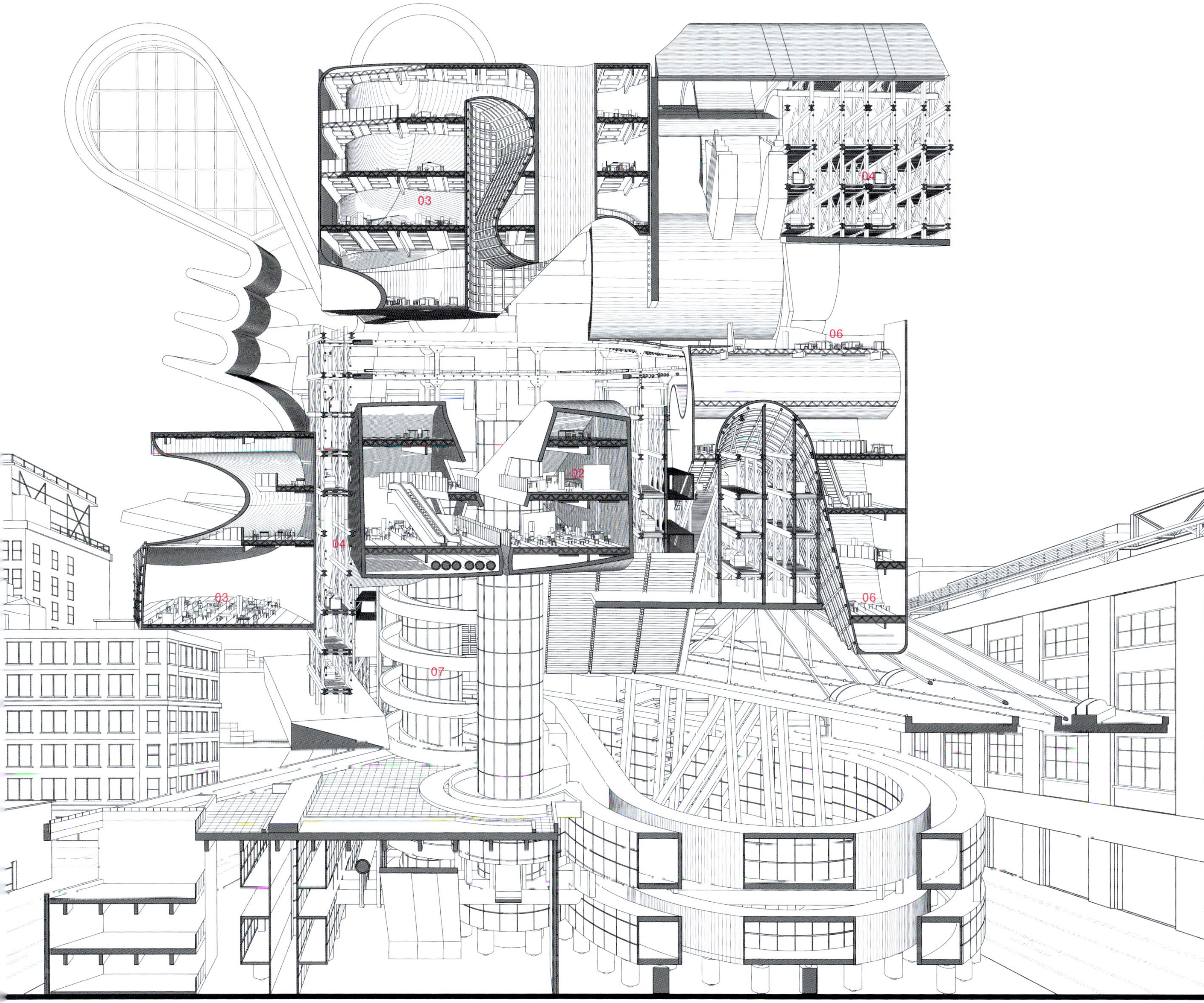

A

A

Right: Physical Section Model, 2'x2'x2', 3D Printed PLA

Left: Physical Section Model, 2'x2'x2', 3D Printed PLA

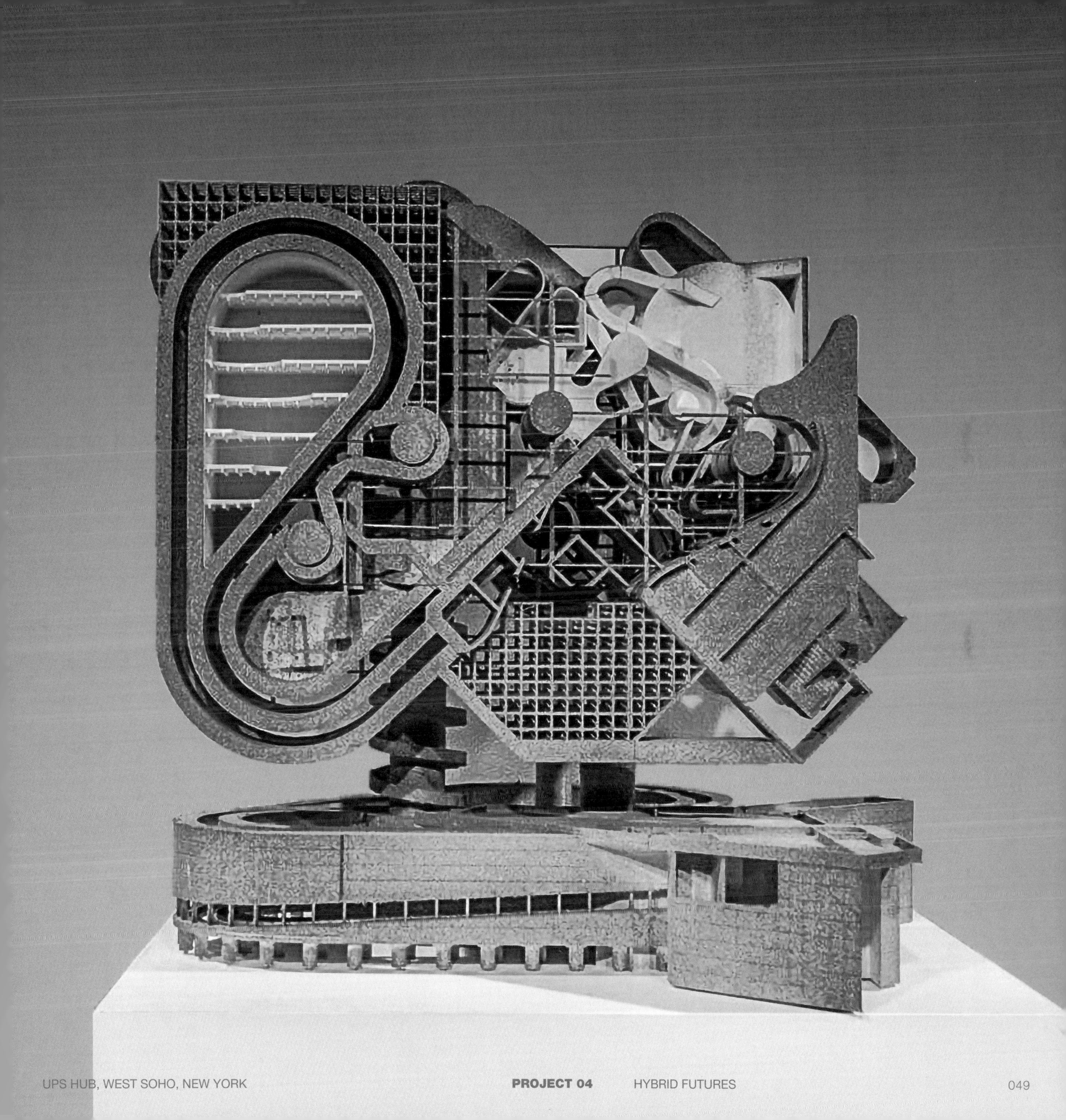

01 THE RELEVANT OFFICE

Verda Alexander

As a climate activist, I've been thinking more and more about adaptation and resilience as I get less and less hopeful about our future. Okay, this essay is not going to be a downer, but we've got to face the fact that we are probably not going to hit our best-case scenario targets for limiting global warming and may well blow past them by a lot. Our world will be a more challenging place to live in the not-so-distant future. As a society, we must not only continue to look for ways to lessen the impact of the climate crisis—and ultimately solve it!—but in the meantime, we will have to learn how to adapt to a more uncertain, hotter, and more volatile planet. We may think it's the job of government agencies and urban planners to button down our cities against sea level rise and heat waves and hurricanes, but we will experience these things as individuals, and it's as individuals (and businesses) that we need to work on our resilience.

The Intergovernmental Panel on Climate Change (IPCC) defines resilience as the capacity of a community, business, or natural environment to prevent, withstand, respond to, and recover from a disruption.

The pandemic was just such a disruption, and the restaurants that survived (to take one high profile industry) were those that quickly implemented take-out services or discovered the fine dining potential of their sidewalks and parking spaces (Fig. 01). It was amazing how quickly we all adjusted to eating with cars zipping by and passing pedestrians checking out our plates. Some of us now prefer al fresco dining, traffic jams included. Restauranteurs will be more resilient when the next pandemic arrives.

We who design and work in offices can learn from their example. The thrust of workplace design since the early days of the Herman Miller action office has been to make it more flexible, more adaptive, more responsive to each user's needs. And that approach changed the office radically over the last one hundred years. But ever since the pandemic sent everyone home, our "workplace" has turned upside down. We are about to see how resilient we truly are as a new hybrid work culture takes root.

Several years ago, I started to look at O+A's corporate office projects through a more critical lens, particularly the amenities and amenity spaces we so painstakingly worked to include in our designs. A well-designed office must have a variety of spaces to work in, but does it really need a video gaming room or ping pong tables or five beers on tap with an artisanal barista in the cafeteria? It's these over-the-top extravagant spaces that I had issue with. In part because I knew these were spaces for the corporate 1%, and very few people had access to such lavish accommodations. We were designing fancy amenities to make people feel good about coming to work, love their companies, and find meaning in the work they were doing. Anyway, that's what we told ourselves. But weren't we also designing space to get them to stay on the job and creating a lot of unnecessary construction and waste in the process? At the time I was reading Cal Newport's *Deep Work*, and I was convinced

01 Outdoor dining on St. Marks Place in Manhattan, 2020. Photography by edenpictures
02 Goldman Sachs building illuminated during Hurricane Sandy, 2012. Photography by erin m

that a more austere, get-down-to-business environment was the real answer to creating collaborative, functional, comfortable workplaces.

The pandemic exposed how quickly our model of the typical office was becoming obsolete. "Work from home" may be delivering mixed business results, but it's been unquestionably popular among employees, and companies competing for talent have little choice but to offer some form of it. This raises some fundamental questions like what do we need the office for now? What is its greatest and best purpose? What's the best place to do heads down work, to collaborate, to build community? How do we justify building new spaces for people to commute to? The mystery of the Great Resignation that hit almost every industry during the pandemic was not why it happened, but whether it represented a temporary or lasting redefinition of work. Would people go back to the old work/life imbalance when the immediate crisis passed, or would they insist on personal fulfillment as a job requirement? I think building resilience and adaptation into our work environments can improve the work experience and increase happiness at work and in life.

And the same holds true for sustainable design. Designing for environmental sustainability, which I believe is a moral imperative, inevitably results in a resilient workplace.

Resilient design addresses future challenges before they become full-blown emergencies. For example, because of climate change, dwindling biodiversity and increasing global population, we know that there will be another pandemic someday. Regionally, here in the Western U.S., extreme drought and heat are already an issue, and we know in the near term they will only get worse. Drought brings more susceptibility to floods, energy disruptions, poor air quality during fire season, and food scarcity. Resilient design must anticipate it all.

One strategy is to design for flexibility. The glut of underutilized and unneeded office space on the market gives designers and planners an opportunity to experiment with mixed-use scenarios, where some floors are repurposed (and more to the point, rezoned) for housing or retail. While local governments may be reluctant to trim lucratively taxable commercial zones, there are few things more destructive to a city's economic welfare than blocks of boarded up storefronts and empty office towers. What if part of a company's office could open up to the community? The extra space could serve as flex space in times of need—a resiliency hub. An office built for resiliency would have systems for redundancy and be equipped with solar micro grids and battery powered generators. Opened up to the public in times of need, these vital spaces could provide air-conditioned oases on days when the power grid fails. In Canada's heat wave of 2021, 595 people died from heat related causes. This amenity could mean the difference between life and death for vulnerable members of the community.

When Hurricane Sandy plunged lower Manhattan into darkness in 2012, the Goldman Sachs building famously remained illuminated (Fig. 02). They caught a lot of flak for it, because hospitals and other essential services did not have the resources of a rich investment firm to keep generators operating through the night. But the incident demonstrated the importance of preplanning in a time of extraordinary climate disruptions and even pointed the way to better corporate citizenship. What if Goldman had opened their bright, warm, and dry space to those in need that night?

In California we are learning to live with poor air quality during fire season which now stretches over many months. Even with air purifiers in every room, keeping the smoke from seeping into our drafty homes is next to impossible. Efficient buildings could better provide sealed spaces with filtered air. Parents would flock to a space where they and their children could breathe fresh air even for an hour or two, and asthma sufferers would have a place of respite. Companies are trying to create a sense of purpose for their employees. Committing resources to the greater community in a time of need would be just such an impactful purpose.

Biophilia is another facet of resilient design with lots of promise. We know it improves air quality, but what if indoor office planting could also address food scarcity? Breakthroughs are happening in intensive vertical farming. The plants creating a visual barrier between you and your neighbor might soon not only filter the air but supply some of the food for your office cafeteria. A Japanese document management firm, Kyocera, surrounds its buildings with "green curtains" of edible plants The purpose is twofold: first to reduce energy consumption by reducing use of air conditioning and second to provide harvestable herbs, fruits, and vegetables for the building's cafeterias. Kyocera's success with this program—they share crops and seedlings with employees—kicked off a green curtain trend nationally, and over 80% of cities in Japan have implemented green

03, 04 "The Water Cooler" installation for Salone del Mobile, Studio O+A, Milan, 2017. Photography by Studio O+A

curtains. How far could this trend go? There's a lot of acreage on building rooftops. What if the top button in every high-rise elevator was FARM?

Rainwater capture is another system that could become a part of every office, with each building devoting a small amount of its estate and infrastructure to capturing rainwater and storing it. In April 2022 the Pacific Institute issued a report titled "The Untapped Potential of California's Urban Water Supply: Water Efficiency, Water Reuse and Stormwater Capture." The report asserts that water reuse and capture efforts combined could be enough to replenish California's aquifers. Several cities in the state are currently looking at how to adapt their infrastructure to capture run off. What if company headquarters and their host cities joined forces in this effort?

Water conservation in the context of a work setting was our theme several years back when O+A was invited by the Italian government to participate in a vision for the Future of Work that would be shown at the furniture fair, Salone del Mobile, in Milan. It was the first time I thought about resilience as a design value. In this case I was projecting out many decades, in the face of extreme environmental collapse, and so my design team began with a dystopian assumption of the future—a scarcity so severe that water had become a precious resource. From that dire starting point, we crafted a positive outcome, and in our design for resilience we transformed the systems for collecting and reusing water. Water containers became translucent walls dividing the work area, and at the center of the space a meditative pool was the anchor. We channeled resourcefulness and saving into a message that would indelibly bind us humans to Earth and created a workplace bringing employees together for that purpose. Water became a metaphor for meditative states, for healing and restoration. The analogy of water as life with its ability to cleanse, nourish, and renew brought those elements into the workspace. It was a place of connection and community, and so we called it "The Water Cooler." As in the office of old—ours was symbolically a place to gather. It's the first time we took on a challenge with a climate message or environmental warning woven into ideas about the future of work (Figs. 03-04).

Rebecca Solnit coined the phrase disaster collectivism: "the sense of immersion in the moment and solidarity with others caused by the rupture in everyday life, an emotion graver than happiness but deeply positive." I think there is opportunity to build community and solidarity around preparation for disaster as well. Right now, when work has lost some of its luster and we are trying to find meaning in a divided world that gets more frightening by the day, our places of work can provide sanctuary while reinforcing a sense of purpose, hope, and safety.

In an article I wrote for *Fast Company* in 2019 I argued that we need more friction in our workplace: "Life is enriched by challenges. To face adversity, to labor is to be human. It's how we find meaning in the world, how we learn and grow. Friction gives us the ability to slow down, to focus, and to steer our attention where we want it to go." Resilience seems to me another product of friction. It's a measure of our fortitude, our capacity for preparedness, and our ability to withstand challenges. It is how we face adversity and thrive.

In 2019 in the midst of experiencing (along with 39 million other Californians) the third year in a row of wildfires, I would have done anything to escape the months of thick, smoky air. It was then that I shifted my work as a designer to tackling the problems of climate change.

I realized whatever design problems I might solve for clients now, the more urgent task ahead was how to keep their workplaces habitable, functional, healthy, and relevant in a problematic future—how to help them build resilience. It's one thing to recognize wildfires as an annual threat. Quite another to plan for how you keep breathing.

02 WORKING FROM HOME[1]

Peter Cappelli and Ranya Nehmeh

Traditionally, workplace design has been focused on physical space rather than the people who would inhabit it (a company's employees). "The office" has been a fixture for centuries now, starting with government and religious administrative buildings and then growing in size and significance with corporations and expansions in service work. It is not only where work gets done but is also the center of work-related intrigue and office politics as well as public failures and successes. It is a source for novels, movies, and of course the eponymous TV show. But, since 2020, the way we perceive the office and what gets done there has been forever altered.

The 2020 COVID-19 pandemic was to date the singular global event of the 21st century. In terms of its global impact across a wide range of sections of society, little else comes close. Since it burst on the scene in February 2020, more than half a billion people have contracted the disease, six million people have died, and millions more have been seriously or debilitatingly ill.

Surprisingly, though, office life continued with fewer dislocations than many expected, in part because of the ability to work remotely. In the U.S., Census estimates suggest that 30 percent of employees were working from home during the early pandemic period, and a Pew Foundation study indicates that 70 percent of those for whom it was feasible to work from home did.

As the most debilitating effects of the virus erode with the introduction of vaccines and some variety of herd immunity, many countries face decisions about what to do next and how to manage moving forward. Considering previous pandemics, societies generally returned to very similar practices and behaviors when infections declined. However, when it comes to the future of offices, the most obvious question is how to manage remote work: should it remain, go back to pre-pandemic norms, or something in between?

Having been away from offices for two years, will workers simply return to them, will they stay away, or will they do something different? Examples from the past shown below suggest that workers will return to work the way they knew it before. However, the reason circumstances may be different now is because remote work appears to have been a success, or, at the very least, much more effective than skeptics anticipated. Employers routinely said as much, especially to shareholders. This is clearly a victory for the Theory Y view of human nature, that employees do not have to be monitored and will not shirk if they are not watched. So, if it seemed to work for employers and employees alike, expanding remote work would seem imminent.

Office work has the chance to be the target of the biggest change from the pandemic. The experiment seemed to succeed, and employees want more opportunities for remote work; so, now the burden has shifted to employers who want to defend a return to the office. In this sense, it would be surprising if companies went back to the old ways. It would be even more surprising if there was a return to the same cold, traditional office spaces that did not reflect what employees have been through over the last two years. Employers are scrambling to deal with the rising trend of humanizing the workplace, which emphasizes redesigning employee experiences to ensure that they can attract, motivate, and retain talent by adapting to employees' changing needs and accommodating a more human-centered office design. Below we identify key issues at play in managing the return and reconfiguring remote work as well as instructive examples of remote work implementation in the past in order to sketch out the horizon of where workplace dynamics are now and where they are going. Throughout, we punctuate with first-person accounts of pandemic work experiences and management techniques among a selection of white-collar workers from different backgrounds.

KEY ISSUES

Despite general declines and fluctuations over the last few decades, companies spend huge amounts of money on offices, in part to show off with corporate campuses, towering buildings, and individual suites to convey prestige. A lot of time and money goes into designs that encourage performance—everything from breakout rooms, interior designs to facilitate collaboration, quiet rooms for individual tasks, and much more. Office real estate is a $1.7 trillion industry that supports $600 billion in the construction industry, which says nothing about all the ancillary businesses that support offices and office workers—what happens to all of those restaurants, gyms, and retail if workers continue to have lunch in their own kitchens?

Office work also has a huge impact on transportation. Many people see remote work as a way to cut down on driving and its associated pollution. Recent evidence suggests, however, that working from home does not cut total driving down as much as one might think, as we tend to drive more when we are home for errands that we might have run during lunch or during office commutes. But, working from home makes it much easier to balance conflicts between the requirements of family and home life, at least in part because the two worlds are physically close together now. Not having a physical space to go to outside of the home has effects on social and mental well-being. Twenty-two percent of married couples reported in recent years that they met and started dating at their offices.[2] If people are not at the office anymore, will this mean more social isolation? Indeed, after two years of pandemic, an epidemic of loneliness emerged among remote workers.

While many employees seem to like at least some level of ability to work from home better than full-time work in an office, employees are not uniform their views. Some want to go back to the office, some want to never go back and to relocate away from their current homes, whose main advantage was proximity to work. Employees want lots of things that they never get, however, and especially in the U.S., they have a small degree of leverage. In this case, what happens will reflect varying individual choices and top-level employer decisions.

REMOTE WORK, THEN AND NOW

These economic, societal, and psychological issues all have their pros and cons, so the history of remote work is illustrative. It is important to remember that "work-from-home" began as a cost-cutting wave aimed at improving shareholder value a generation ago. New accounting practices demonstrated how much capital had been tied up in unproductive offices, warehouses, and other locations. The size of a typical office shrank by about one-third between the 1970s and the early 2010s.[3] Companies also redesigned their office spaces to make them more standardized and modular, making downsizing quicker and cheaper.[4]

A more dramatic approach was to get rid of offices altogether. IBM claimed to have cut real estate costs by 75% in one division by cutting the offices of consulting employees and having them telecommute. They further claimed to have 40% of their employees working remotely and that they were saving $100 million in real estate costs as a result.[5] Other employers cut offices as well, especially for staff who dealt with clients elsewhere. AT&T moved 10,000 account executives to virtual status, taking back their offices, for example.[6]

When it was impossible to get rid of an office, employers still found ways to cut space for those who required office space on a temporary basis. This was the move to "hoteling," the concept of temporary offices for employees modeled after guest rooms in a hotel. The idea of "sharing" an office seemed haphazard, so, instead, employees were able to "reserve" a space when they were in town. In Europe, this became known as "hot-desking;" an employee who needed to come in could have a temporary office or desk space. Ernst & Young were early pioneers of this concept in 1993 with their consultancy office in New York. One problem with this approach, noted by most observers, is the simple supply chain challenge: if all the virtual employees show up at the same time, there will not be enough desks. The high-water mark, though, for hoteling and remote work was the Chiat advertising agency, where Jay Chiat believed that the physical structure of the office was both unnecessary and stifling to creativity. He gave all employees laptops and cell phones and told them that they could work virtually, wherever and whenever they wanted (Figs. 01-02). Then he created an extreme version of an open office with no private space, lockers where employees could store personal items, and clusters of couches and tables in place of desks. While critics loved it, employees did not. When the agency was sold, the new owners brought back offices for the executives, added a desk and landline phone for each employee, and tried to create an environment to get people to stay in the office.[7]

Interest in cutting office space did not abate, but concerted efforts stopped accelerating in the 2000s and 2010s. In 2020, the pandemic brought remote work back to life due to public health restrictions that required office workers to stay home. Initially, some companies struggled to figure out how to organize and coordinate, but eventually the new reality of full-time remote work was more effective than expected. As we describe below, remote work became much longer-lived—so much so that for many it became a new normal. The open question now is how much remote working for office workers will persist? Will it slide back, and if so for whom?

The primary argument as to why remote work may persist at present seems most strongly tied to the fact that many employees prefer it, or at least prefer a "hybrid" model, which in practice means something less than losing your office and never returning. Given this key factor, we believe it is important to develop a richer sense of worker experience than simple survey preferences.

To get a sense of the work-from-home experience of the pandemic, we share the first-person perspectives of several white-collar employees in different roles at different organizations. All of them were required to work from home. We begin with their initial transition:

The VP: *"Unless you were an entrepreneur or working in a creative industry, the 9 – 5 office job seemed like the norm to me. I never considered there was any other way of working. During my 15-year professional career, I was always used to*

01, 02 Chiat/Day Advertising Agency interior design, Gaetano Pesce, New York, 1995.
Photography by Donatella Brun, Courtesy of Gaetano Pesce office

setting my alarm, commuting for thirty minutes to the office, working a full day, and back at home by 6 p.m.

"The first day we had to work from home, there was a general confusion, not just for me but the whole office. I spent that first morning using the instructions that our IT team had emailed everyone on how to login to our virtual desktop and what Apps to download to be able to receive office calls. On the one hand, it was fun, well, because I was literally on my couch, in pajamas in the middle of the day, a completely new experience for my professional career, but, on the other hand, it just seemed impossible that we were going to get any work done that way."

We can see in this account the lack of structure that leaving the office created for many people.

The HR Professional: *"Our decision-making process is extremely cumbersome, usually taking weeks even months to approve a policy or procedures. Usually, our HR team drafts the policy, which is then submitted to Management for their review and feedback, before it is approved by the President. Yet, when the pandemic hit, the remote working policy was drafted in the morning, approved in the afternoon, and communicated to all employees by the evening. They managed to do all the steps in a matter of hours. It was the quickest decision ever made in our company, and a clear indication that when things needed to move fast, the Management was capable of doing so."*

This example shows how organizations can adapt and move quickly and raises the question about what they learned from it, whether it will mean a different pace and way of operating going forward. We return to that issue below.

The Consultant: *"Years of being a consultant, and travelling the world to work with different clients, always being on the go, has made me more attached to the stability of being in an office. I like to see our employees, chat with them, brainstorm; this collectiveness as a team is what gives us energy and also leads to the successful completion of our projects. We have always had a solid and robust IT structure in place. We employ mostly consultants who are used to working out of the office, usually in client offices. Being connected off-site is part of their normal ways of working. We were therefore not concerned about how to get all our employees up and running effectively with the right IT tools. Our main concern was to ensure business continuity and that the level of productivity would be maintained."*

This example reminds us that not everyone was in the office before the pandemic. Many people were working partially out of the office before the pandemic. Pew Research Center polls indicate that as many as 20% percent of regular employees in the U.S. were at least occasionally working from home before the pandemic.[8] We also see here that the limited time they were together in the office was even more important as a result.

The Banker Turned Start-Up Employee: *"I converted over a decade ago from being a banker in a traditional sector, a typical 9-to-5 job with all the perks and benefits one could want, to joining the startup world. I had desperately needed a challenge to get out of my stable comfort zone. Since then, I have worked for three startups. They have a much more flexible approach to working, which was a positive development from my previous job. Instead of creating the work and home boundaries like in my banking role, here it was all integrated. Between this mode of working and almost never having to wear suits again, I got hooked to the startup world."*

It is important to remember that the notion of flexibility at work was already significant to many people long before remote working became popularized, as a result of the COVID-19 pandemic.

EVALUATING REMOTE WORK

Because of experiments with remote work by some companies in the 1990s, there are a fair number of studies as to how it worked out. The simplest effects to measure are those for employees: What happens to the person working remotely and their performance? With respect to life outside of work, the answer is that it probably improved, but that is complicated to assess because, in most cases, they were choosing to work from home, so it would be surprising if those who chose to do it did not like it better. On the career outcome side, the conclusion of the vast literature on these employees was, in summary, "not good."[9] They seemed to be worse off in many dimensions associated with their jobs. It was also challenging for supervisors and coworkers to navigate and make successful.[10]

The explanation for these outcomes is, arguably, not so much remote work as such but the fact that other employees and possible competitors were in the office on a permanent basis. This was not the case in the pandemic, where entire offices went remote. An important conclusion, therefore, is that the pandemic experience does not reveal much about what remote work will be like when companies are not forced into it.

Research in economics regarding organizational performance, as opposed to a focus on individuals, suggests much more positive outcomes. The most carefully done studies show improvements in productivity. The caveat is that the jobs in question, such as patent attorneys and call center employees, were individual contributor roles that did not require interaction with other employees. Additionally, they do not offer insight into longer-term implications of remote work, which are especially important because studies of individuals show that remote work leads to higher rates of quitting.

There is no doubt that most all surveys show that a majority of employees liked remote working during the pandemic; however, how much of that is because they were glad to still have a job and a pay check is hard to know. Many employees had already been furloughed or actually laid-off, others wondered whether they would be, and few people wanted to be exposed to infection in crowded offices or commutes. This, though, still does not explain why they would want to continue working remotely after the pandemic, of course. As the VP highlighted:

"I can't say the first few days of working from home were easy or productive, we were all just figuring out how we should communicate with each other. Everything started to blend in together: very late start to the morning followed by no lunch breaks, often working late into the evenings and no exercise, which was very important to me. The structure was lacking, the day started to become a blur. I also noticed that my eating and sleeping habits became very irregular."

It is no surprise that offering choices to work remotely is desirable, as there are always benefits to having options: those who do not want to do something do not have to. But we really do not know why they liked working from home. There is often an assumption that it is simply because it cuts commuting time, but in some cases, they are working more hours, so the assumption that not commuting—which is not a burden for everyone—just makes for more free time is not necessarily true.

A critical insight here is that employees reported that they felt better about their supervisors and employers during this period. Not commuting is unlikely to be a cause. Many other things changed during the pandemic—the sense that workers were all in the same boat of having to work from home; that they were trying to keep their employers and, in some cases, society afloat; perhaps especially that employers trusted employees more to get their work done when and how they chose. Some of these developments cannot be replicated, some of them could be replicated in the office, and some could be ruined even with remote work. The introduction of "tattleware," software that monitors what employees are doing when they work, is an example of the latter, something that became increasingly popular with employers as remote work continued.

The experience of remote work depends on how it is organized. To get a sense of that, we turn back to our case interviews. A central issue here has to do with how employees managed their own workspace.

The Banker Turned Start-up Employee: *"Three months after starting my new job, the pandemic hit. During the first week, I was patiently listening to all my friends, who were transitioning to the home office in complete shock and frustration. To me it made no difference at all to my work. Not only had I been working flexibly for the last decade, but specifically in the last months I hadn't even had an office to go to at all. My current company operates as a fully distributed one, which means there is no headquarters, or office, over 500 employees working globally across time zones. What all my friends were experiencing in terms of learning how to operate in these new, remote, flexible ways, I had already been privy to for the last years.*

"My office at home is fully equipped. After leaving banking and joining my first start up, I had already bought myself proper office furniture and equipment. The current company provides new joiners with a home office stipend for a one-time purchase to re-create a constructive office environment at home. I used that to upgrade my ergonomic chair and purchase better quality web cams and other technology items. My home office is a No Zone for my children; the only boundary that I have created is to physically close the door of that room by the end of the day to create a distance where work ends, and family starts. Perhaps because I had spent a decade in an office, clicking my time attendance in and out, my mind still worked by compartmentalizing different parts of my life."

The VP: *"After the first week, my supervisor instituted daily morning video calls for our team. This meant we had to be dressed and ready to be productive by that time. These calls helped to create structure to the day. I went back to setting an alarm and the 30-minute morning commute was replaced by a 30-minute workout. Most of our meetings were scheduled in the mornings or early afternoon, so I started to take my lunch breaks at the same time as if I was in the office and would shut down my computer at the latest by 6 p.m."*

"By the end of the second week, my productivity levels had vastly increased. Unnecessary meetings that would have taken hours were no longer happening, neither were pointless calls or other distractions. The main challenge I had was creating an office space. I didn't have a spare room and spending the day working from my kitchen counter or working with my laptop in bed was not ideal, so I carved myself a small space in the corner of my living room. I added a small table facing my terrace so I could overlook an open space and the outdoors with a plant in the corner of the table, some pads and pens to use when on calls, a water bottle, and a small rubbish bin under the table. Without realizing, I had placed everything in the same way as it was in my office. Carving out a space to work helped to create a boundary of what was my office space and what was my living space. That was necessary; otherwise, as I experienced in the first week, there was too much of an overlap, and consequently, I neither felt productive by day nor relaxed by night."

The Consultant: *"During the pandemic, I was still going into the office occasionally. It's not that I prescribe to the notion that when you work from home, you are not working, but I just don't believe you are working as hard or as effectively because there are so many distractions. In the office, I see my employees, I see who is present, I hear the discussions taking place, I know what everyone is working on. If I have a question, I pop round and get an immediate answer; I don't need to wait for a call back or an email. It is my responsibility as part of the senior management team to ensure that our efficiency does not suffer, and consequently, this requires a certain level of employee work monitoring. On a different note, I can't assess employee morale or the general vibe of the office from behind the screen; this is only something I can gauge in person."*

The HR Professional: *"At home, I have a spare room, which has always been used by either my husband or myself as an occasional office, but during the remote working period, it became my personal office space. My husband preferred working in other parts of the flat. Being a visual person, I printed out working from home tips and stuck those on a board in front of me, along with a list of projects I had to complete and deadlines. I printed out personal photos that always gave me joy to look at of my family, the sea, close friends, nature, adventures. It was important to make this room into a warm, comfortable, cozy, colorful, and lively space, very much in line with my personality. Surprisingly, this was opposite to my actual office setup, which was cold, plain, sterile, paperless, with no pictures anywhere. I had consciously created a boundary between work and home."*

In short, we see employees and their organizations settling into new routines, and different people, perhaps based on their backgrounds, have different comfort levels doing so.

Managing space at home seems to be a major concern for everyone. While we notice the importance for some in personalizing their space, for others it provides structure and helps to create a clearer work/life boundary. The need for humanizing the workspace is therefore becoming pertinent for employers. The above example of our HR Professional highlights the difficulty of creating a physical boundary between where work ends and life begins: *"In the office I had never added any personal touches to my desk, I had created a clear boundary where my work-self ended and my private-self started, whereas, in my home office, I had treated it as an extension of myself,"* she had commented. If employers want their employees back in the office, they have to do their best to cater to these changing needs and perspectives, one of them being a work space that encourages collaboration and communication, builds comradery, and creates more in-person dialogue.

This would adhere to the concept of "neighborhood offices" which consist of more informal meeting areas, breakout spaces, and relaxation spaces as well as less boardroom-type spaces or the "death of the boardroom" shift. Furthermore, with employee well-being as well as diversity and inclusion initiatives rising to the top of employers' agendas, workplace design can severely impact employee happiness and feelings of belonging in the workplace. While studies have not fully confirmed this yet, recent research suggests an initial linkage between a more humanized workplace and positive employee engagement and job satisfaction.

REMOTE WORK, MOVING FORWARD

Both employees and employers seemed reasonably comfortable with new remote arrangements during the COVID-19 pandemic. By 2022, when effective vaccines were readily available in Western countries, it was no longer necessary or required to work from home for public health reasons. These circumstances created a conundrum: there was no urgent reason to stay remote, and there was also no urgent reason to return to in-person work.

"The distributed workforce is the future. The technological advances of the last decade and the collective mind-shift of remote working over the last two years have shown us that work can be experienced in different ways. With this new way of working and its promise to make us happier, healthier, and feeling more alive, while still growing in our careers, I just don't think any company can un-see this anymore, and if they do, they will be the real losers."

Silicon Valley companies tried to monetize work from home outright. After telling employees that they could work remotely on a permanent basis, they then imposed a cost: employees would have to be paid less to do so, as much as 20 percent less. One explanation for this practice is that these employers offered it anticipating that their competitors would do the same. When they discovered that was not the case, rather than just walking back the offer, they priced it at an uncompetitive level. A recent survey of employers found that a majority who offered remote work options felt that it was saving them money by allowing them to hire more cheaply and retain more employees.[11] Whether the market will settle down in some way, allow employers to offer it or not, and create competitive advantages in the job market, remains to be seen.

Another issue is whether technology or our ability to use it has improved enough to compete with the efficiency of face-to-face interactions. Although companies clearly improved their use of technology over the shutdown period, the fact that time spent in meetings—not just in communications—appears to have increased and that companies have implemented tattleware monitoring software suggests that they have not found truly better ways to manage remotely. The evidence so far is not encouraging.

A longer-term drawback is evidence from neuroscience on the lack of engagement in the relationship-building aspects of our brain when we are interacting virtually. Real eye contact and proximity is an important factor.[12] Remote workers require more from supervisors as well to ensure that they are up to date on tacit knowledge in the organization that affects their work. Where that extra time will come from given how stretched most supervisors are already is not clear. It is easy to say that they should just specify what outcomes they want from employees and then let them do it from home, but that only works for well-defined individual contributor roles.

An additional factor for employers to consider is the notion of humanizing the office, not just in its physical structures but also to remember the actual employee at the center of this concept. At the end of the day, even with numerous technologies in place, people are working together who have unique characteristics that require interaction and collaboration as well as a degree of recognition to promote engagement and productivity.

A further challenge is how to maintain an equal and fair working model in a hybrid setting based on issues arising from proximity. As our VP highlighted:

"...several employees, mainly females, have felt excluded in this hybrid model because while they have taken advantage of the working from home option, their supervisors have remained in office, so a kind of favoritism bias has developed towards employees who are in office, and who they see more often. Being "out of sight, out of mind" has unfortunately impacted them negatively in terms of annual promotions."

Distance also impedes spontaneous communication, the exchanges of information that happen when a worker crosses paths with a manager in the corridor or in the watercooler. These encounters are great chances for managers to gather feedback regarding a task in which the worker is involved and for workers to make their managers aware of a potential problem they may be encountering (be it personal or with their team members) and that may be the reason for a delay in task execution. The transmission of this information is harder to do

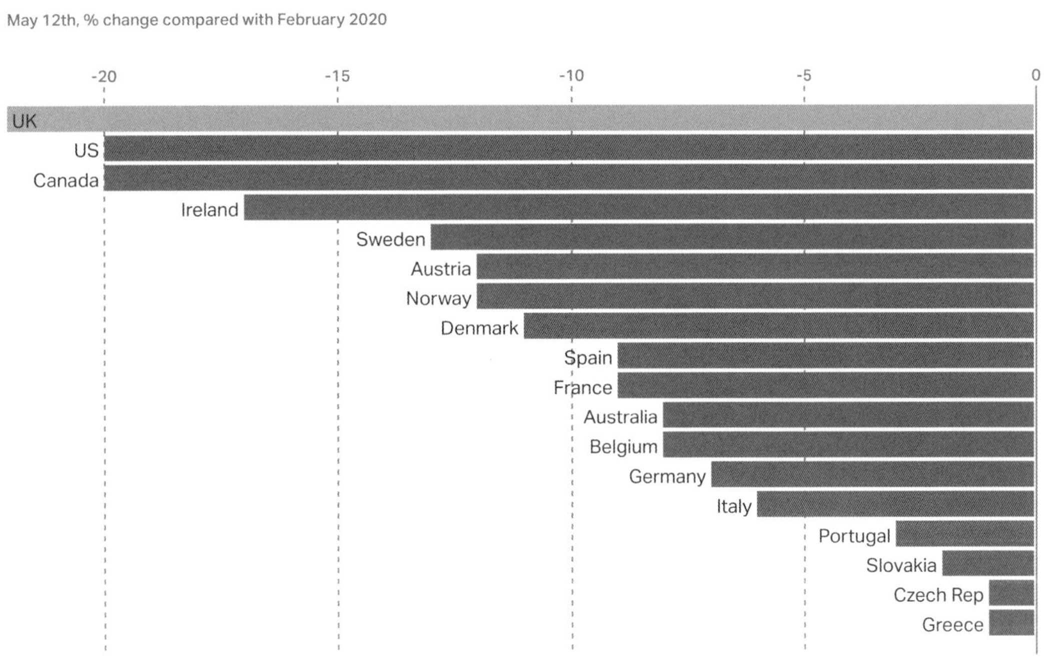

03 Office Occupancy levels in mid-2022 vs. the average level in 2020. Source: Google Mobility Data found in Valentina Romei, "UK Ahead of European Peers on Shift to Working from Home," Financial Times, May 15, 2022.

remotely. It may also be harder for managers to learn about workers' skills, ability, preferences, working styles, and behaviors.

EMPLOYER VS. EMPLOYEE DECISIONS

The implicit view in many news stories is that a move to permanent remote work is more or less inevitable because employees want it. But all employees know that they do not get something just because they want it. Especially in the absence of union power, employers make these decisions unilaterally, and if the practices do not have a payoff, they do not happen. Before deciding how much remote work is sensible, it is important to have answers to the following questions.

First, how well did things actually work when employees were at home. Were there things that they missed? The list to check includes hiring, bringing on new employees, tasks that were not routine, and similar criteria. If the list is short, then it will be difficult not to continue with some remote options.

Second, what did employees like about remote work, and what does the variation look like? Employees with children might very much appreciate the ability to meet their kids at home when school is out, which implies a regular schedule of remote work from their home. Those without kids might appreciate the opportunity to travel and work from new locations, which precludes a regular location and might not require a regular schedule. An issue to consider is how many people will like, and how many will not see any benefit from, the proposals we are considering.

Third, how independent is the work being done by the people who want to work from home? The more independent contributor does, of course, more easily work remotely. The more our work is done in real teams as with projects, the more difficult it is to miss the face-to-face and ready ability of interaction of being in the office.

Fourth, a topic rarely considered is how proximate are the possible remote employees from those who will have to remain on site? As an obvious point, it would be very difficult to have a supervisor work at home when they cannot make direct reports because of perceptions of fairness.

Fifth, a related question is what, if anything, are employers willing to do for those employees who cannot work remotely, if they allow others to do so. If the answer is nothing, it will likely create perceptions of unfairness.

Sixth, how much hiring will a company do, and what are the anticipated rates of turnover? Remote work is much easier to pull off when we have a reasonably tenured workforce as opposed to a steady stream of new hires trying to figure out what to do with few experienced employees around.

Seventh, how can an employer design a physical workspace that caters to the needs of employees and creates a harmonious, comfortable, and community-like environment that helps to break the boundaries between home life and office life?

Eighth, a question related to turnover, how strong is the company work culture? It is hard to establish and maintain a culture without seeing other people. If it is important to the way the organization runs, then face-to-face time is important.

The answers to these questions will determine the best option for in-office and remote work balance. The subject that gets the most attention, but which survey evidence suggests has the least interest among employees, is permanent remote work. The upside for employers is immediate savings: offices for those workers are taken back as are parking spaces, office perks such as cafeterias, and so forth. The downside is less measurable control—those remote employees are akin to independent contractors in that it is difficult to engage them with the rest of the organization on project work, to have them be part of company culture, and so forth. There are successful examples, however; for instance, the U.S. Patent Offices have operated this way with its patent attorneys successfully for some time.

Hybrid models propose everything in between fully back to the office and permanent at home work. The devil is obviously in the details. Hybrid models lose the cost advantage of permanent remote work. Some organizations think they can move to a "hoteling" or "hot-desk" model where hybrid workers only borrow a desk at the office when they need to come in, cutting the need for office space and adding more flexibility. This was a popular idea in the dot-com era, but it largely disappeared because employees disliked it so much. The downsides of hybrid vary. The more control individual employees have over their schedule, the more they arguably like it, but the more complicated it makes management tasks

	Wed 8/10	Wed 8/17	% Change	
Dallas metro	50.4 %	52.0 %	**1.6 %**	▲
Philadelphia metro	38.0 %	37.1 %	**0.9 %**	▼
Houston metro	54.7 %	55.4 %	**0.7 %**	▲
New York metro	38.3 %	37.6 %	**0.7 %**	▼
San Jose metro	34.0 %	34.8 %	**0.7 %**	▲
San Francisco metro	37.8 %	38.4 %	**0.6 %**	▲
Los Angeles metro	43.0 %	43.5 %	**0.5 %**	▲
Austin metro	58.2 %	58.5 %	**0.4 %**	▲
Chicago metro	40.1 %	40.5 %	**0.4 %**	▲
Washington D.C. metro	37.5 %	37.1 %	**0.4 %**	▼

04 Kastle Systems Back to Work Barometer Summer 2022.

such as scheduling. For example, early reports suggest that when meetings are held in which some people are coming in by video, even those in the office go on video, which defeats some of the main reasons for scheduling an in-office meeting and even being in the office altogether.

The problem for employers who think it makes sense to go back to the office permanently, or at least to pull back on the current arrangements, is that most of them have asserted at some point that working from home turned out well. Not continuing with a successful arrangement could be bad business or worse, be perceived as spiteful or ideological. Think: we cannot trust employees in the long term even if we had to in the short term. If that is the case, the return will not go well. The upside for employers is that because many employees like the idea of hybrid arrangements, it is possible that those practices may retain employees or allow employees to be hired at lower wages than they might otherwise demand. But those advantages are relative and go away if other competitors follow.

MANAGING SOME KIND OF RETURN

As of the end of 2022, we see very different approaches to the return to the office question. At the country level, the variance across Western countries is extraordinary. European Union countries, which are thought to be the most sympathetic and supportive to employee demands, have nearly twice as much or more employees in the office than the U.K. and the U.S. (Fig. 03), where employers have more power and employee interests have traditionally received less attention. It is difficult to explain this puzzling pattern.

We also see variance within the U.S. Card swipe data, which indicates that offices are about 43 percent full, which may not sound like much, but they are typically not much above 70 percent—some employees are out on business, others on vacation, out sick, and so forth. But the variance across regions is considerable. Offices in Houston, Texas, are getting closer to typical levels, while New York City offices remain 16 percentage points behind and are not filling up quickly (Fig. 04). It is tempting to see these differences as a Red State (Texas)

vs. Blue State (New York and California) divide, and no doubt state government policy differences played a role, with the Blue States mandating remote work much longer than, for instance, Texas, where they were lifted in 2020.
It would help the transition to acknowledge worker experiences during the pandemic. Spending some structured time in work groups and teams talking about what it was like trying to work from home and what happened to us during the pandemic humanizes the workplace. It is also an opportunity to transition back to work and to talk about what we learned and what we could do differently going forward. Other aspects of a return campaign should include highlighting what employees liked about being in the office—perhaps the social connections, or maybe the food—and to do more of that, especially at the beginning of the return.

To better illustrate these issues, it is helpful to return to what our interviewees experienced in 2022, when the pandemic receded to a slow smolder. Did they keep going remote or bring employees back?

The HR Professional: Their experience anchored one end of the spectrum and was reflected by the fact that the company's leaders continued to go into the office even when it was officially closed:

"After a few months we received notification that all those considered essential staff (30% of the workforce) had to start coming into the office. Soon after, all employees were called back. The minute the world started going back to normal, the company went back to their old ways, the "old normal" as I refer to it. I had held out hope that we would be adopting some kind of hybrid working model, but from one day to the next I was back in the office full time, sitting at my desk, which seemed alien to me, stressing about who would be taking care of my child for the rest of the week, as the daycare hours were still limited. During that time, HR was tasked by Management to come up with a remote working policy, but over the course of the next three months, the proposal was presented several times to Management, and each time, there were more questions, revisions, and obstacles, so we were back to square one; slow decision-making, with no approved flexible working policy. Long gone was the quick decision-making we had experienced at the beginning of the pandemic.

The Consultant: *"The minute they started to ease restrictions we asked all our employees to return to the office. It was not about control but about being more efficient; we did not want the work to suffer. The interactive and dynamic way we operate is also reflected in the way our office is structured: it's an open plan with over twenty desks, so you can just plant yourself wherever you find space. In this open space, knowledge on projects is shared openly and is very transparent, so you really get a feel for what is happening in the company. With time, the whole office becomes involved in certain projects and anecdotes arise about the peculiarities of some of our clients. These shared commonalities have contributed toward the company's culture. How would we be able to re-create this, if our employees continued to work from home?"*

This is perhaps the most surprising of the four responses given that a significant part of the company was already organized remotely to facilitate work done in the field. They believed that the work required employees to be back in the office.

The Former Banker: Their start-up was already remote, and here the conclusions were that the problems they anticipated did not appear:

"One of the challenges I thought I would face with the distributed model was working across time zones, as I had a team operating from different geographic locations. But through asynchronous communication this worked very well. We were able to collaborate effectively and stay in touch through so many different platforms.

"Another challenge I thought this type of company setting would face would be its corporate culture. In the bank, the culture was very dominant, it was a driver for everything, and as is typical in that sector, it was formal, conservative, hierarchical, and top-down. I wondered how a culture could be created operating in a virtual space without having anyone physically present. The success lay in its leadership team. Every day the intranet page was flooded with messages from the co-founders about the benefits (and joys) of distributed work. Often, they attached pictures of the locations where they were currently working, encouraging everyone to share pictures and stories. There were morning virtual coffee sessions with team members and lots of new branded merchandise sent to new joiners—e.g. sweaters, t-shirts, stationery, water bottles, mouse pads, tea mugs, caps—so by the time you create your office space at home with all these company goodies, you can't help but feel connected to the company wherever you are."

The VP: *"Six months after the first lockdown, our company adopted a hybrid model of working, so we could come into*

1 Much of this text draws on Peter Cappelli, *The Future of the Office: Work from Home, Remote Work, and the Hard Choices We All Face* (Philadelphia: Wharton School Press, 2021).

2 John T. Cacioppo, Stephanie Cacioppo, Gian C. Gonzaga, Elizabeth L. Ogburn, Tyler J. VanderWeele, "Marital satisfaction and break-ups differ across on-line and off-line meeting venues" *Proceedings of the National Academy of Sciences*, June 18, 2013, https://www.pnas.org/doi/10.1073/pnas.1222447110.

3 For the new accounting, see I. V. Mahlon Apgar, "Uncovering Your Hidden Occupancy Costs," *Harvard Business Review*, May 1, 1993, https://hbr.org/1993/05/uncovering-your-hidden-occupancy-costs. For evidence of space cuts, see June Langhoff "Does Place Still Matter? The Role of the Workplace in a Distributed World" *New Ways of Working Network*, May 1, 2007, http://www.westerncontract.com/wp-content/uploads/Does-Place-Still-Matter.pdf and Nikil Saval, *Cubed: A Secret History of the Workplace* (Knopf Doubleday Publishing Group, 2014).

4 C.C. Sullivan, "Earn as You Churn: Minimizing Outlays for Corporate Layouts," *Buildings*, September 1, 1993.

5 Sarah Kessler, "IBM, Remote Work Pioneer, Is Recalling Thousands to its Offices," *Quartz*, March 21, 2013, https://qz.com/924167/ibm-remote-work-pioneer-is-calling-thousands-of-employees-back-to-the-office/.

6 Michael Considine and Kurt Haglund, "Reworking the Work Space," *Journal of Management in Engineering* 11, No. 2 (March 1, 1995): 18–20, https://doi.org/10.1061/(ASCE)0742-597X(1995)11:2(18).

the office 2-3 days a week. I had gotten so used to my home setup, I hadn't missed being in my office one bit. I no longer associated these four walls with the job, given that I could now do the job from anywhere. This hybrid model is now the norm for me and the ideal situation, because I can have a mix of in-person meetings, when needed, but it also provides the flexibility to continue working at home, at my pace, in my environment, in my own time The benefits of working from home were witnessed on a larger scale, because the company's profit last year was one of the best in the last decade."

This is the only one of the four whose organizations made a change. Whether the company's superior profit was actually caused by remote work is not so clear, but it did not appear to hurt the business.

In reflecting on their experiences, our four subjects noted the importance of the mindset of the leaders, and how they thought people should be managed was arguably the key factor in determining where they ended up. Only one in the end was a true believer that remote work was the wave of the future—the former banker—perhaps because they had already made that choice themselves a few years before. We see reluctance to spend time on managing employees, but the return from the most important and traumatic experience in a generation certainly merits it.

Employers are under immense scrutiny to strike a fine balance between company performance and management of employee expectations concerning the future workplace. Remote work is a big part of that conversation, one that will have a profound impact on keeping the workforce engaged and productive. If remote work is implemented right, this could mean the decline or even the end of physical office spaces. If it doesn't work out, then we will be back into office space and more commercial real estate renovations. In the end, companies opting for the more hybrid approach need to ensure that work spaces are designed with the spatial flexibility in mind that will also be mirrored in the way employees work, interact, and produce.

---

7 For an extensive discussion of the Chiat experience see Warren Berger, "Lost in Space," *Wired*, February 1, 1999.

8 Kim Parker, Juliana Menasce Horowitz, and Rachel Minkin, "How the Coronavirus Outbreak Has—and Hasn't—Changed the Way Americans Work," *Pew Research Center*, December 9, 2020, https://www.pewresearch.org/social-trends/2020/12/09/how-the-coronavirus-outbreak-has-and-hasnt-changed-the-way-americans-work/.

9 For examples, see C. D. Cooper and N. B. Kurland, "Telecommuting, Professional Isolation, and Employee Development in Public and Private Organizations," *Journal of Organizational Behavior* 23 (2002), 511–532.

10 For evidence on the former, see W. F. Cascio, "Managing a Virtual Workplace," *Academy of Management Executive* 14 (2000): 81–90; and on the latter, see T. D. Golden, "Co-workers Who Telework and the Impact on Those in the Office: Understanding the Implications of Virtual Work for Co-worker Satisfaction and Turnover Intentions," *Human Relations* 60 (2007): 1641–1667.

11 Jose Maria Barrero, Nicholas Bloom, Steven J. Davis, Brent H. Meyer, and Emil Mihaylov, "The Shift to Remote Work Lessens Wage-Growth Pressures" *National Bureau of Economic Research*, Working Paper 30197, July 2022.

12 For a review of this work, see Michael L. Platt, *The Leader's Brain* (Philadelphia: Wharton School Press, 2020).

03 DISNEY HEADQUARTERS

Colin Koop and Qiyao Li

In a burgeoning Manhattan neighborhood, a one-of-a-kind company headquarters is on the rise. The iridescent green terracotta panels installed on the facade suggest that this is no ordinary building; yet the most innovative aspects are located inside, where state-of-the-art studios are configured around social, administrative, and amenity spaces that consolidate all of the functions of a media production studio into the footprint of a single Manhattan block. This is the future New York headquarters for the Walt Disney Company (TWDC): an ambitious building project that responds to the changing nature of media production and distribution. In a shifting media landscape—where production facilities have become increasingly decentralized, while development pressures have led to a densification and urbanization of studio lots—Disney's New York headquarters puts forward a bold and decidedly urban model for the future workplace.

Disney's decision to create a dense, centralized hub was very much intentional, driven by the benefits of proximity in fostering corporate culture. Moreover, the company sought to embed this hub within a dynamic neighborhood at the heart of one of the most energetic cities in the world, a place where talent thrives. For the first time, all of TWDC's New York-based businesses will be under one roof, sharing one front door and a single address. The design of the new Disney headquarters explores the ways that architecture and design can not only serve a company's aspirations, but also express and shape its unique culture, and to do this in a way that conveys an innate sense of place. It will be a place where content is conceptualized, created, edited, and distributed to the world, mirroring both the production pipeline and the way media is consumed today—a true 24/7 campus.

REINVENTING THE "PRINTING DISTRICT" FOR 21ST-CENTURY MEDIA

When Disney announced that it would consolidate its headquarters in the formerly industrial neighborhood known as Hudson Square, the location might have seemed surprising. Most of New York City's premier, ground-up commercial developments over the past decade have been concentrated further north, in and around Hudson Yards, and along Park Avenue following the rezoning of Midtown East. For more than a decade, however, the Hudson Square district—surrounded by TriBeCa, SoHo, and the West Village, but less well known than these neighborhoods—has quietly been emerging as a destination of choice for media and creative industry companies. In 2013, this trend was accelerated through the rezoning of Hudson Square, which allowed for the creation of a denser, mixed-use district in keeping with the historic industrial character of the neighborhood.

Hudson Square was once known as the Printing District. After the construction of the West Side Highway, the Holland Tunnel, and the Sixth Avenue extension in the 1920s, the area became attractive to the printing industry because of its proximity to these major transportation arteries. The neighborhood is characterized by large masonry buildings with robust frames and deep floor plates, constructed to accommodate heavy

Historic photographs of the Printing District in New York.
01 Holland Plaza Building, 75 Varick Street, New York. Photography by Jim Henderson *(Top Left)*
02 131 Varick Street, New York. Photography by Percy Loomis Sperr *(Top Right)*
03 Maltz Building, 225 Varick Street, New York. *(Bottom Left)*
04 Butterick Building, 159 6th Avenue, New York. Photography by George P. Hall & Son *(Bottom Right)*
05 Pressroom of the New York Times newspaper, 1942. Photography by Marjory Collins *(Bottom)*

commercial printing equipment (Figs. 01-05). Generally 12 to 15 stories tall, these warehouses represent a classic style of New York City architecture, rising flush with the street wall up to about 10 stories in height, with terraced setbacks at the top. Notable examples include 1 Hudson Square, the former home of Astoria Graphics, Macmillan Publishers, the American Book Bindery, and the Royal Typewriter Company; and 345 Hudson, the onetime headquarters of the historic printing house Bowne and Co. These buildings have proved highly adaptable to new uses as the city's economy has evolved.

During the 1980s, media companies, creative industries, and nonprofit organizations began to move into the neighborhood as the printing industry went into decline. The Hudson Square BID, formed in 2009, has been instrumental in the neighborhood's repositioning: In 2012, the BID launched a streetscape improvement plan, which introduced more open spaces, street trees, and improved pedestrian and bike access. The next major step was the new zoning regulation, enacted in 2013. It sought to preserve the neighborhood's distinctive architectural character, while also allowing for the growth of residential and retail uses—supporting the transformation of Hudson Square into a vibrant mixed-use district.

The new zoning includes height limitations for new buildings, in order to prevent out-of-scale development, and also to encourage a continuation of the commercial and manufacturing uses that have defined the district for more than a century. In late 2018, the possibilities of this zoning envelope attracted Google to initiate a major new building project just two blocks away from the Disney site. More digital technology and start-up companies have since followed suit.

Today, about 70 percent of the workforce based in Hudson Square—more than 40,000 people—are employed in creative industries. As financial services companies and large corporations have asserted their presence in Hudson Yards and Midtown, occupying newly constructed skyscrapers with expansive views and floor-to-ceiling windows, Hudson Square presents an alternative that is uniquely attractive for the creative industry: lower rent, industrial character, active street life, waterfront access, and proximity to the most lively and storied neighborhoods in the city. For tech companies especially, the large floor plates of older industrial buildings provide not only the capacity to introduce expanded workplace amenities, but also the ability to combine traditional workstations with collaborative spaces suited to creative work.

We quickly realized that it was no coincidence that Disney picked this particular site. It presents a rare opportunity to accommodate the programmatic needs for large studio spaces and their adjoining supporting functions, all within a full-block site in the heart of downtown Manhattan.

Hudson Square is also a uniquely appropriate cultural fit, giving Disney, a historic company that has reinvented itself over a century, a chance to make its new home in a district that has also undergone constant reinvention as a center for creative media and technology. Our design takes inspiration from the district's classic industrial architecture. A building type that was invented for print media becomes the ideal home for new media production, a modern warehouse with maximum connectivity and flexibility.

CONVEYING CULTURE AND IDENTITY THROUGH ARCHITECTURE

As the company's Burbank headquarters has continued to grow, it has maintained a strong culture and identity that is rooted in Disney's history and origins as an animation studio. Later additions to the campus have reinforced this identity; the most notable example is the Team Disney / Michael D. Eisner Building, an administrative facility designed by Michael Graves and completed in 1990. The building's postmodernist facade, in a playful homage to the studio's past, features a pediment supported by towering figures of the Seven Dwarfs. References throughout the campus to iconic characters and productions celebrate an inimitable legacy, while asserting a singular identity: this could be home to no other company than Disney.

Disney's existing premises in New York, however, do not express such a strong and cohesive identity. For the new headquarters project, the company seeks to take a different approach than on the Burbank campus. The new headquarters will bring together

06 "Toward tomorrow with Lehigh Cement" the imaginary skyscraper, 1925. Drawing by Hugh Ferriss

07 Study model of Disney Headquarters design highlighting setback massing. Disney Headquarters, SOM, New York, 2020. Photography by SOM

a diverse range of creative professionals, and also an expanded suite of media brands. All of these people, divisions, and departments must find a home under the “Disney” umbrella.

We explored the question of how to express a “New York” identity through architecture—how to create a sense of place that is irreducible to the city and its downtown neighborhoods—through many different lenses. Many of our reference points come from our lived experience in the city, while others emerged from the way it has been imagined and portrayed in the movies, literature, and music: the bustling streetscapes of lower Manhattan, the energy of the restaurants and bars that spill out to the sidewalk, and the iconic silhouettes of rooflines and water towers. The street life and the rooftops define the downtown experience in our memories. If we were to define the essence of New York that we wanted to embrace, we wanted to design a building with a story about its roof and its street.

As with most development projects in New York, the building maximizes the allowable floor area, and the zoning envelope defines its shape and massing The design, with its nested volumes and set-back roofline, embraces the zoning envelope and the massing of classic New York City buildings that the architectural illustrator Hugh Ferriss evocatively captured in his images of the 1920s, and which still today characterize the historic masonry buildings of the neighborhood (Figs. 06-07). While the majority of the building adheres to a subdued palette, the subtle change of facade module and material articulates a more porous and animated ground floor, bringing the energy of the street in. At the cornice line of the surrounding buildings (around 135 feet in height), the podium roofline is marked with a series of green terraces, surrounded by amenities, exhibiting the excitement of the building out to the city.

It was clear that the new headquarters needed an identifiable “heart,” a place that would bring employees from all across the campus together and create a sense of community. We envisioned a social hub that would become employees’ first and last stop of the day, and that would encourage staff from various divisions to mingle. Instead of distributing separate amenities throughout the building, we proposed gathering them into a central amenities floor with access to cascading terraces, positioned at the 10th floor, where the neighboring buildings just start to set back, opening up views out to the distinctive surrounding roofscape and waterfront. At the center of the floor, surrounded by greenery and activity of the amenity spaces, is a column-free pavilion that spans the block from north to south. Measuring 100 feet by 120 feet with north-facing skylights, this space can function as an informal production stage, screening room, or event space. It will be a mixing chamber, creating opportunities for people to connect and cross paths.

The planning of vertical transportation infrastructure (stairs and elevators) is designed to further encourage commingling. The expansive horizontal floor plates, by nature, make for a highly walkable workplace. Egress stairs are designed with elevated finishes, sometimes strategically located at the building perimeter with natural daylight and views, promoting the use of stairs for between-floor communication as much as possible.

Social and environmental responsibility also play an essential role in Disney’s corporate culture, and we sought to express these commitments in the design of the New York headquarters. The design places an emphasis on resilience and environmental responsibility, with a progressive approach to sustainability beyond LEED Platinum certification. As an all-electric building, it exceeds the current code requirements for energy efficiency by 25 percent; features including a high-efficiency DOAS system, high-performance facade, and cogeneration plant contribute to the building’s exceptional energy performance. The plumbing system targets 40 percent indoor water use reduction, zero potable water use for irrigation, and management of the 98th percentile storm event onsite. Gender-neutral bathrooms along with traditional bathrooms are provided on each floor. The plumbing layout allows for conversion of the remaining traditional bathrooms in the future.

For typical office buildings, built on spec, users exist in the abstract as “prospective tenants”; the design accounts for generalized notions such as market trends, desirable lease spans, amenities, and sustainability and wellness certifications. Conversely, the design of the Disney headquarters building is tailored to the company’s specific purpose and culture. This headquarters not only has to function as a workplace, but just as importantly it should tell a story of the people who reside within. Once complete, the complex’s 1.2 million square feet of space will become a vertical city within a city, and an emblem for all things Disney.

A MODEL FOR CONTEMPORARY MEDIA PRODUCTION

When Disney began the construction of its new Burbank headquarters in the late 1930s—flush from the success of its first animated feature, *Snow White and the Seven Dwarfs*—

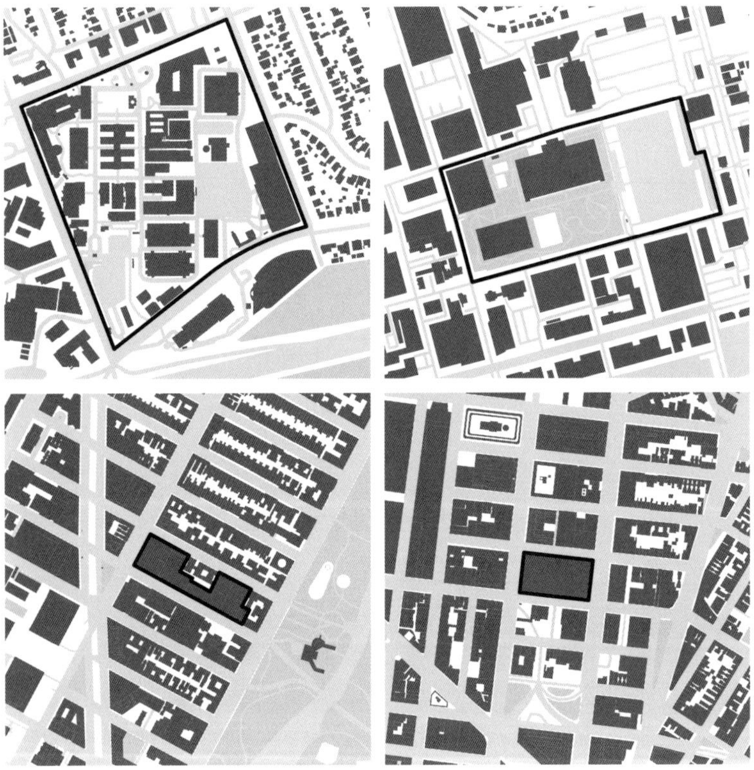

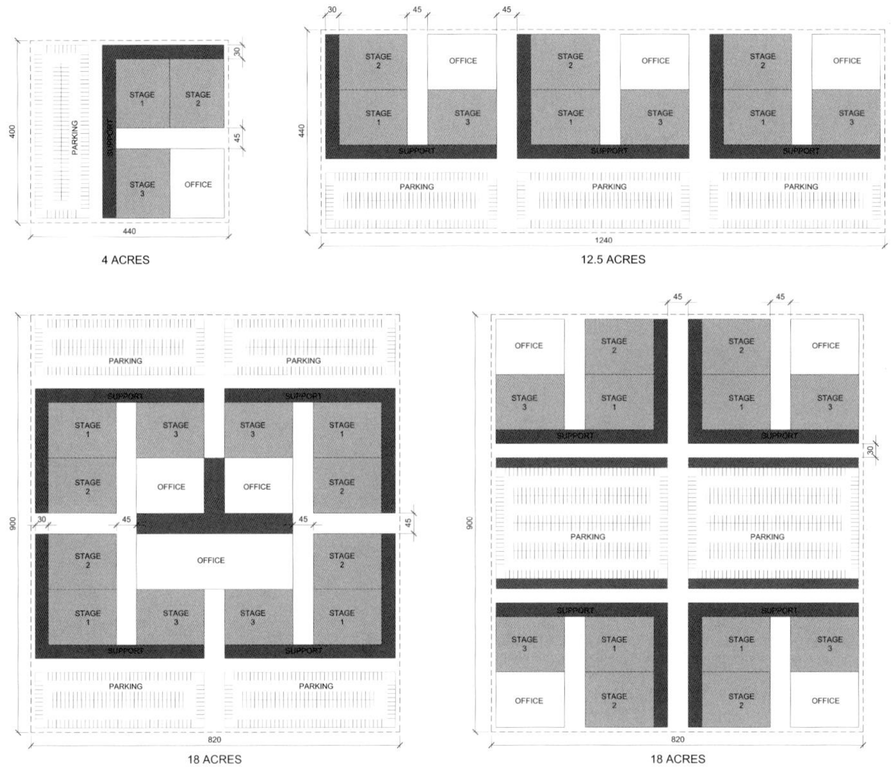

Diagrams showing backlot layouts in contrast with vertically dense new design for Disney Headquarters.

08 The Walt Disney Studios Burbank. *(Top Left)*

09 Pixar Animation Studios. *(Top Right)*

10 ABC Studios, 77W 66th Street, New York. *(Bottom Left)*

11 Disney Headquarters in Hudson Square. *(Bottom Right)*

12 Typical backlot production studio module. *(Right)*

the typical model for media production resembled a walled city. Movie studios would acquire a large lot and fence it off in order to build an internal world that encompassed every aspect of production. The Disney Burbank headquarters was originally built on this model, and structured around the animation process. The three-story Animation Building, at the center of the campus, served as the creative and administrative hub. Surrounding it were buildings dedicated to specific functions: the ink-and-paint department, the camera building (where animation backgrounds and cels were photographed onto film), the "cutting building" (where editing took place), and other production aspects of the studio. These buildings were connected by tunnels, which allowed workers to transport animation materials without exposing them to the elements.

In recent years, as large-scale urban and suburban lots have become scarcer, and each aspect of production has become more specialized, we have seen a trend away from the classic studio lot model toward the decentralization and densification of media production spaces. Accelerating this trend is the intensifying competition between streaming platforms, which has increased demand for both on-location and stage based production. Existing studio campuses are being updated and densified to accommodate more production needs, while new soundstages are being constructed in more urban environments such as Los Angeles, New York, and Toronto. A new typology of "spec studio" (analogous to the spec office), led by developers and investors, is popping up across the country (Figs. 08-12).

Unlike the older campus model, where functions were loosely connected and grew organically over time, the new backlot studios are designed around maximizing efficiency and modularity. It takes the essential components in the production process (usually including the soundstage, its support space, and the workplace for post-production) and compacts them into an efficient singular module. Each module maintains and optimizes the critical adjacencies between components, acting as an independent mini-campus. Then these modules are arrayed across the site, sometimes grouped together to allow doubling in size if needed. These more compact forms not only allow product studios to exist in more urban environments closer to resources and talent, but also greatly reinforce the vertical integration between departments.

At the arc of this trend, the design of the Disney Headquarters presents a compelling model for a densified media production center. It aims to bring the discrete pieces together to form again the connective tissue that ties the media production line within a single city block. Architecturally, each one of them requires a different type of workplace. The question of how we efficiently fit them in one building, exploiting possible synergies in integrating them into one ecosystem, poses an interesting challenge. In Disney's New York headquarters, the walled kingdom of studio lots has been reinvented as a vertical village, with all the efficiency, production intensity, and urban sociality of a city.

A typical live studio ranges from 6,000 to 8,000 square feet, while a news studio is slightly smaller—roughly 4,000 square feet. Every square foot of the studio requires roughly an equal part of support space. While they don't need access to daylight, they require a highly controlled environment with robust mechanical systems and vibration separation, and direct access to various support programs. The massive podium floors at the Disney headquarters are perfectly suited to host the studios. With floor plates of over 80,000 gross square feet, it can accommodate three to four studios with their support spaces on the same floor. Studios are grouped together to allow for larger production spaces when combined.

News studios are embedded in the center of the podium floors, surrounded by tech and production supports, and sandwiched by newsrooms above and the mechanical infrastructure directly below. It serves as a three-dimensional production hub operating with high efficiency. The more public-facing live studios are situated below grade, closer to the ground floor, with separate sets of infrastructure and direct access from the loading dock. Building infrastructure, including cooling and heating, is designed with redundancy and located above the floodplain to maintain critical operations such as news broadcasting through extreme weather events or power outages. The studio floors are also equipped with extensive, uninterrupted power and emergency power generators, enhanced fire protection, and blast prevention.

Up in the towers, floor plates that range from 13,000 to 15,000 gross square feet provide the ideal workplace for smaller business segments and executive floors, with quick access to production studios through elevators and stairs. Unlike the massive studio floors, these smaller workplace floors have ample daylight from all sides and views toward downtown and the waterfront. Additional access to power and cable infrastructure is provided at street level and on the terraces and amenity spaces, anticipating that every corner could become a stage for content creation.

13 Disney Headquarters is under construction. Disney Headquarters, SOM, New York, 2022. Photography by SOM

The new headquarters will house the New York broadcasting and technology divisions with approximately 5,000 employees. Disney wanted limited signage on the building, in order to differentiate it from the more public-facing retail stores and theaters in the city. The building will serve as a creative, efficient, and environmentally responsive workplace, and a unified campus for many business divisions—a singular yet diverse home for The Walt Disney Company in New York.

BEING A GOOD NEIGHBOR

As media production shifts to urban typologies that prioritize efficiency, density, and social interaction, it confronts the inherent politics of urban development. Here, rather than creating an iconic, brand-driven identity, Disney seeks to create a workplace that harmonizes with its urban surroundings and is imbued with a sense of place. Architecture, rather than characters and brand elements, should set the tone; it was clear from our first conversations with Disney that the New York headquarters should be defined by the architectural and urban identity of the neighborhood and the city. This was largely reflected in the design of the facade.

Unlike the Financial District or Hudson Yards, the neighborhoods around Hudson Square are traditionally masonry blocks with unornamented rhythmic facades and deep punched windows, with only a few new buildings challenging the existing palette by presenting all glass towers with tight curtain wall modules. Cognizant of the scale, the design of the facade seeks to sympathize to the urban context with the art of effortless elegance that would allow it to stand out while fitting in. To achieve this goal, we believe the building needs a facade with depth and shadow, with rhythm and texture, with the diversity and resolution in details found in a hand-laid masonry facade but the performance of a modern curtain wall envelope (Fig. 13). The warehouse buildings in SoHo were an inspiration. The generous facade module maintains floor-to-ceiling windows for daylight, yet gives the building a sense of scale and depth that can be lost with all-glass facades.

The resulting design is a romanticized historic masonry facade reinvented in a classic Manhattan fashion. Terracotta was an apparent choice of material from the beginning. As part of the natural oxidation that happens during the firing process, the imperfections give the material a rich expression and variation within subtle shades of color and texture. Since being used in New York City architecture in the early 1900s, terracotta has undergone many industrial and material innovations. It is now able to be rapidly produced at scale and easily integrated into unitized curtain wall assembly thanks to automation in the industry.

During the design process, we examined hundreds of samples, experimenting with variances in color and transparency. The final choice, a dark turquoise green tile with a semi-glossy finish, best evokes the modernized aesthetic of the Printing District's history we sought to echo. The color of the glaze shifts in the sunlight, making for a more dynamic facade throughout the day.

The glass design and selection also take advantage of technological advancements. Each typical glass unit, approximately 7.5 feet wide and 9 feet tall, is a triple pane glass unit delivering high energy performance (Fig. 14). Coated on the outer surface of the glass is a thin layer of bird-safe coating that is barely visible to the human eye. It is estimated that anywhere from 90,000 to 230,000 birds die each year, colliding into glass buildings in New York City. Shortly after the building was designed, in an effort to reduce bird strike fatalities, a new local law came into effect which mandates bird-friendly glass design in all newly constructed or altered buildings in the city. The selection of glass (and building materials) has evolved to encompass aesthetics, human comfort, energy performance, and also the living things around us.

From the original World Trade Center to the United Nations headquarters to Lever House, workplace design in New York has a legacy of leading technological innovation, especially in the building envelope. The facade represents not only the way people work but also the value of the workplace. Interestingly, in the past years, the city has been gradually shifting away from the all-glass facade, accompanied by the increasing popularity of masonry materials such as terracotta or brick veneer panels. One apparent driver is New York City's new energy code.

The other driver we have noticed is companies' increasing desire to "be a good neighbor," a phrase Disney has invoked throughout our design process. It is also worth noting that thanks to technological advancements, manufacturers now have production lines that can produce unitized facades with these more traditional materials at a competitive price. The cost of an ornamented and "crafted" facade has and will continue to decrease. It opens up many more opportunities for new constructions to take into consideration the urban fabric that preceded the design.

14 Building facade close-up. Disney Headquarters, SOM, New York, 2022. Photography by SOM

FUTURE WORKPLACE

In its nearly century-long history, Disney has witnessed a continued evolution of the workplace. The design of the New York headquarters reflects the forces that are shaping workplace design today, as many companies are embracing the transition from offices with assigned desks to a dynamic workplace model with expanded amenities. The building was largely designed before the COVID pandemic; in fact, the pandemic has only accelerated trends in the evolution of the workplace that we took into account in our design. Density and desk-to-amenities ratio may have been driving forces in the past 10 years, but what the design of Disney's headquarters has presented is a more complex picture of how today's workplace is changing organizationally, technologically, environmentally, and culturally.

The modern workplace is not just a place for production, but also a place for social interaction. Its design represents the workplace culture and the pressing need to address social equity issues. Besides the employee working inside, there is also a rising sensitivity to what it projects to the people outside (being a good neighbor), and how it impacts the living world beyond us.

In the context of climate change, beyond the basic needs of light and air and human comfort, the system design needs to embrace the urgent challenge of energy efficiency and resiliency. Just like the building facade, technology will continue to push every single building element to get smarter and less carbon-intensive. All these things together push the limits of architecture to be richer in content, more diverse, and more sensible.

The new Disney headquarters is just the beginning of a new paradigm of workplace evolution.

PROJECTS: METABOLIC FUTURES

Manufacturing is being critically reshaped by technological advancement in the areas of AI, additive manufacturing, 3d modeling, and cloud computing. If the 20th century model of production was the assembly line, the 21st century model is the 3d print farm. While it could be modified to swap out different parts and processes, the assembly line was by and large designed to a product or type of product as efficiently and cheaply as possible. Manufacturing plant architecture was essentially a form for containing such singular processes and other key administrative functions. The 3d printing farm implies a new spatial distribution wherein products are estranged from the particular manufacturing methods, spaces, and circumstances from which they derive. In this condition, the print farm's ability to nestle into and boost existing exchange nodes and networks is paramount. This section speculates on new synergies between architecture, additive manufacturing, logistics, and what has been termed "the internet of things" (ioT) to create new typological considerations for work and production. Here the building is configured to take on new productive capacities, making it a spatial locus for part or even whole aspects of a distributed manufacturing apparatus. The aim is to enable local nodes and networks to have more influence over production flows and to respond better to global supply and demand pressures. These projects imply a new, more nimble, and more flexible approach. They imagine new distributed forms of production wherein direct to consumer/direct to business exchange is boosted by the building as a productive and logistical urban actor. Decentralization of manufacturing processes take the workplace into unchartered territory, wherein products from multiple different companies can be developed under one roof, much like the model of a print business where jobs from different clients are processed through the same basic workflow. In the scenarios that follow, this is keyed into other rapid prototyping and research facilities as well as distribution mechanisms. In this model, the paradigm of "just in time" manufacturing is questioned and reconfigured by positioning manufacturing technology that can serve as stable yet flexible infrastructure while reducing production risks and disruptions.

PROJECT 05

MAINFRAME

UPS Hub, West SOHO, New York

Yuxuan Liang, Xuechen Chen, Yue Pan

Mainframe reimagines the traditional office building by combining highly articulated manufacturing, packaging, storage, and distribution mechanisms into a single, seamless system. This amalgamation of functions creates a new form of architectural productivity that emphasizes local production and on-demand manufacturing, promoting a more sustainable and efficient model for the work environment. To achieve this, the project introduces human-centered workspaces that merge and interface with production spaces, creating an environment that supports rapid prototyping and collaborative work. The result is a workplace that integrates technology, design, and manufacturing, offering a new paradigm for architecture that is both functional and aesthetically striking.

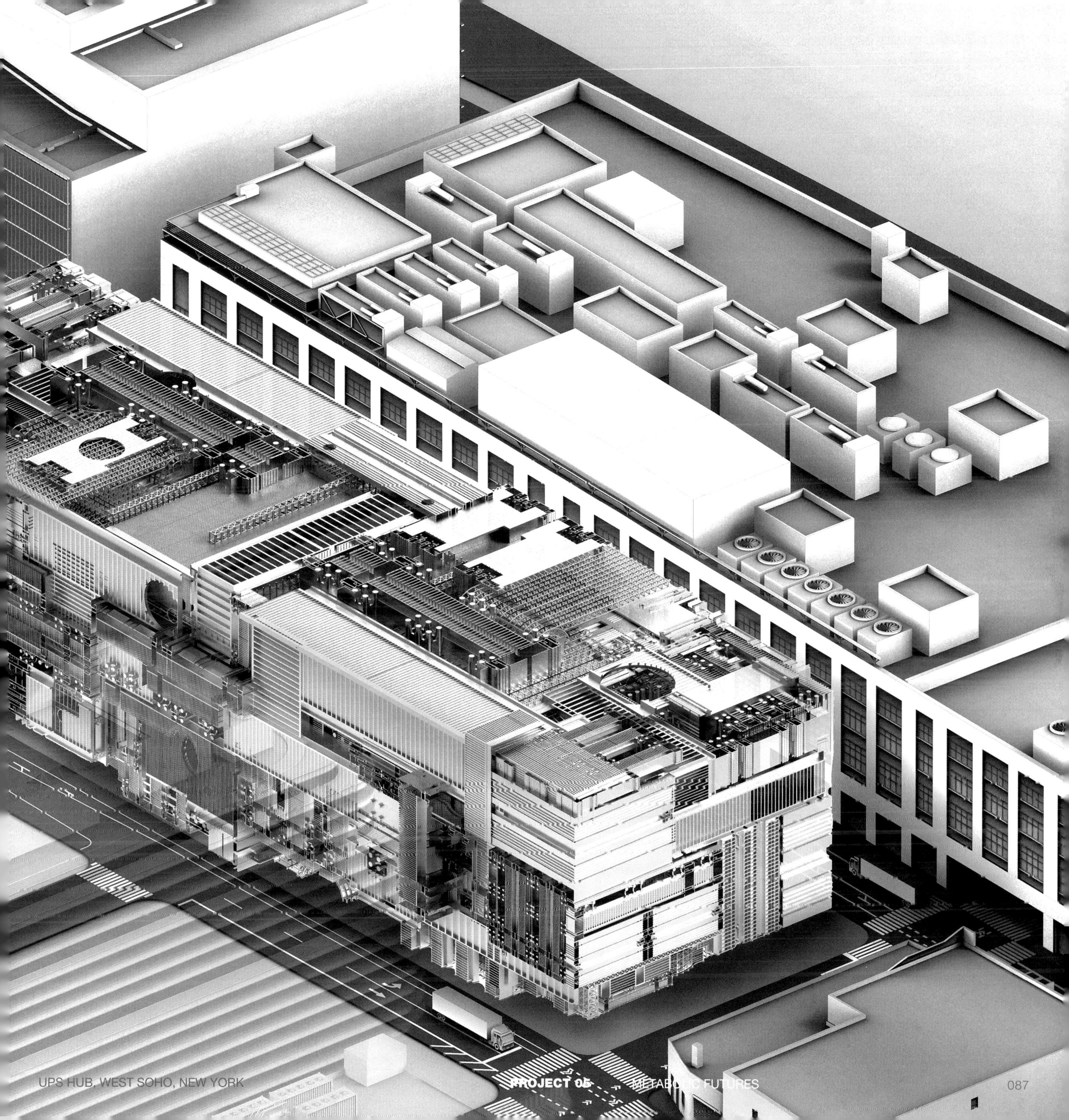

Elevation Drawing

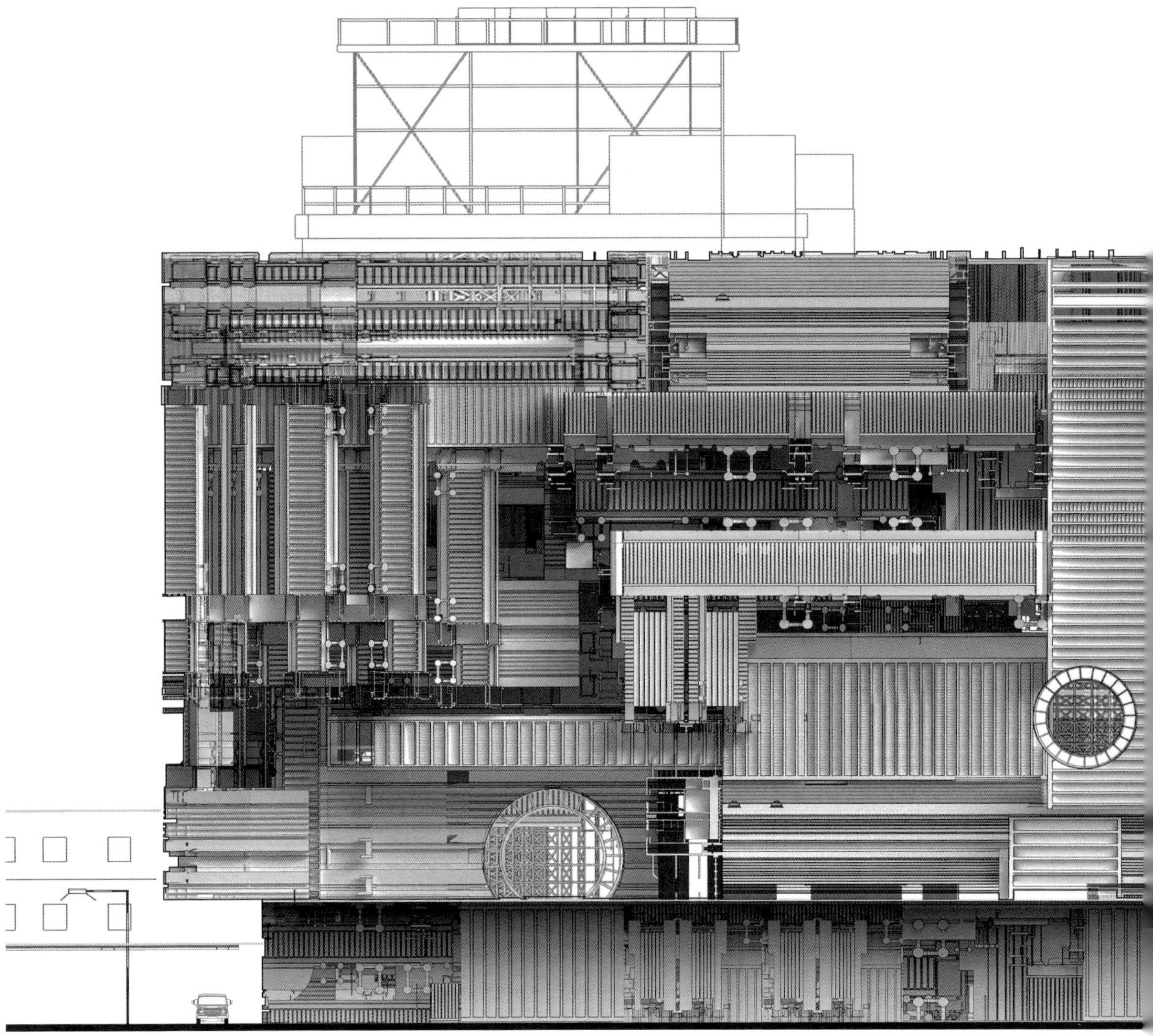

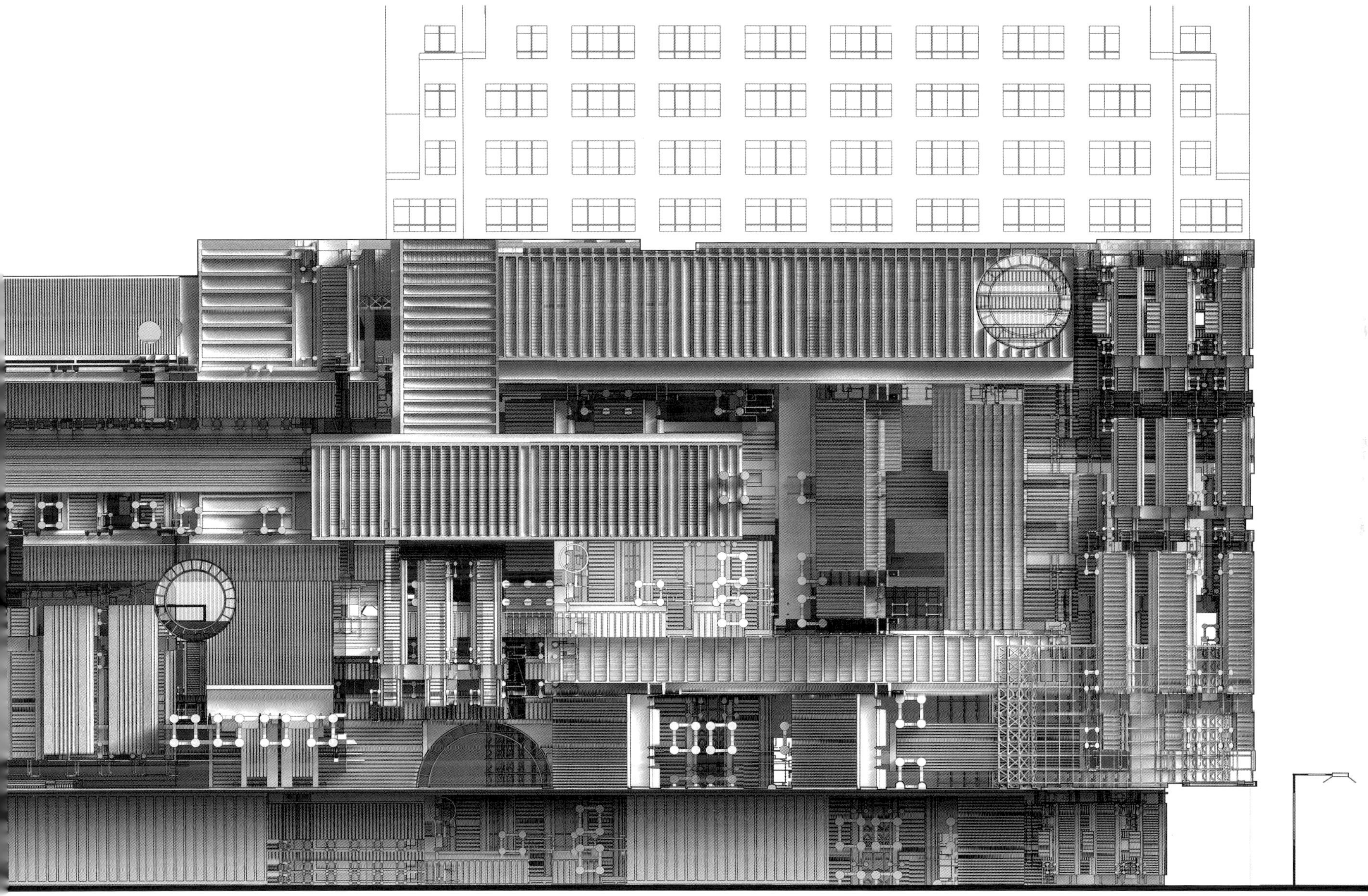

Typical Floor Plan

01 Atrium
02 Board Room
03 Package Distribution System
04 Cargo Drop-off
05 Hall
06 Information Desk
07 Meeting Area
08 Restrooms
09 Package Storage
10 Offices

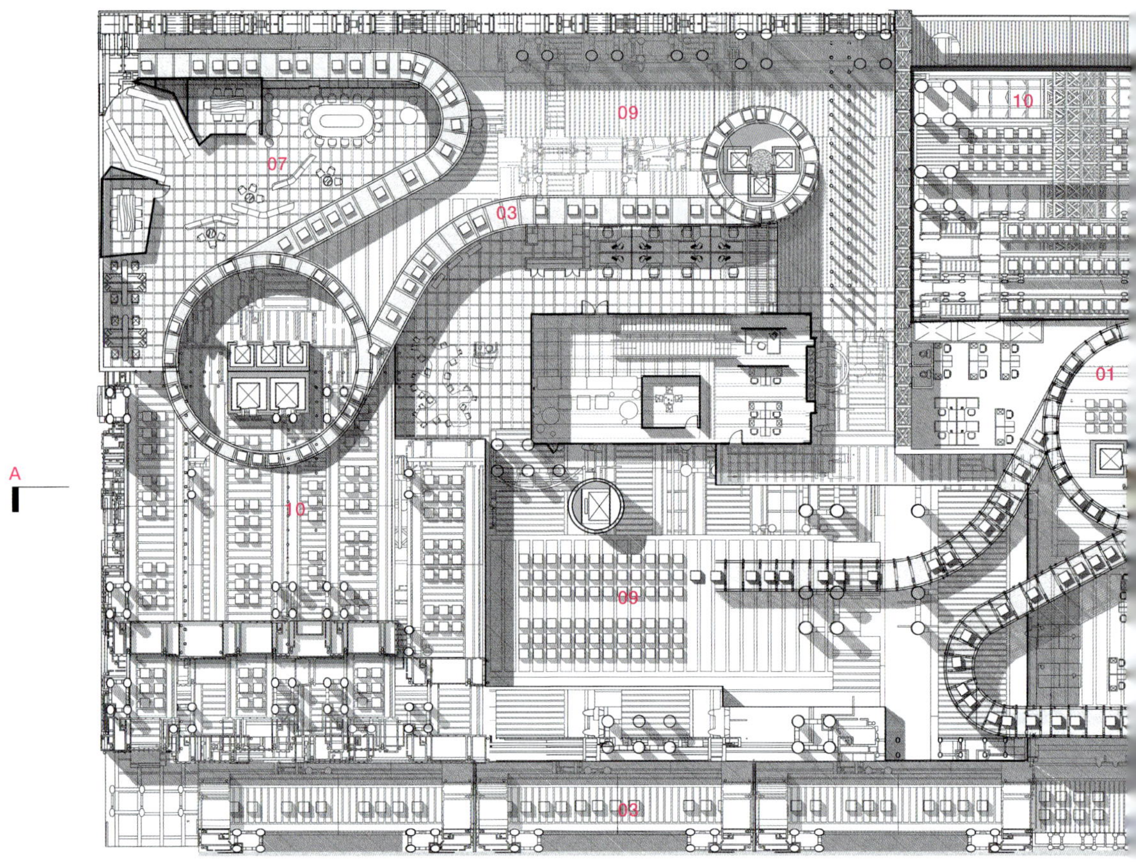

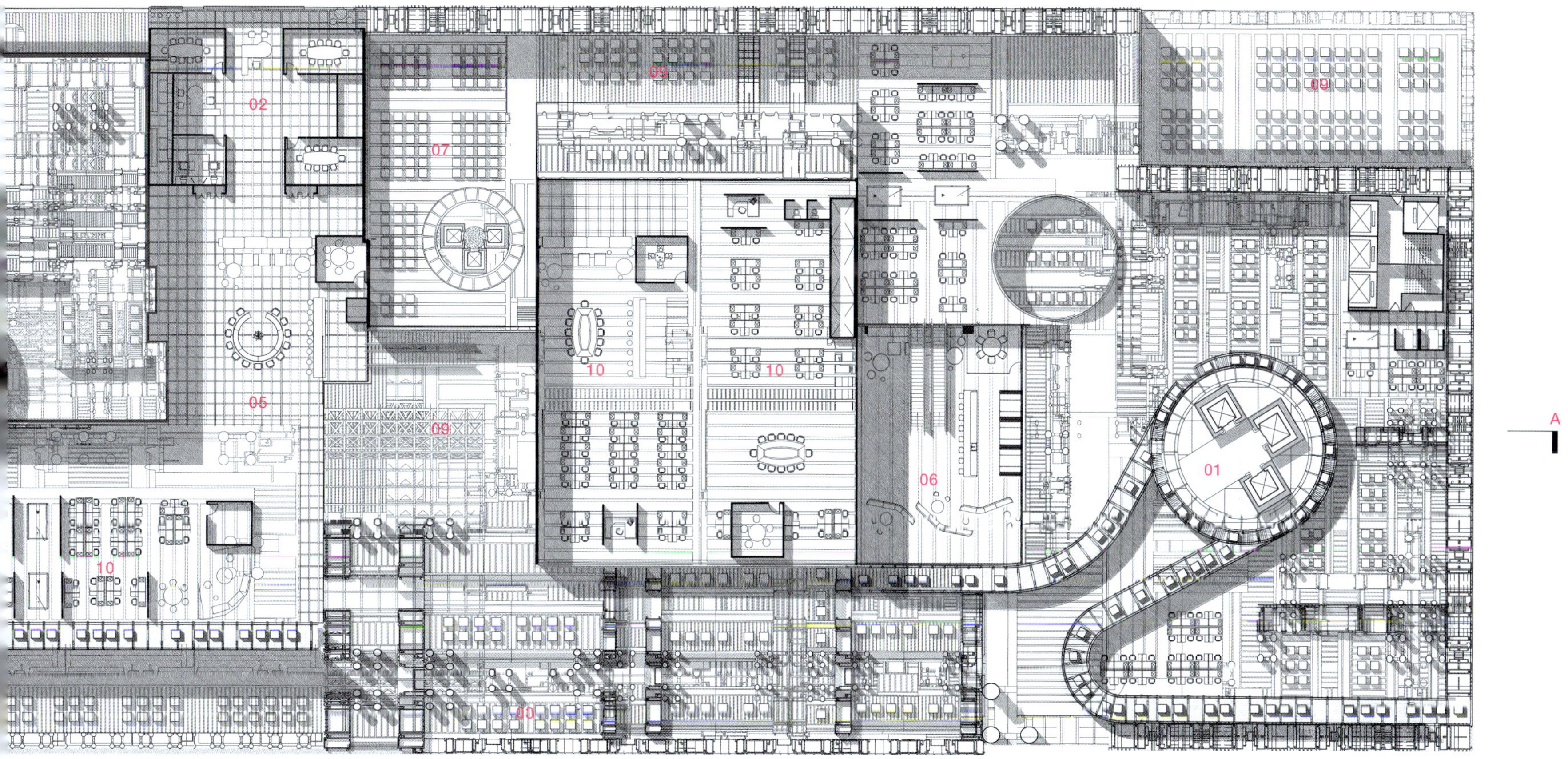
02
07
09
09
10
10
05
09
06
01
10
09
A

Top Right: Ground Floor Plan

Bottom: Long Building Section

01 Atrium
02 Board Room
03 Package Distribution System
04 Cargo Drop-off
05 Hall
06 Information Desk
07 Meeting Area
08 Restrooms
09 Package Storage
10 Offices
11 Rest Area

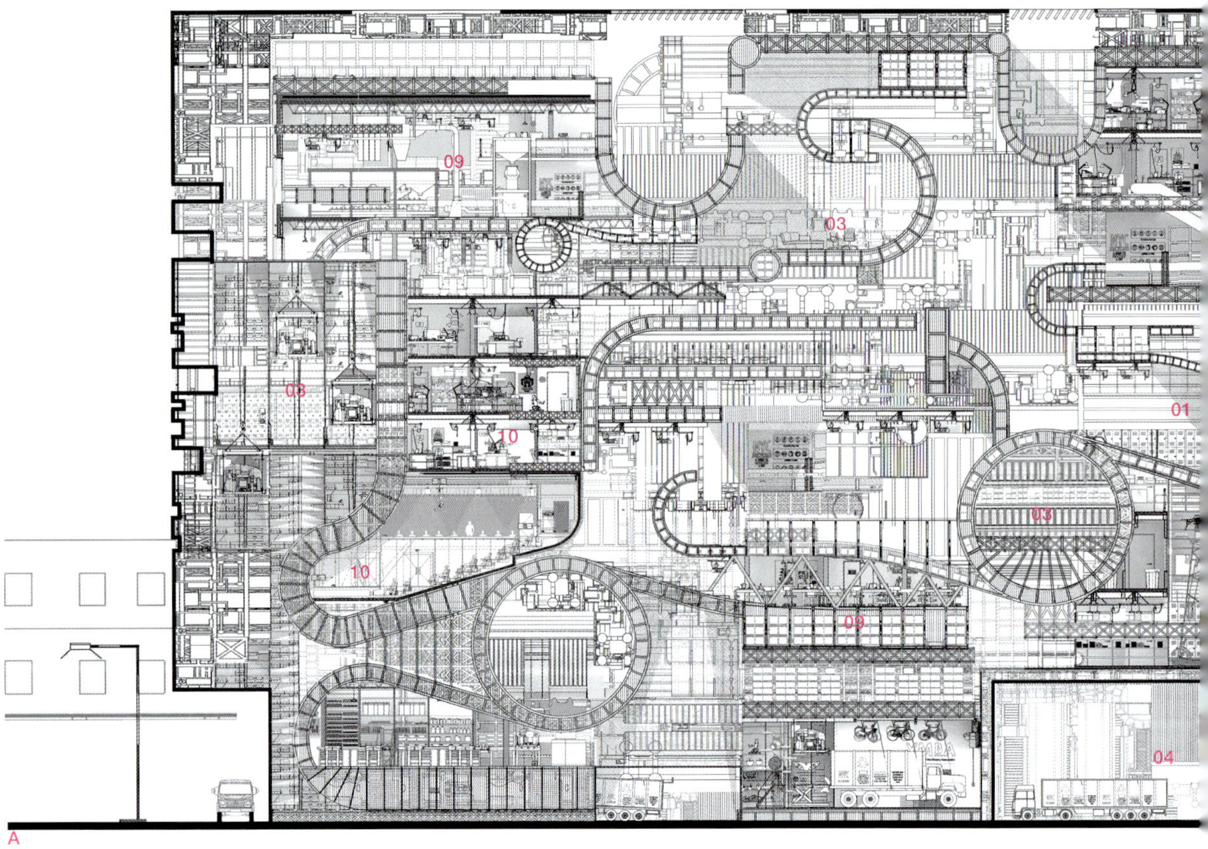

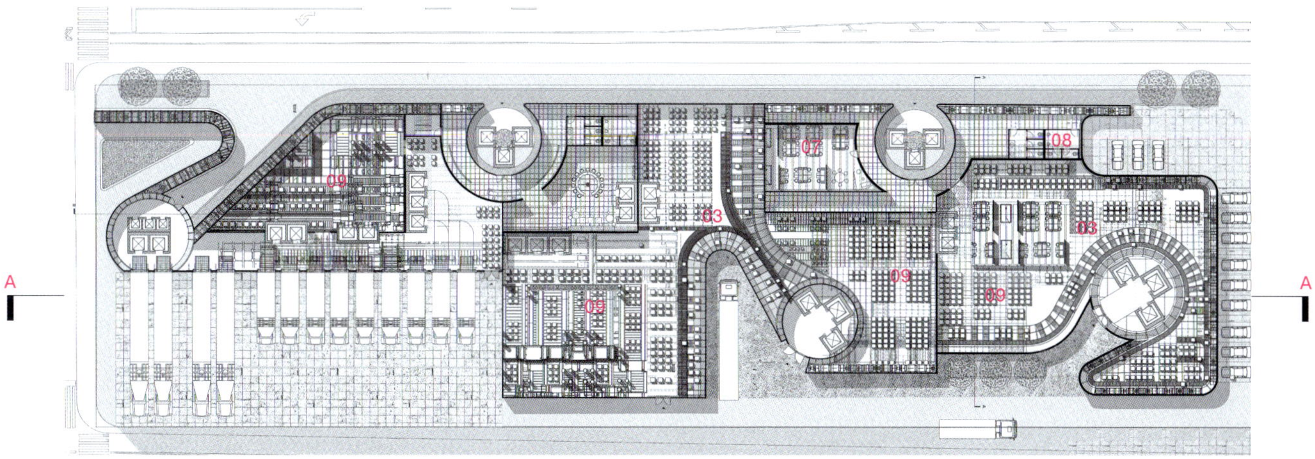
A
09
07
08
03
03
09
09
09
A

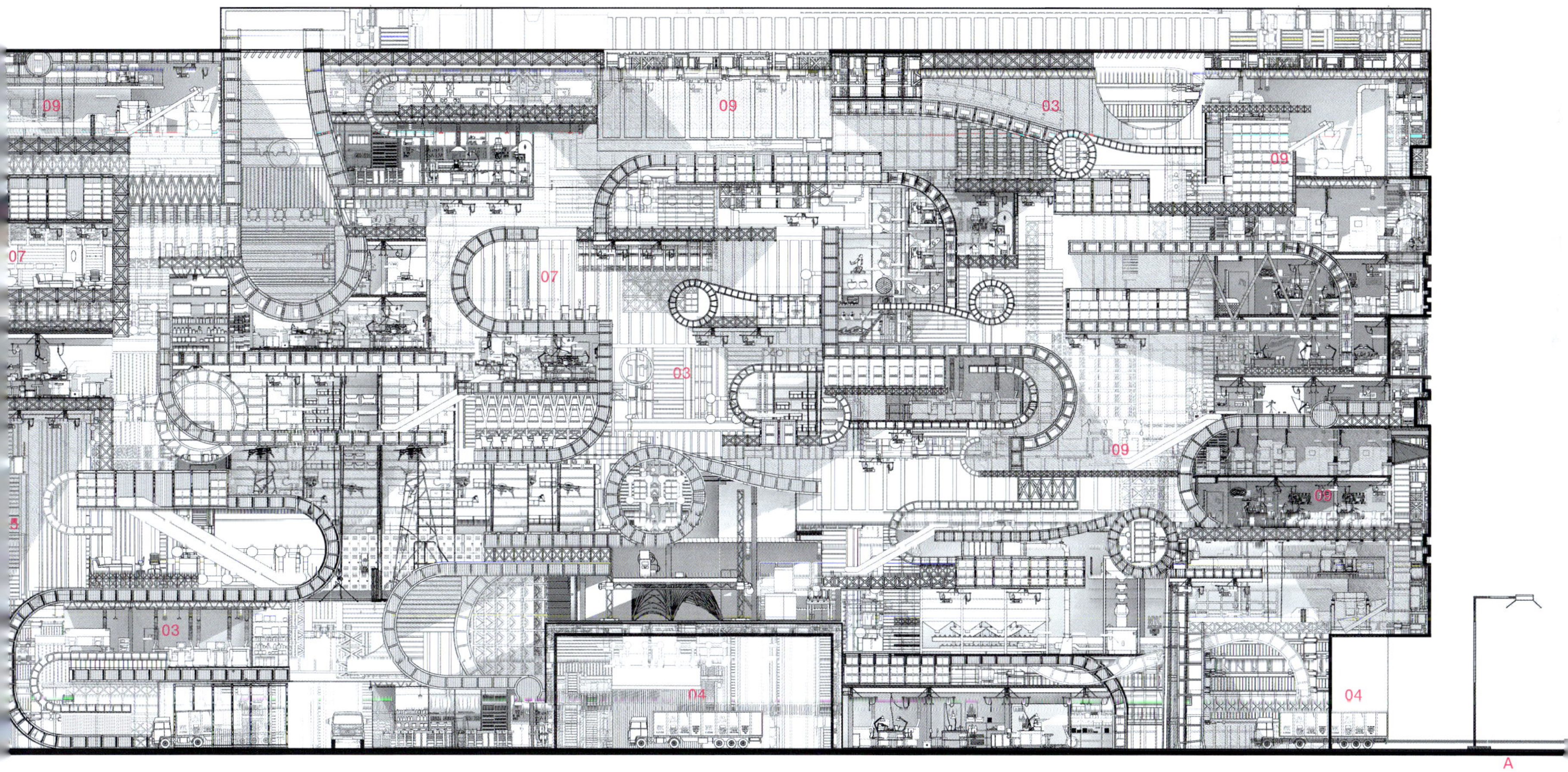
09
09
03
09
07
07
03
09
09
03
04
04
A

Right: Physical Section Model, 2'x2'x2', 3D Printed PLA

Left: Physical Section Model, 2'x2'x2', 3D Printed PLA

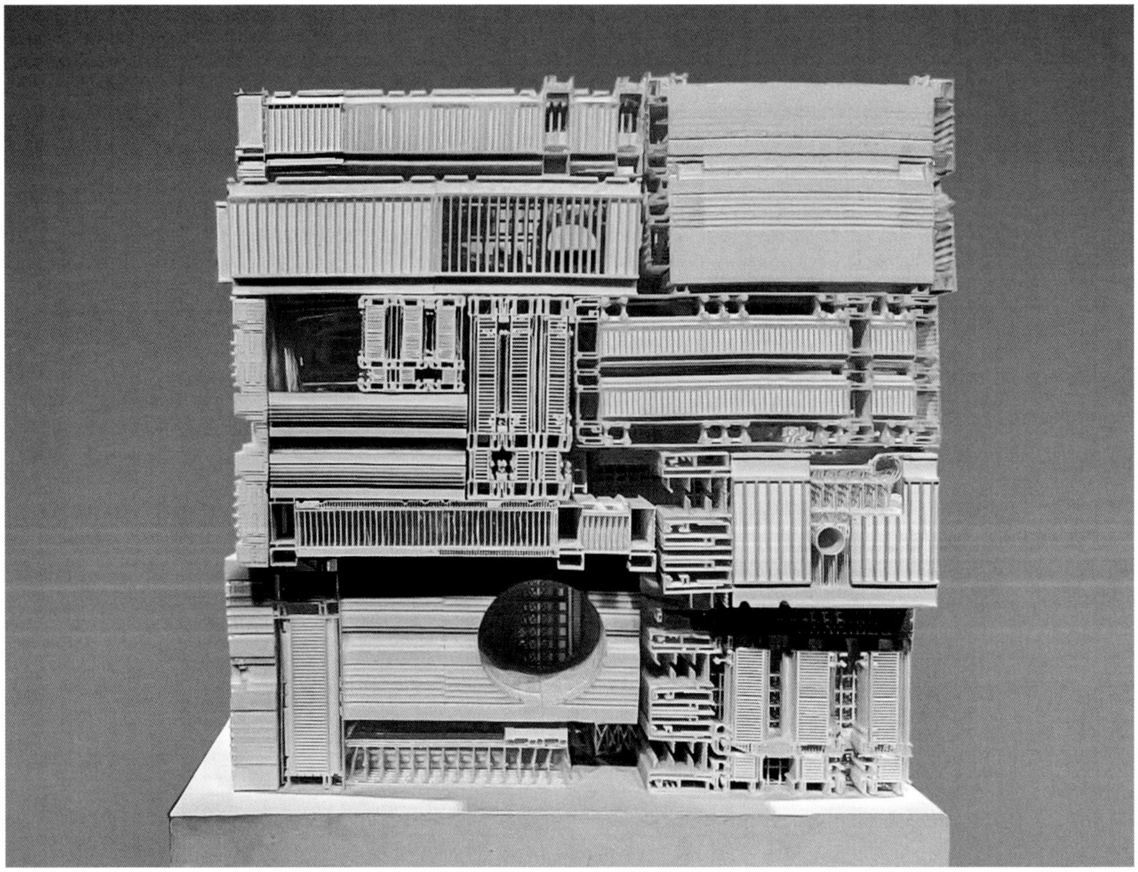

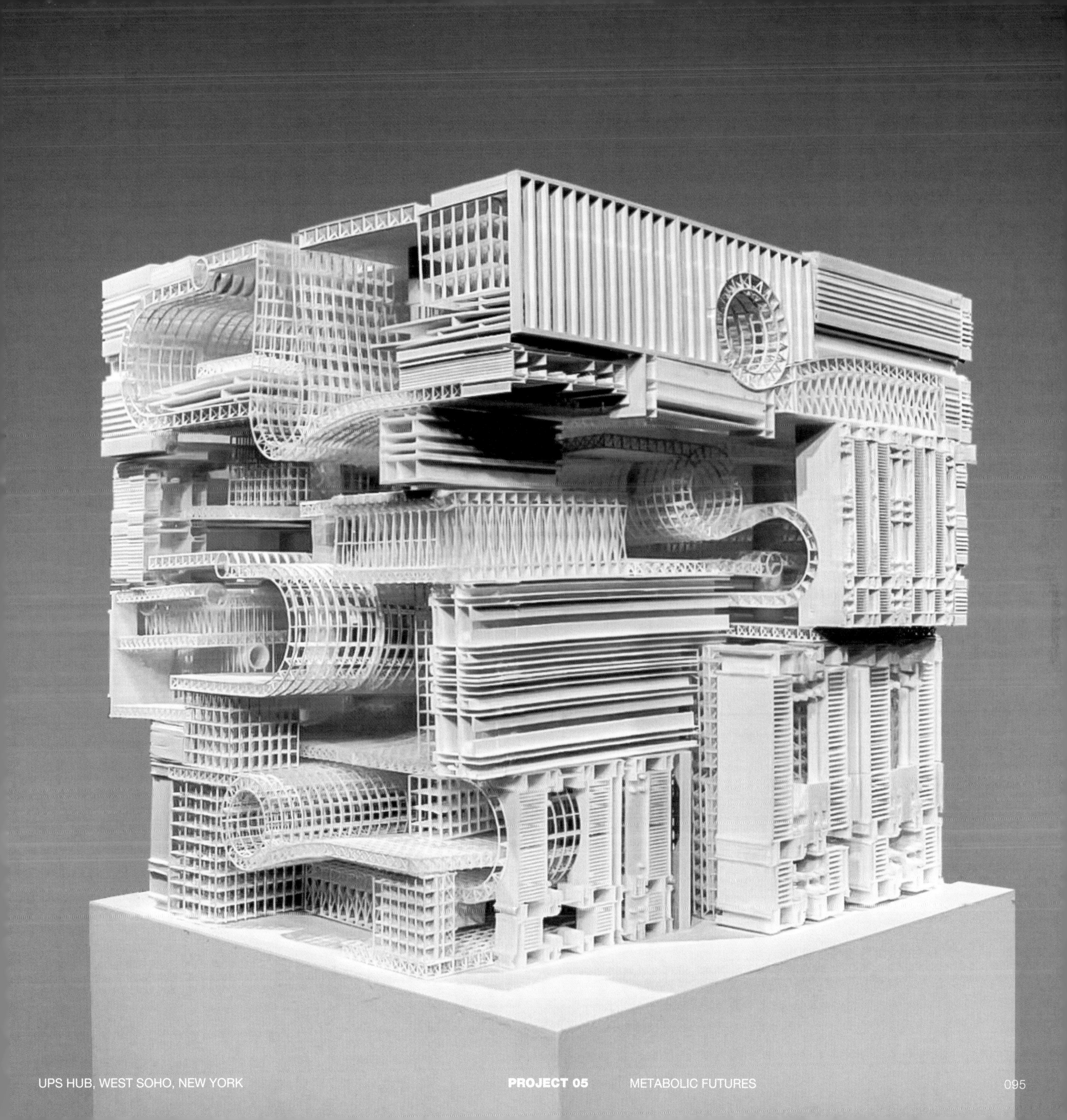

PROJECT 06

SUPERMOD

UPS Hub, West SOHO, New York

Bingkun Deng, Ming Jiang, Yang Yang

Supermod combines a series of three-dimensional grid-like structures with large round atria and transverse tubes to create a flexible yet highly curated spaces that can accommodate a range of programs. The scaffold volumes not only serve as a superstructure but also can be adapted to a variety of functions, from logistical operations like storage and distribution of goods to modular office spaces and larger manufacturing and fabrication areas. This versatility is achieved through the modulation of the grid-like structures, which allows for a range of sizes and shapes that can be customized to suit different needs. The tubes and atria play a critical role in the building's performance, providing both natural light and circulation through the building for truck loading and unloading. This design strategy not only enhances the functionality of the space but also creates a unique and memorable aesthetic experience.

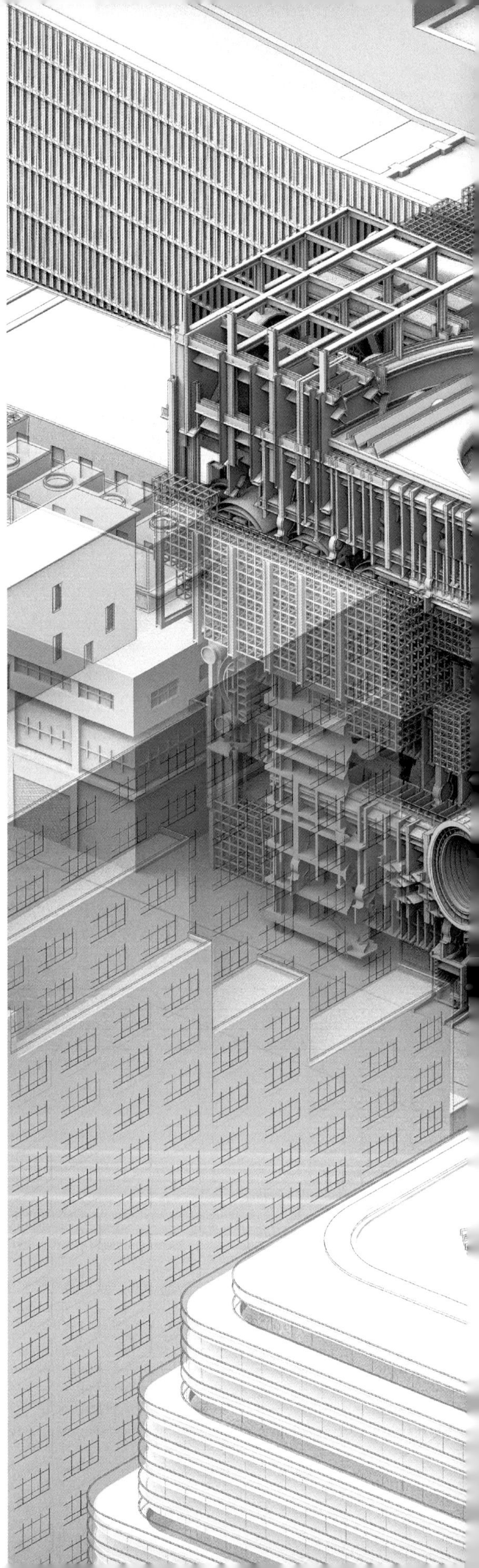

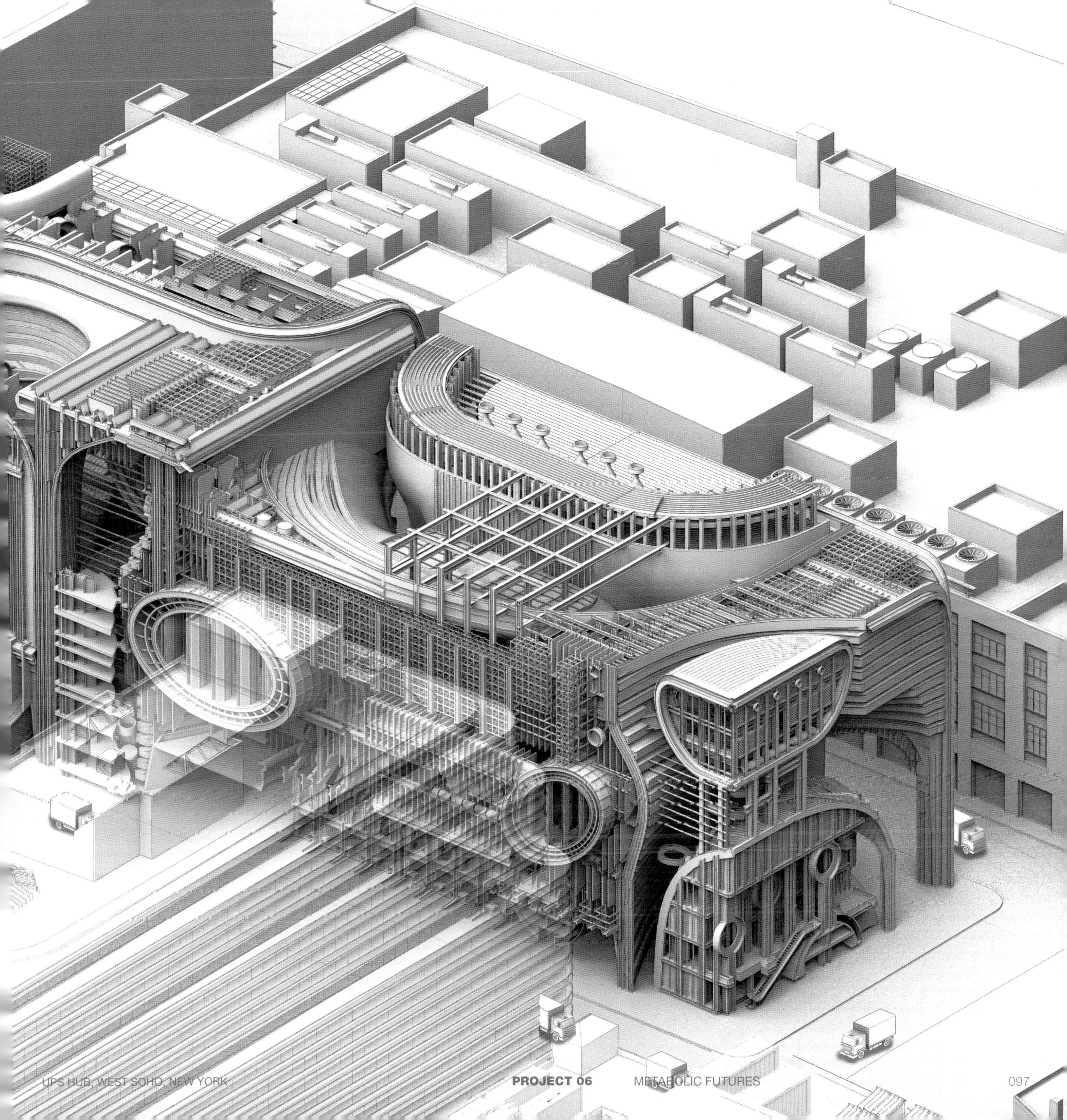

Elevation Drawing

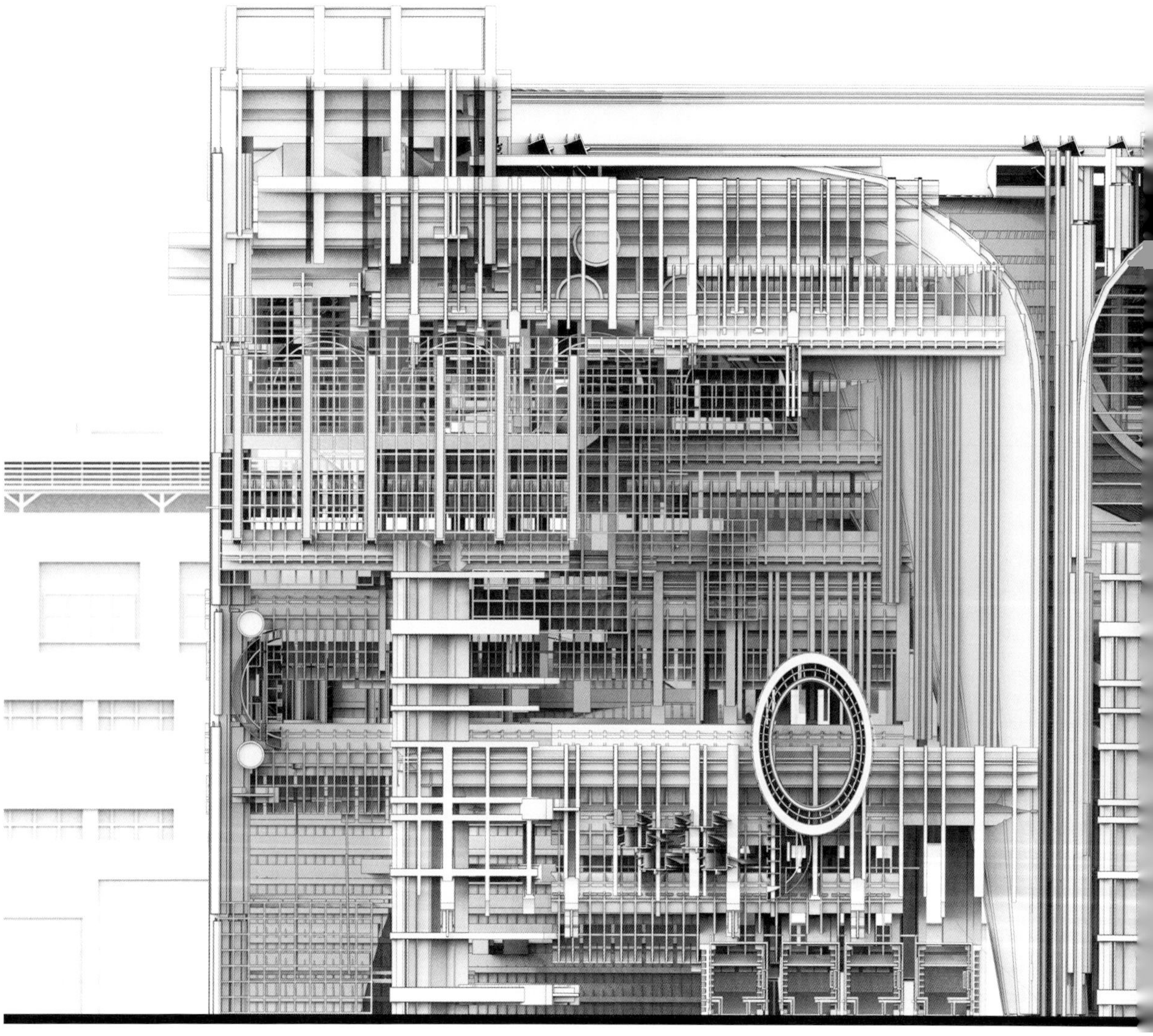

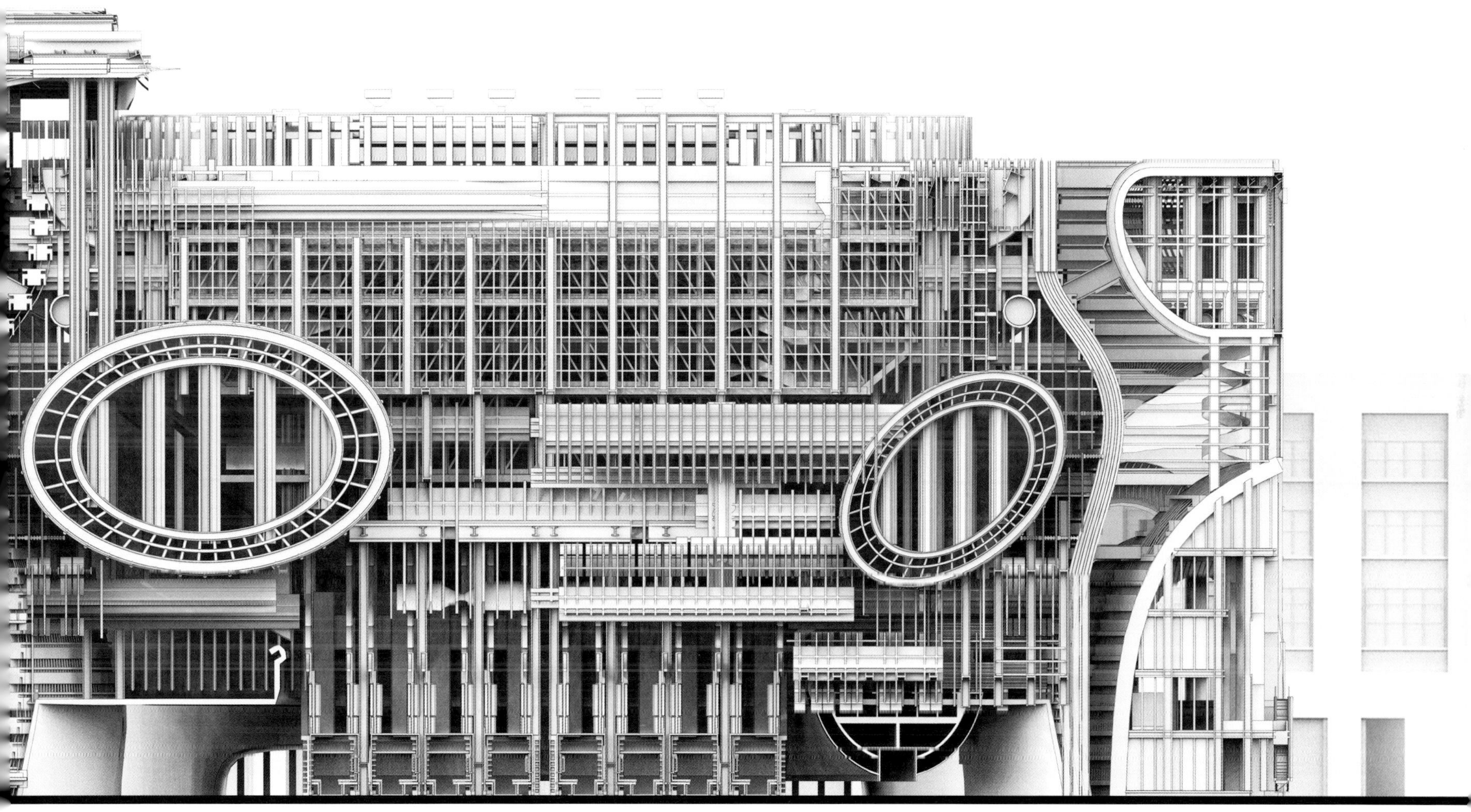

Top Right: Typical Floor Plan

Bottom: Long Building Section

01 Package Claim
02 Package Shooting Tunnel
03 Package Sorting Area
04 Package Pick-up Area
05 Package Transportation
06 Package Storage
07 Pedestrian Bridge
08 Offices
09 Lounge Space
10 Meeting Room
11 Atrium
12 Truck Dock

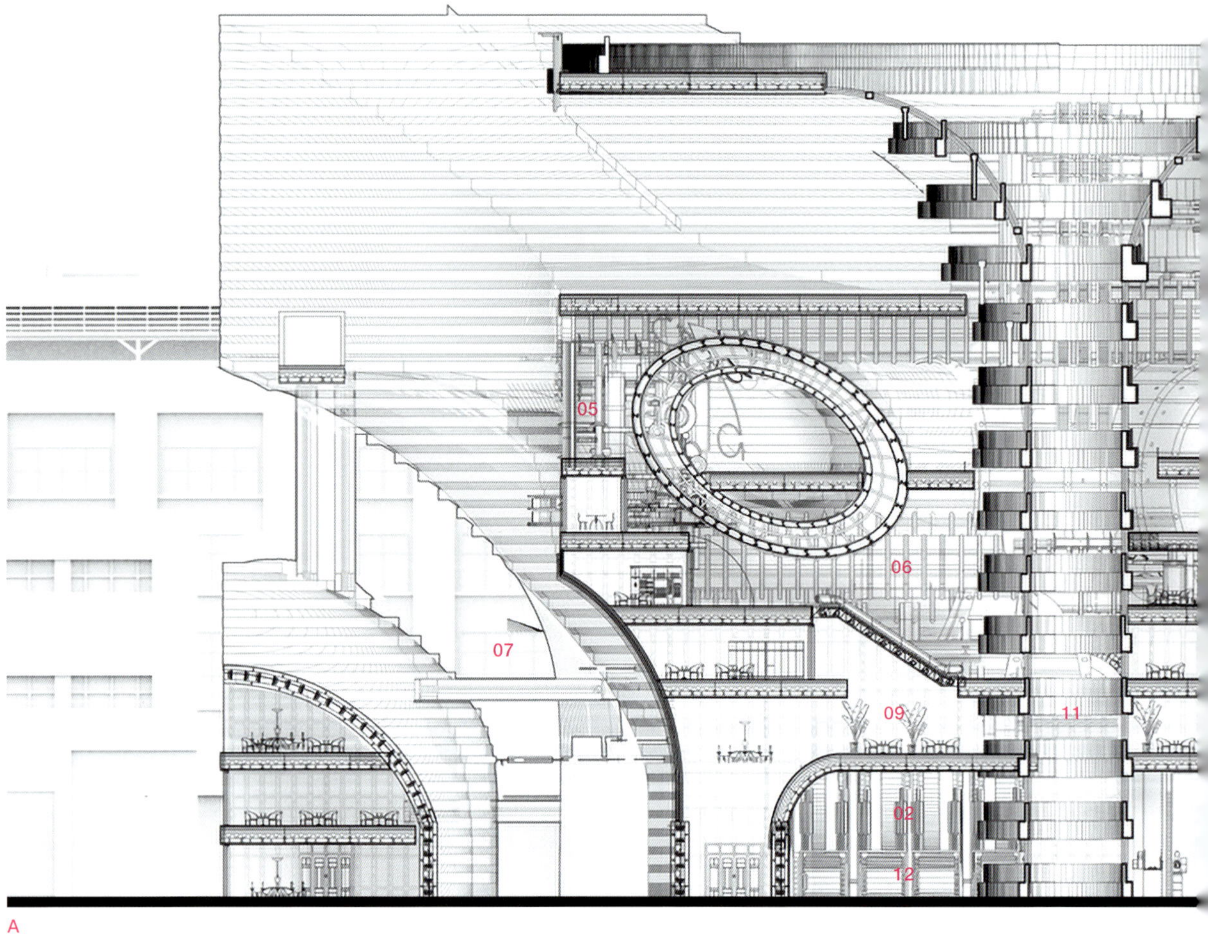

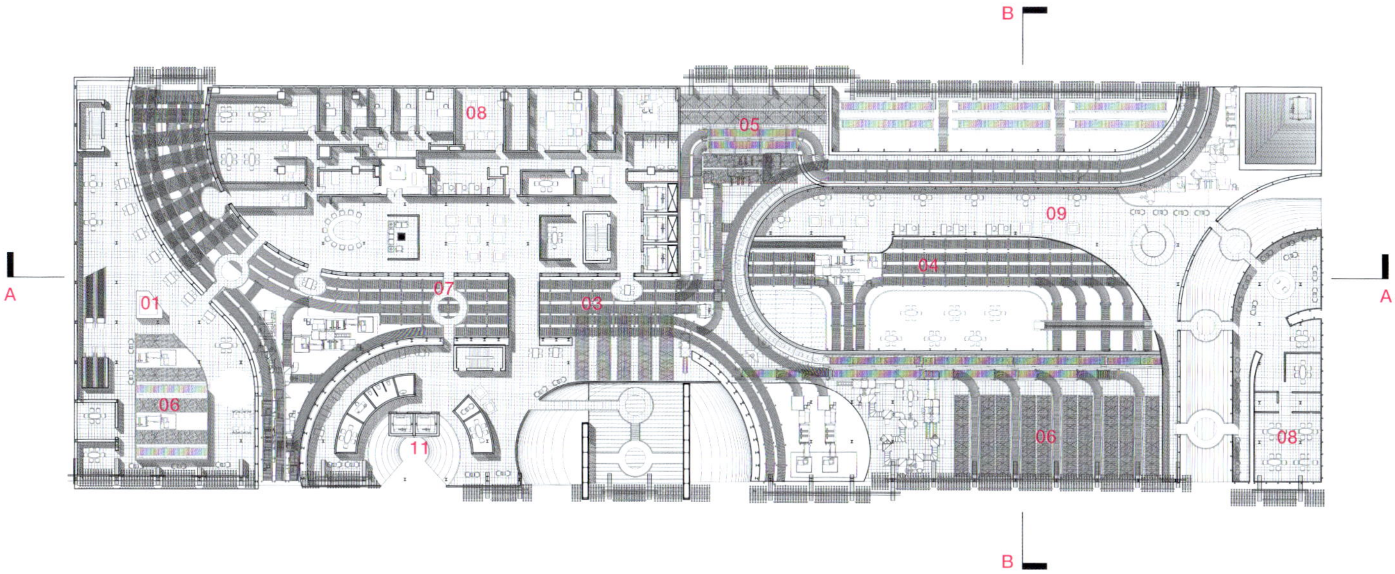
B
08
05
09
04
A
01
07
03
A
06
11
06
08
B

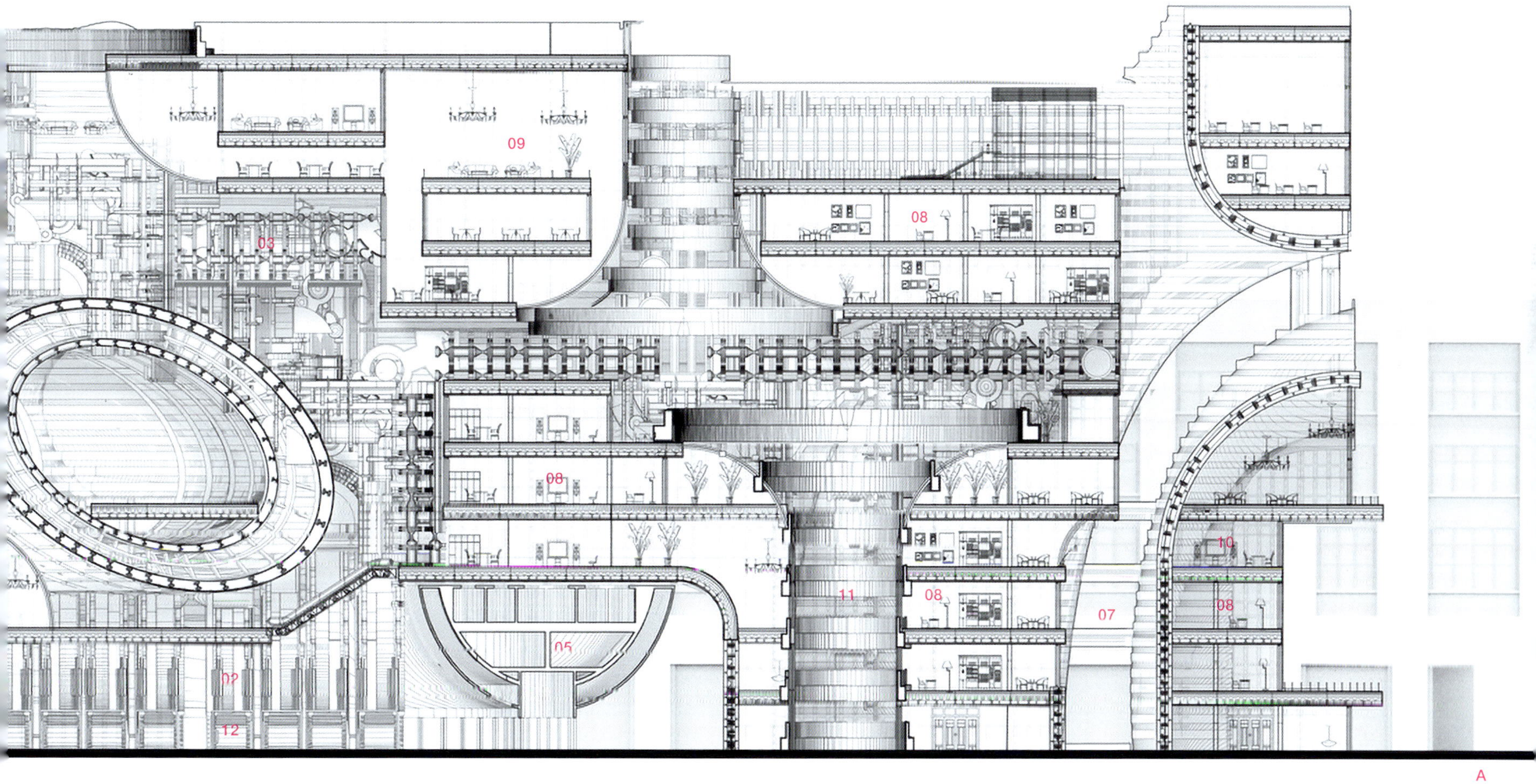
09
03
08
08
08
11
08
07
10
08
05
02
12
A

Right: Physical Section Model, 2'x2'x2', 3D Printed PLA

Left: Short Building Section

01 Package Claim
02 Package Shooting Tunnel
03 Package Sorting Area
04 Package Pick-up Area
05 Package Transportation
06 Package Storage
07 Pedestrian Bridge
08 Offices
09 Lounge Space
10 Meeting Room
11 Atrium
12 Truck Dock
13 Outdoor Auditorium

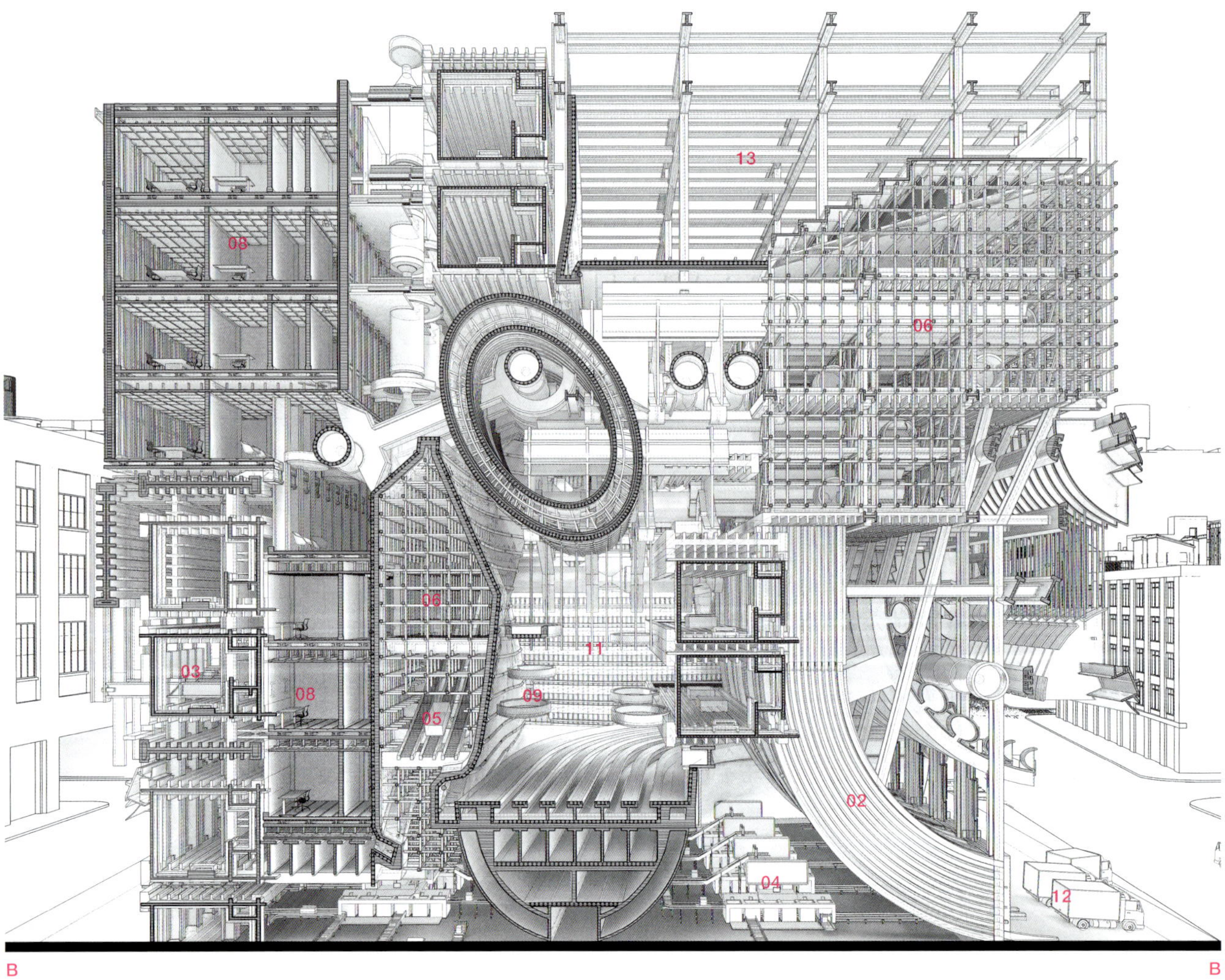

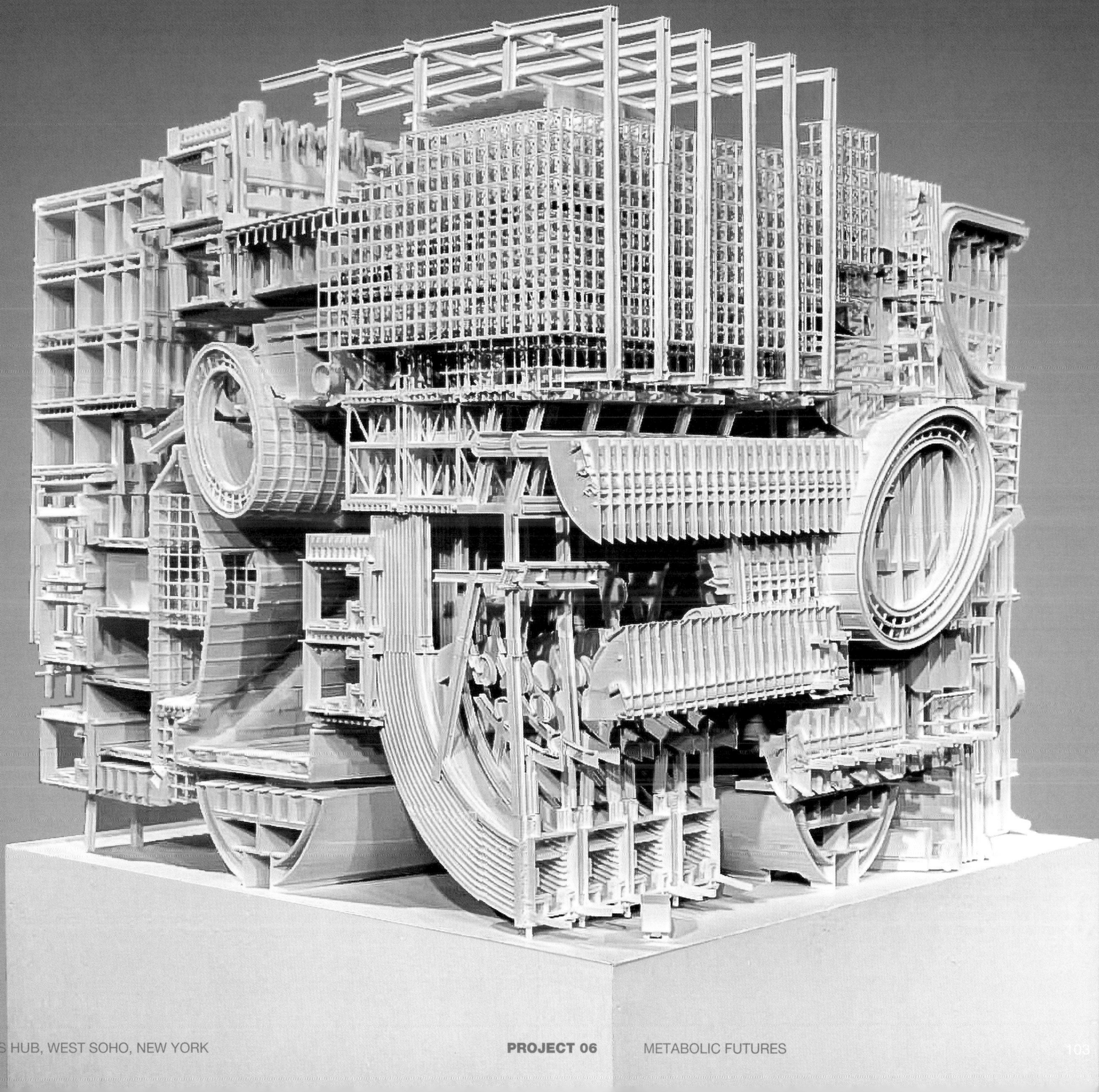

Physical Section Model, 2'x2'x2', 3D Printed PLA

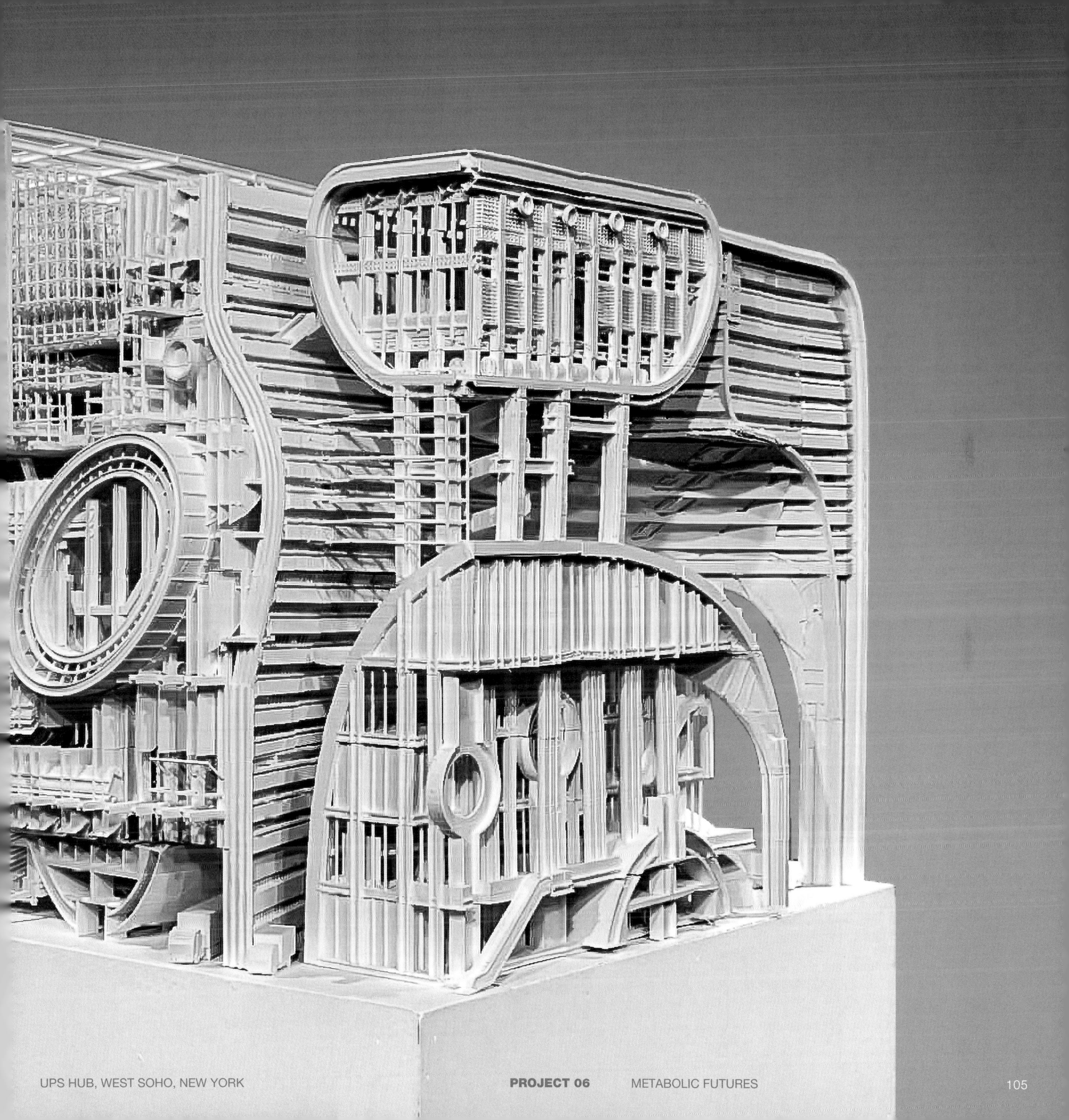

PROJECT 07

MITOCHONDRIA

UPS Hub, West SOHO, New York

Yanpeng Wang, Jiayun Zhang

Mitochondria explores a new office typology inspired by the structure and function of mitochondria, which are the powerhouse of cells. The project imagines an office building that is organized around autonomous zones, each devoted to specific functions related to manufacturing and logistics. These zones include large, automated fabrication, packaging, and product circulation systems that serve as the core of the building. Flexible workspaces varying in scale from the intimate and private to hall-like gathering spaces meander around large automated systems. The project emphasizes the concept of the building as infrastructure, meaning that the building itself becomes a crucial component of the business processes and operations of the companies that occupy it as well as its greater urban context.

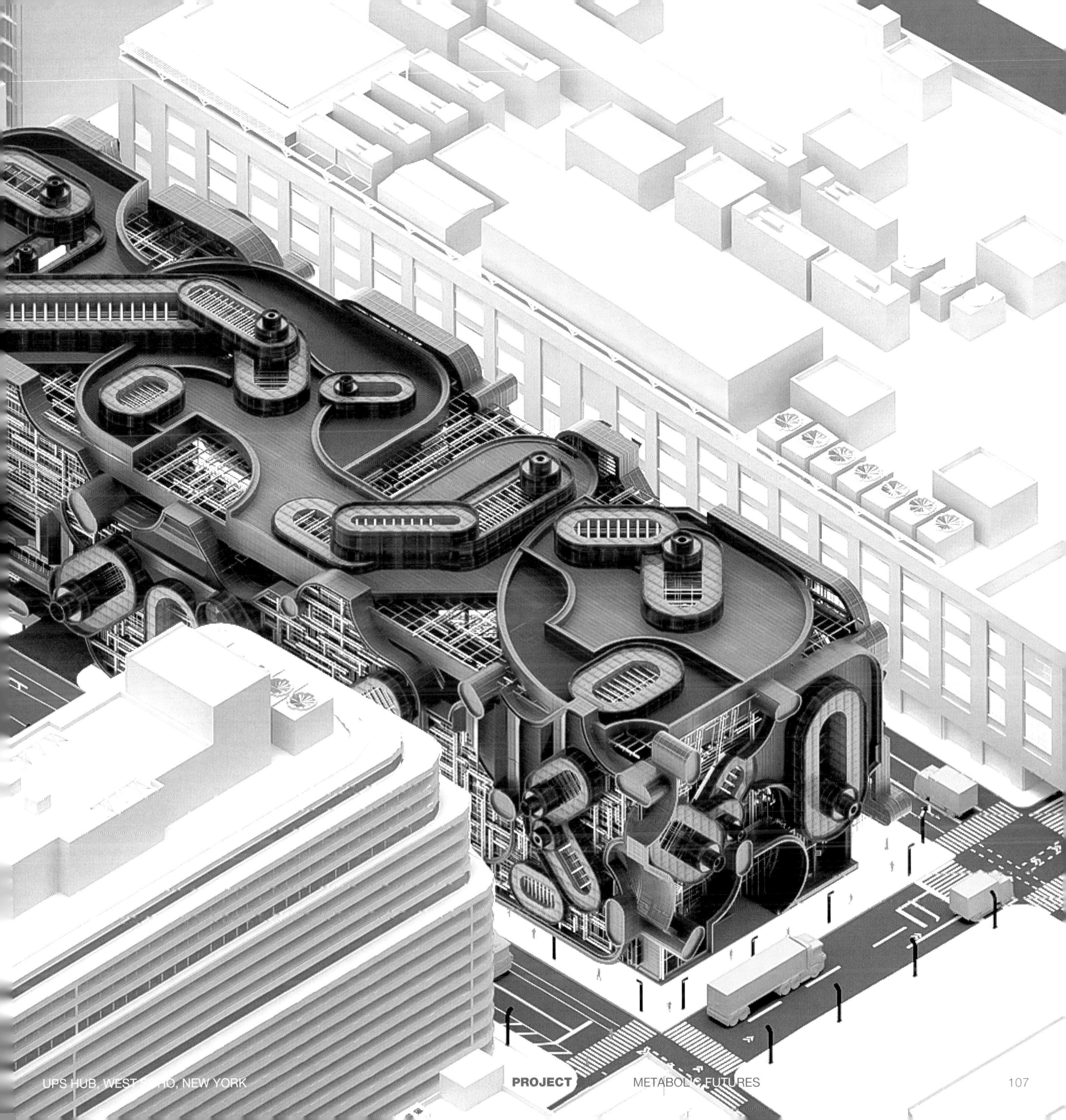

Elevation Rendering

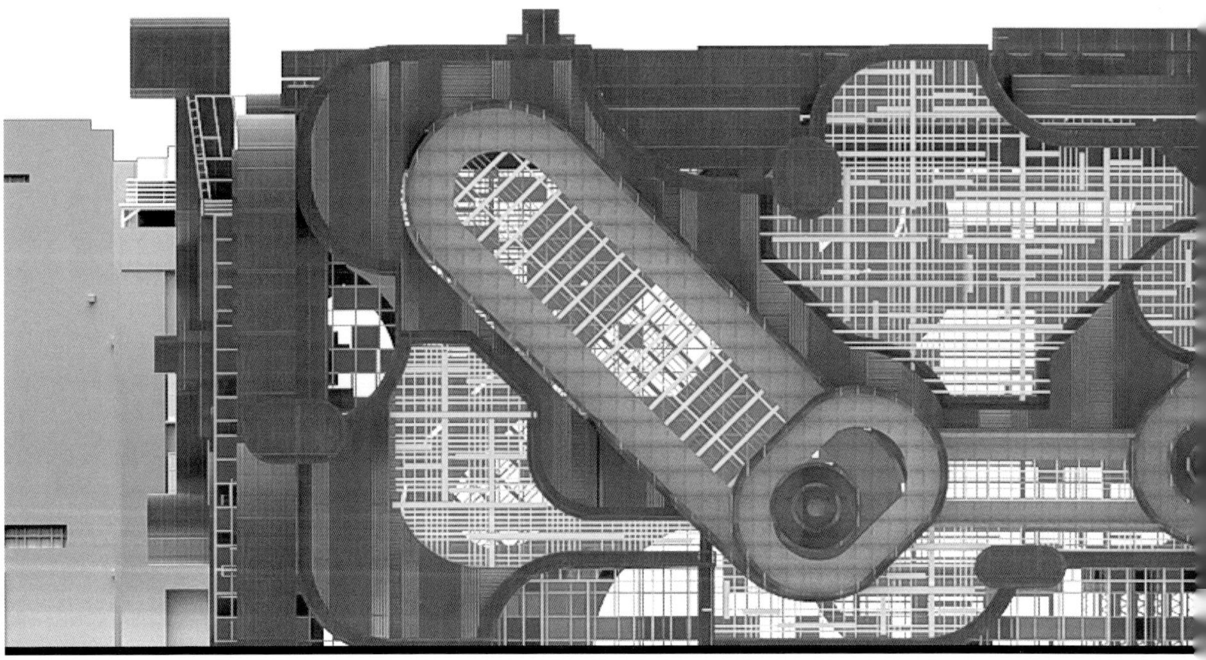

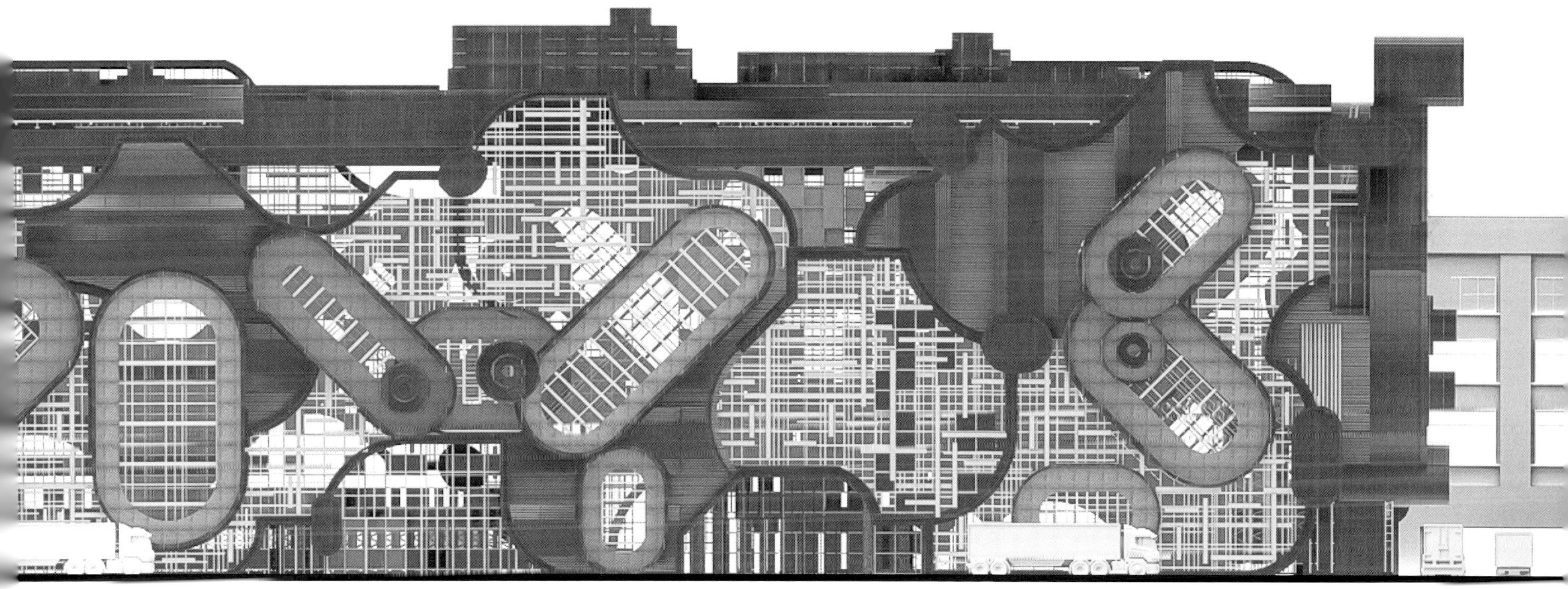

Right: Section Model Rendering

Left: Typical Floor Plan

01 Lounge
02 Conveyor Belt
03 Offices
04 Package Storage
05 Meeting Room
06 Board Room
07 Training Center
08 Restroom

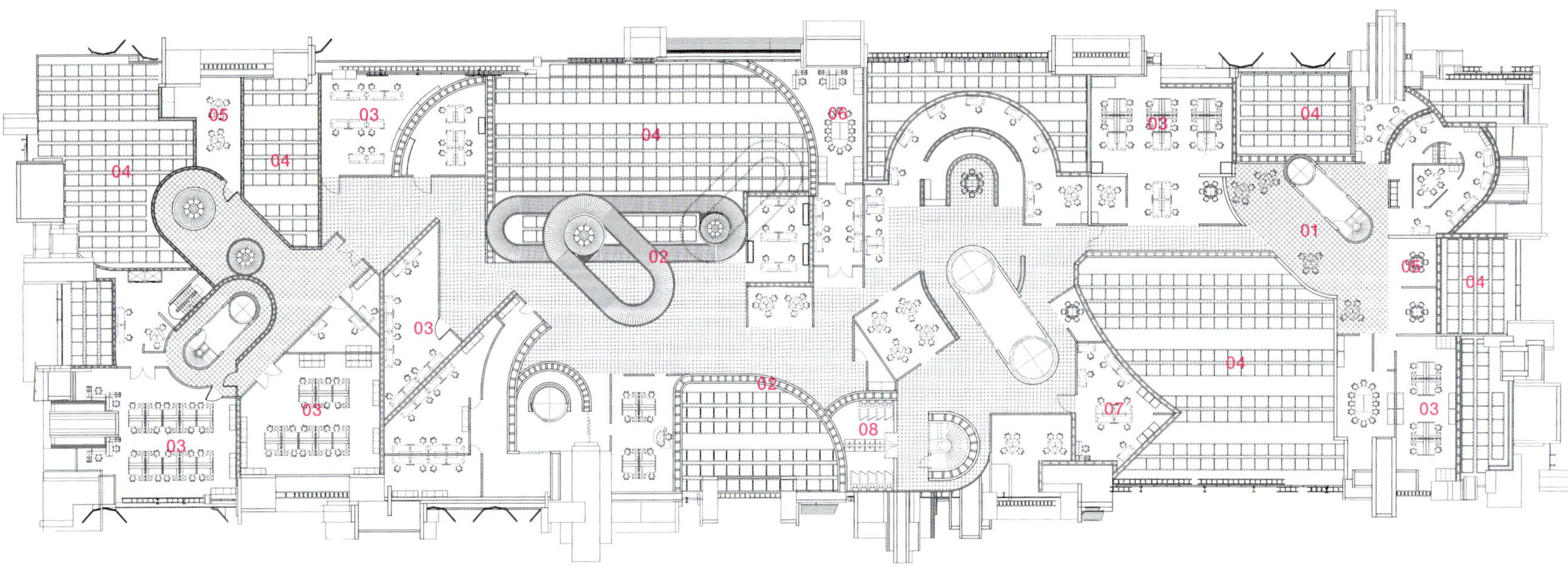

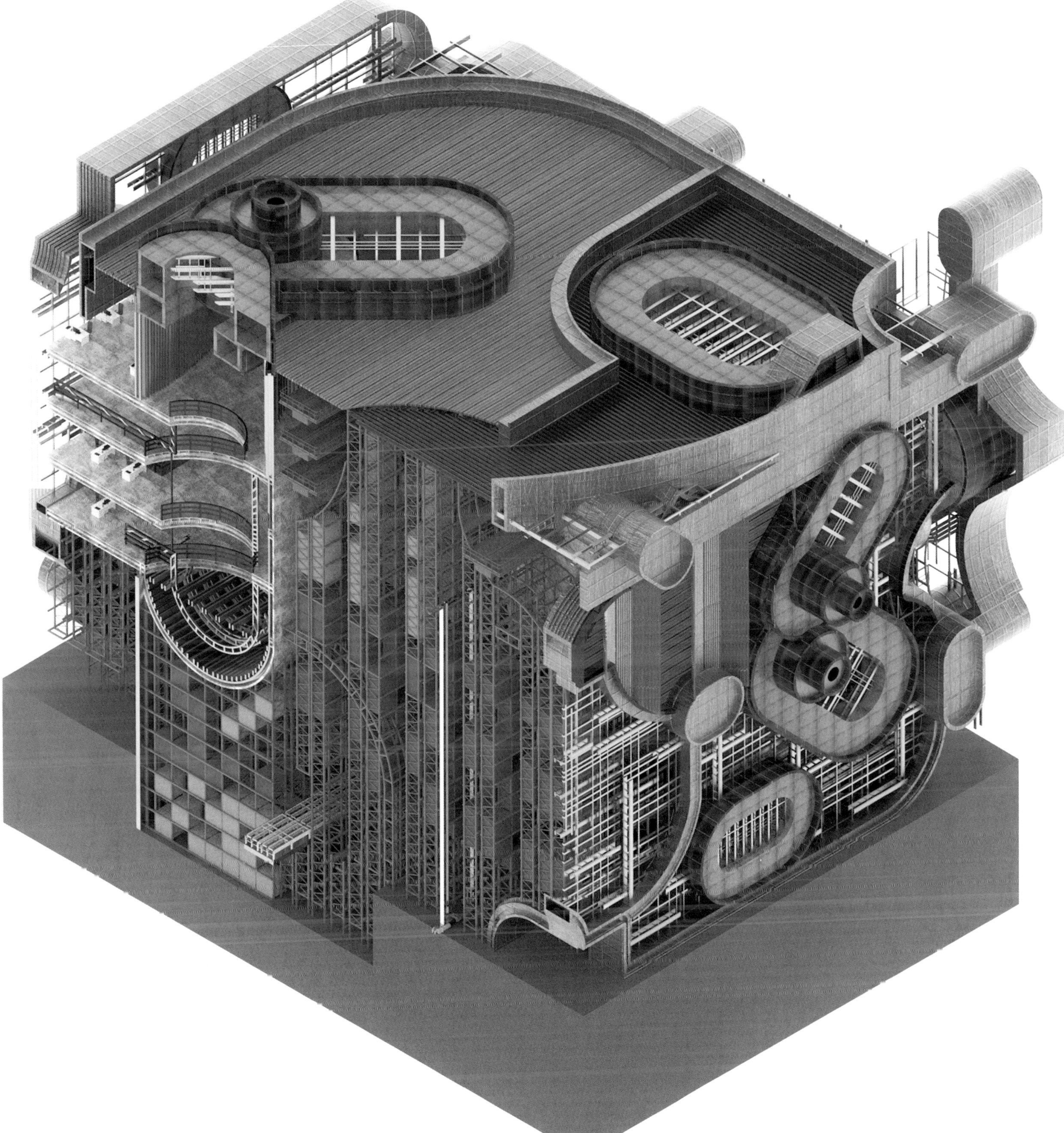

Physical Section Model, 2'x2'x2', 3D Printed PLA

Physical Section Model, 2'x2'x2', 3D Printed PLA

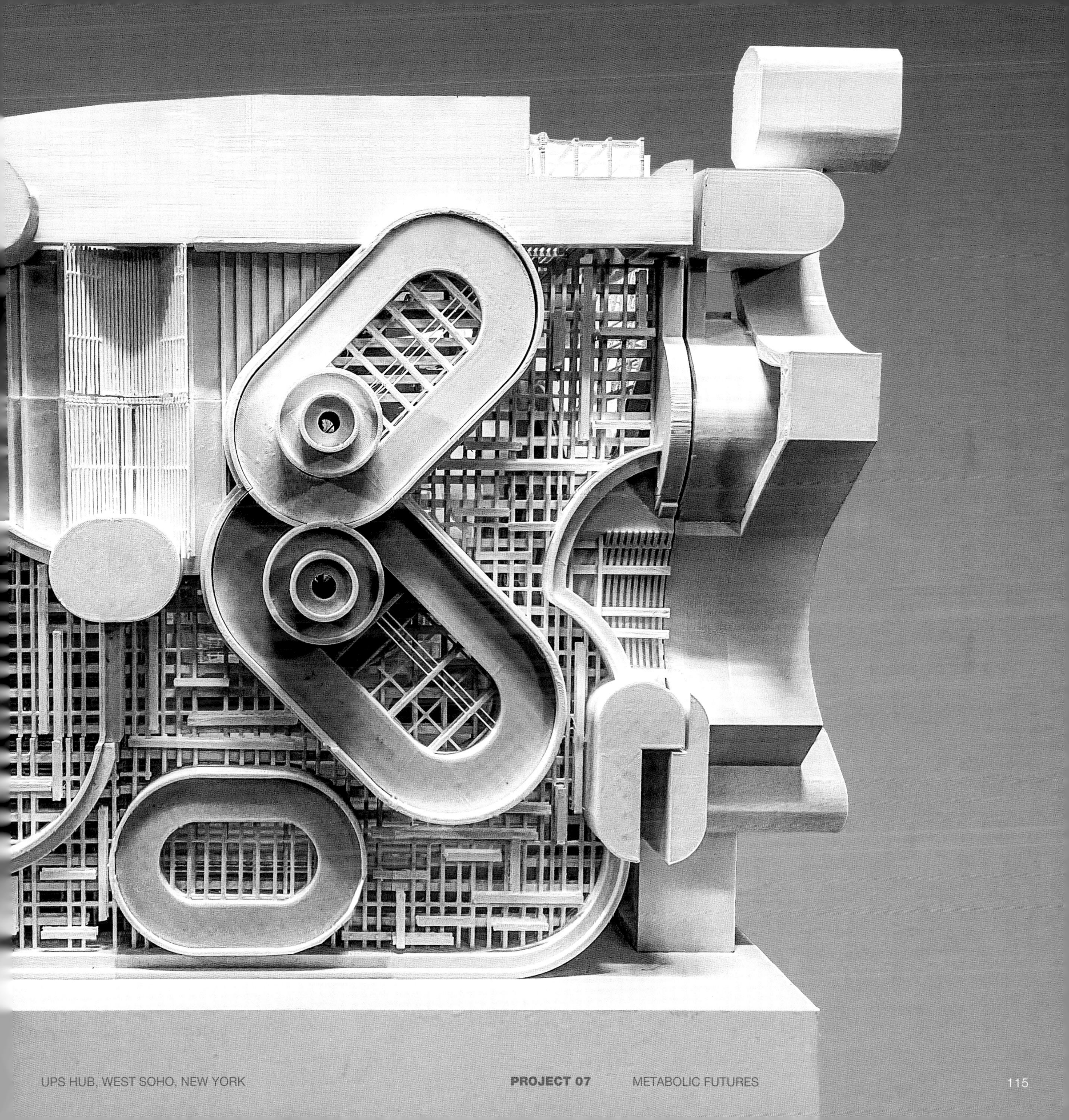

PROJECT 08

APPARATUS

UPS Hub, West SOHO, New York

Weihang Huang, Sina Lee

Apparatus places logistical operations at the forefront of its design. Rather than treating these operations as a functional afterthought, they are tightly integrated into the building's overall structure and aesthetics, creating a dynamic and efficient workplace. This integration is achieved through the building's unique façade, structural, and circulatory systems, which link external loading to internal processing seamlessly. The project is designed to meet the needs of modern businesses that rely on a combination of human and machine-centered programs. To achieve this, a diversity of flexible workspaces is strategically positioned throughout the building to foster productive relationships between workers and machines. Overall, Apparatus represents a new direction in workplace design, one that seeks to amplify the relationship between technology and human labor, creating an environment that is both efficient and comfortable for all workers.

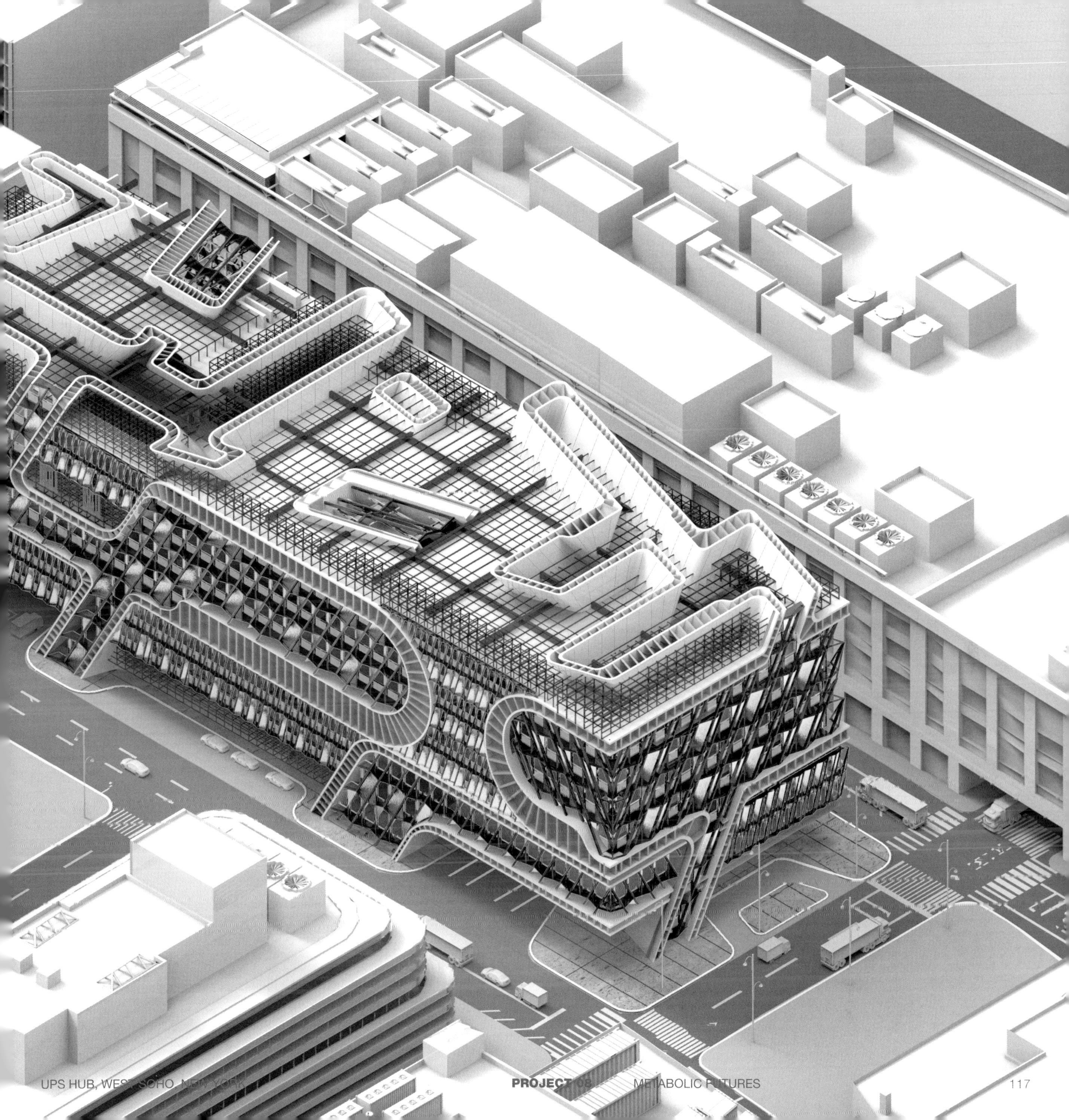

Right: Section Model Rendering

Left: Typical Floor Plan

01 Lounge
02 Conveyor Belt
03 Offices
04 Elevator
05 Package Storage
06 Cargo Drop-off Area
07 Meeting Room
08 Board Room
09 Lobby
10 Package Sort Area
11 Truck Dock
12 Training Center

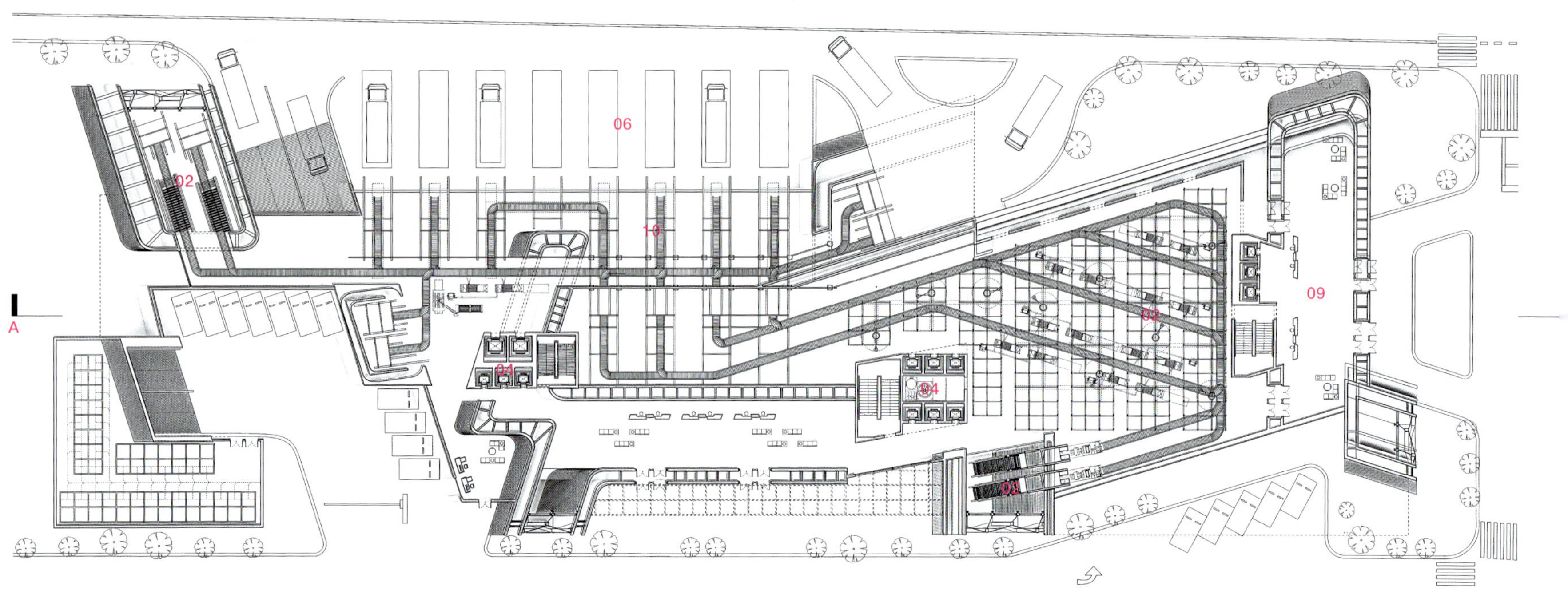

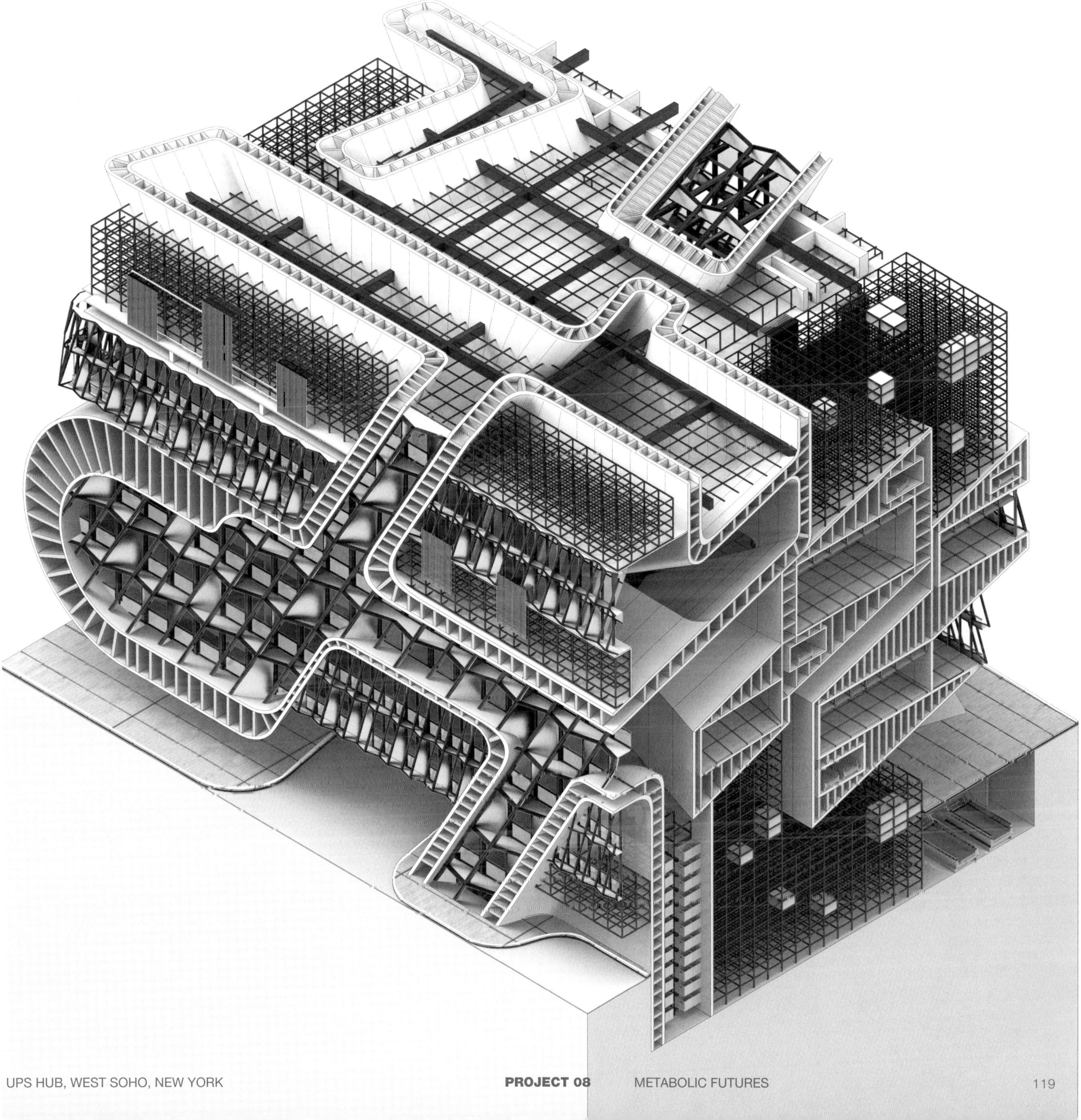

Elevation Drawing

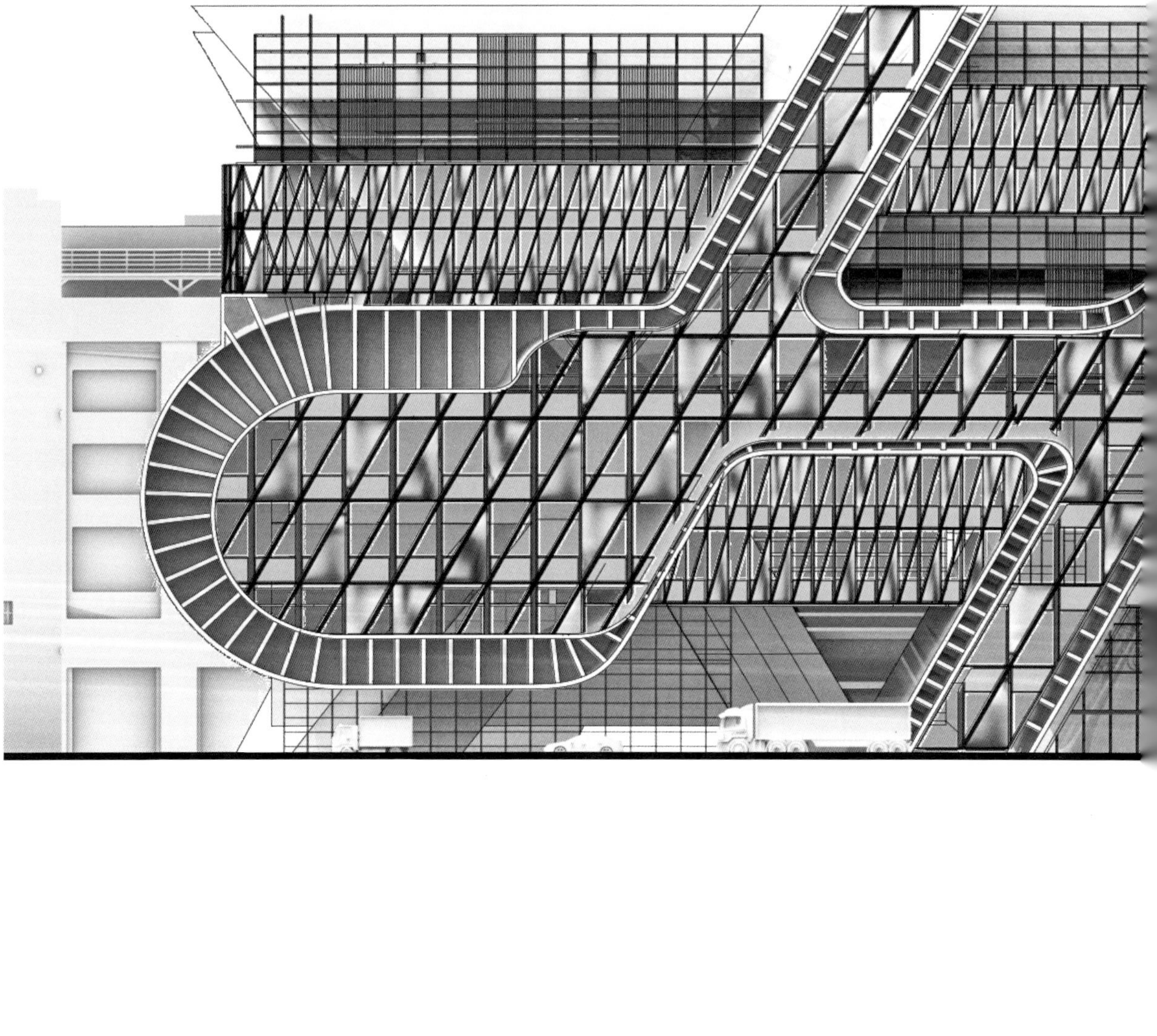

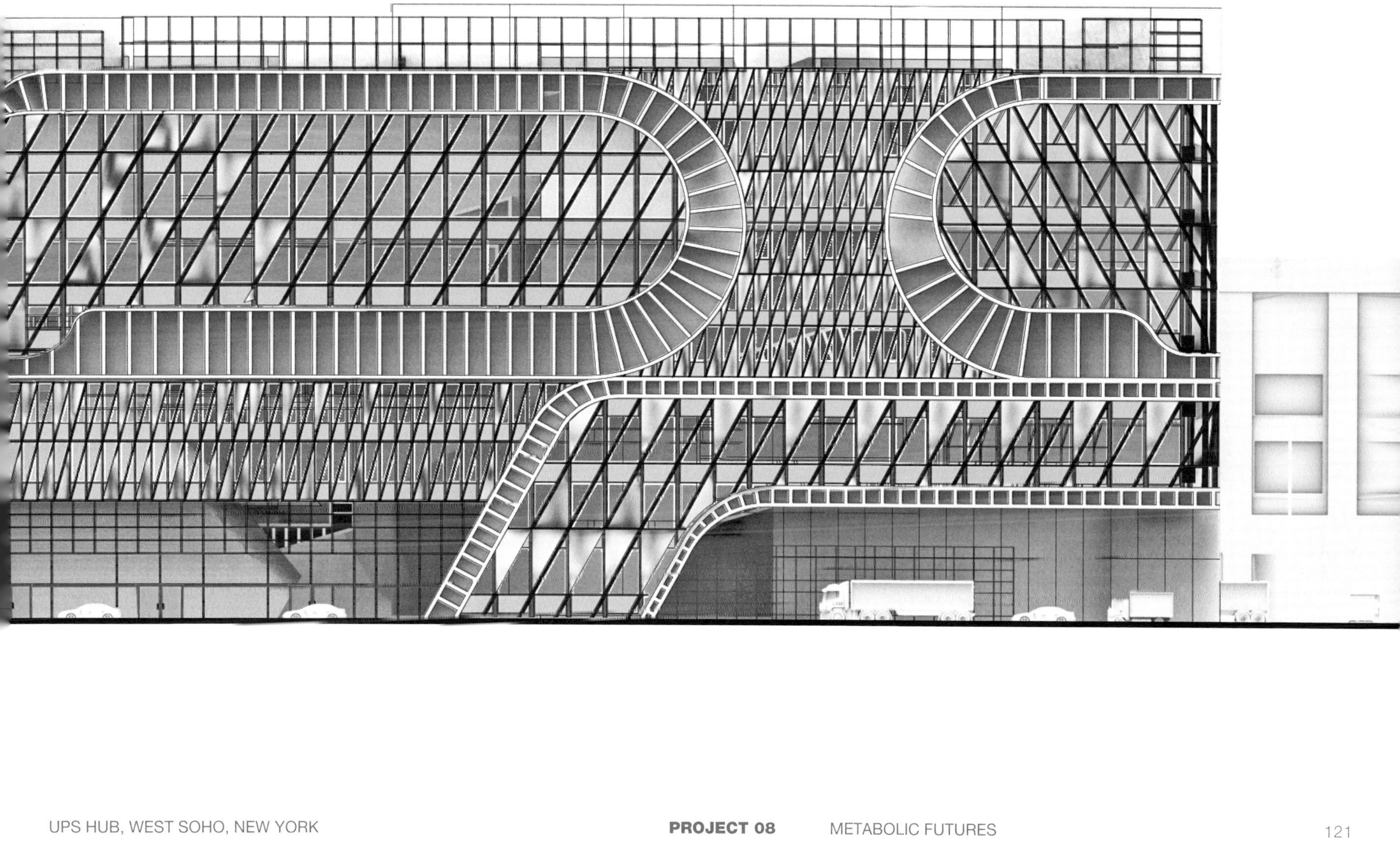

Long Building Section

01 Lounge
02 Conveyor Belt
03 Offices
04 Elevator
05 Package Storage
06 Cargo Drop-off Area
07 Meeting Room
08 Board Room
09 Lobby
10 Package Sort Area
11 Truck Dock
12 Training Center

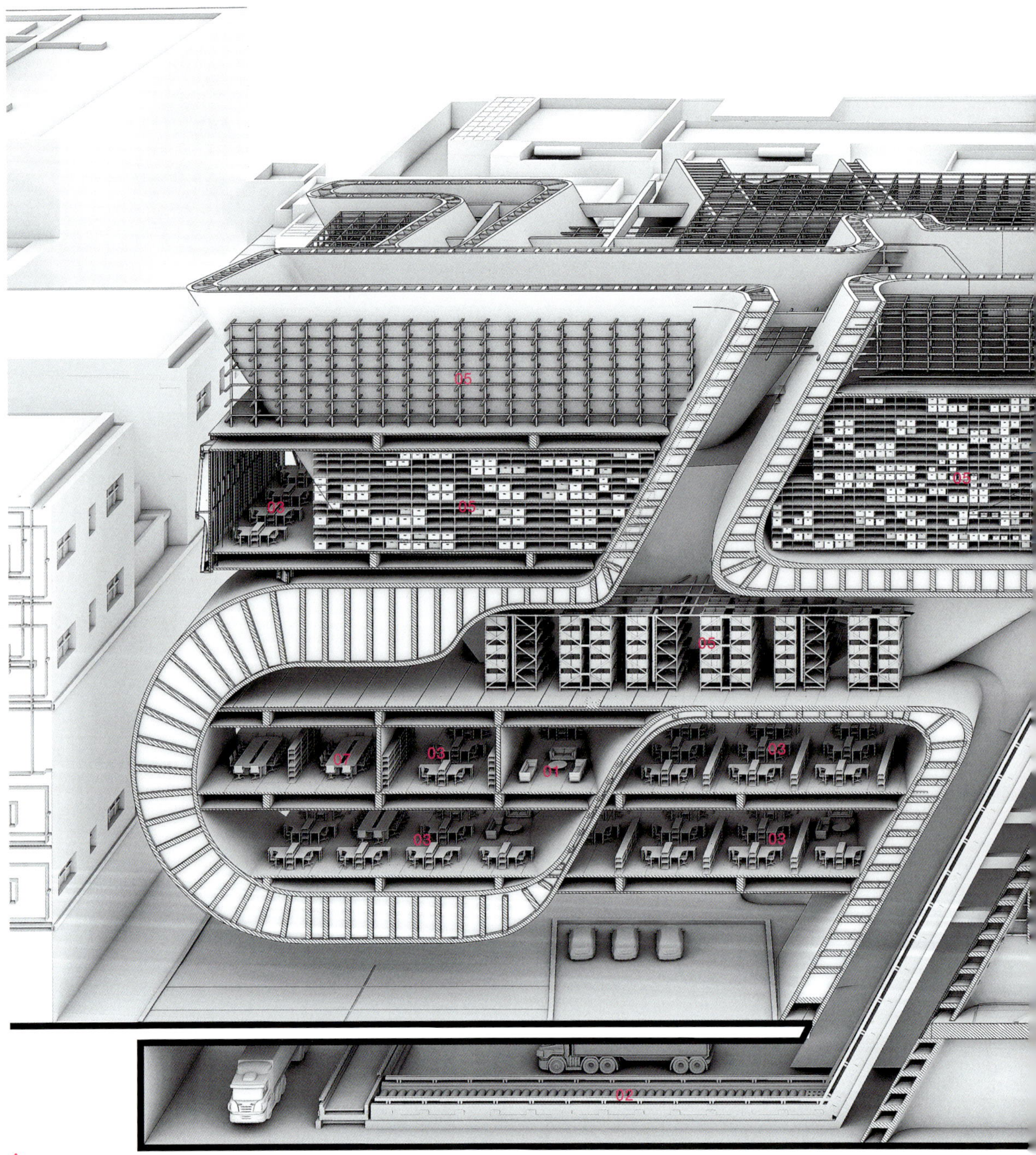

A

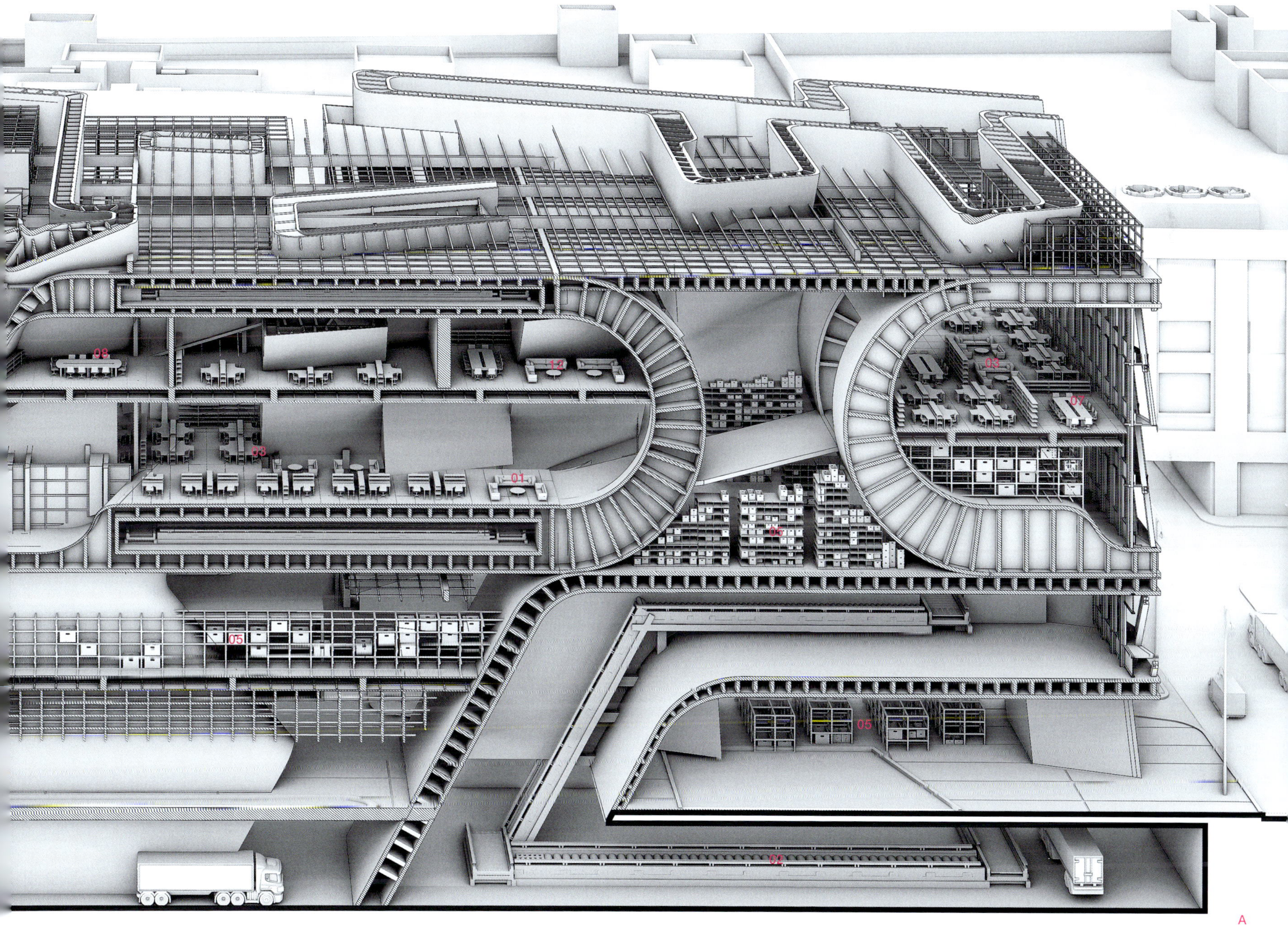
08
12
03
07
03
01
06
05
05
02
A

Right: Physical Section Model, 2'x2'x2', 3D Printed PLA

Left: Detail View of Physical Section Model

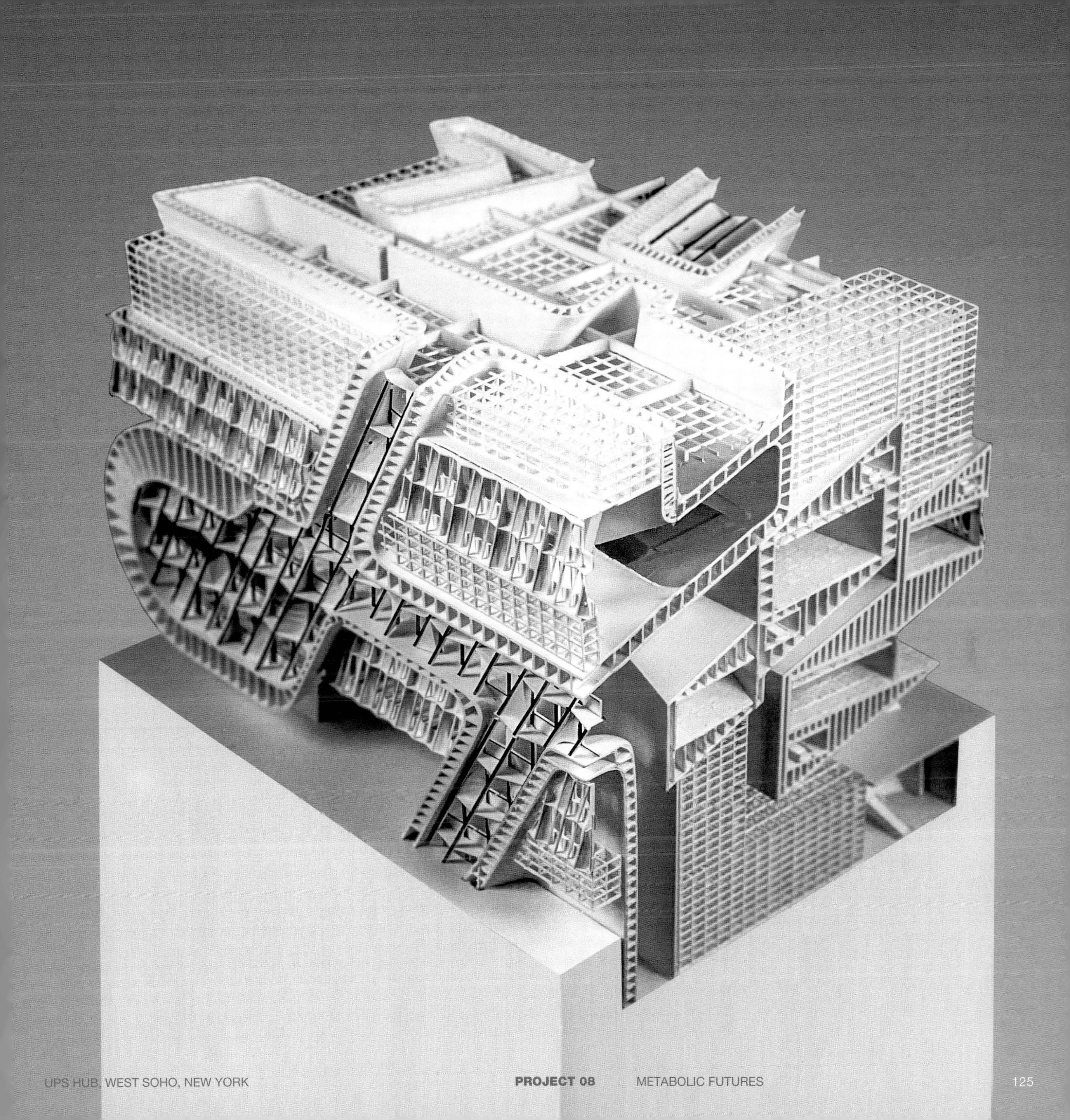

PROJECT 09

ENGINE

UPS Hub, West SOHO, New York

Yichi Zhang, Ruiwan Wang

Engine is an innovative and forward-thinking architecture project that aims to revolutionize the industrial landscape of the city. At the heart of the project is the idea of creating a high-tech, cutting-edge industrial complex that seamlessly integrates research labs and advanced manufacturing equipment and spaces. This unique approach brings together the creative and analytical aspects of the industrial process, fostering a culture of innovation, collaboration, and productivity. The labs are strategically placed in direct relationship with the manufacturing equipment and spaces, creating a fluid and efficient workflow that allows for rapid prototyping, testing, and production. Moreover, Engine is designed to be a sustainable and eco-friendly project, incorporating the latest green technologies and practices. From energy-efficient lighting to renewable energy sources, the project is built with the goal of minimizing its environmental impact while also creating a healthy and comfortable work environment for its occupants.

Right: Section Model Rendering

Left: Long Building Section

01 Lounge
02 Conveyor Belt
03 Offices
04 Stair
05 Package Storage
06 Cargo Drop-off Area
07 Meeting Room
08 Board Room
09 Roof Garden
10 Package Sort Area
11 Truck Dock
12 Mechanical Room
13 Package Distribution System

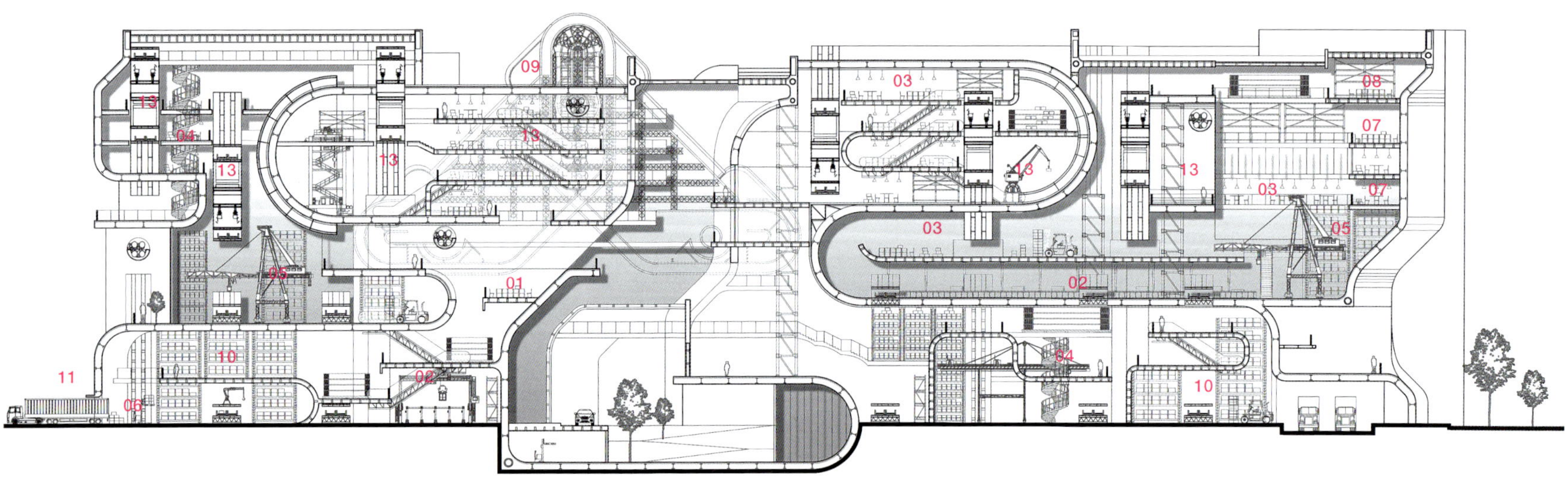

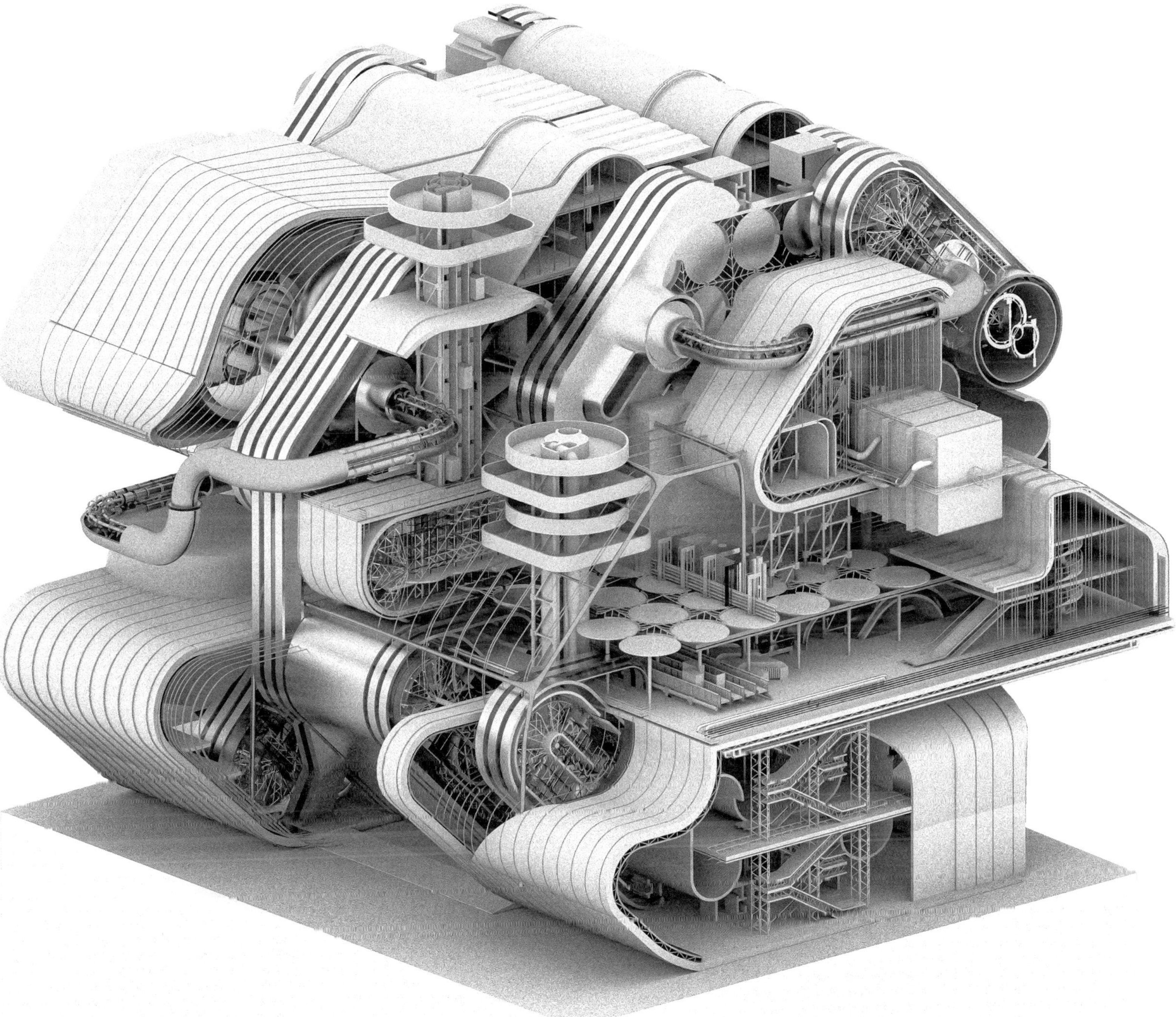

Elevation Rendering

Short Building Section

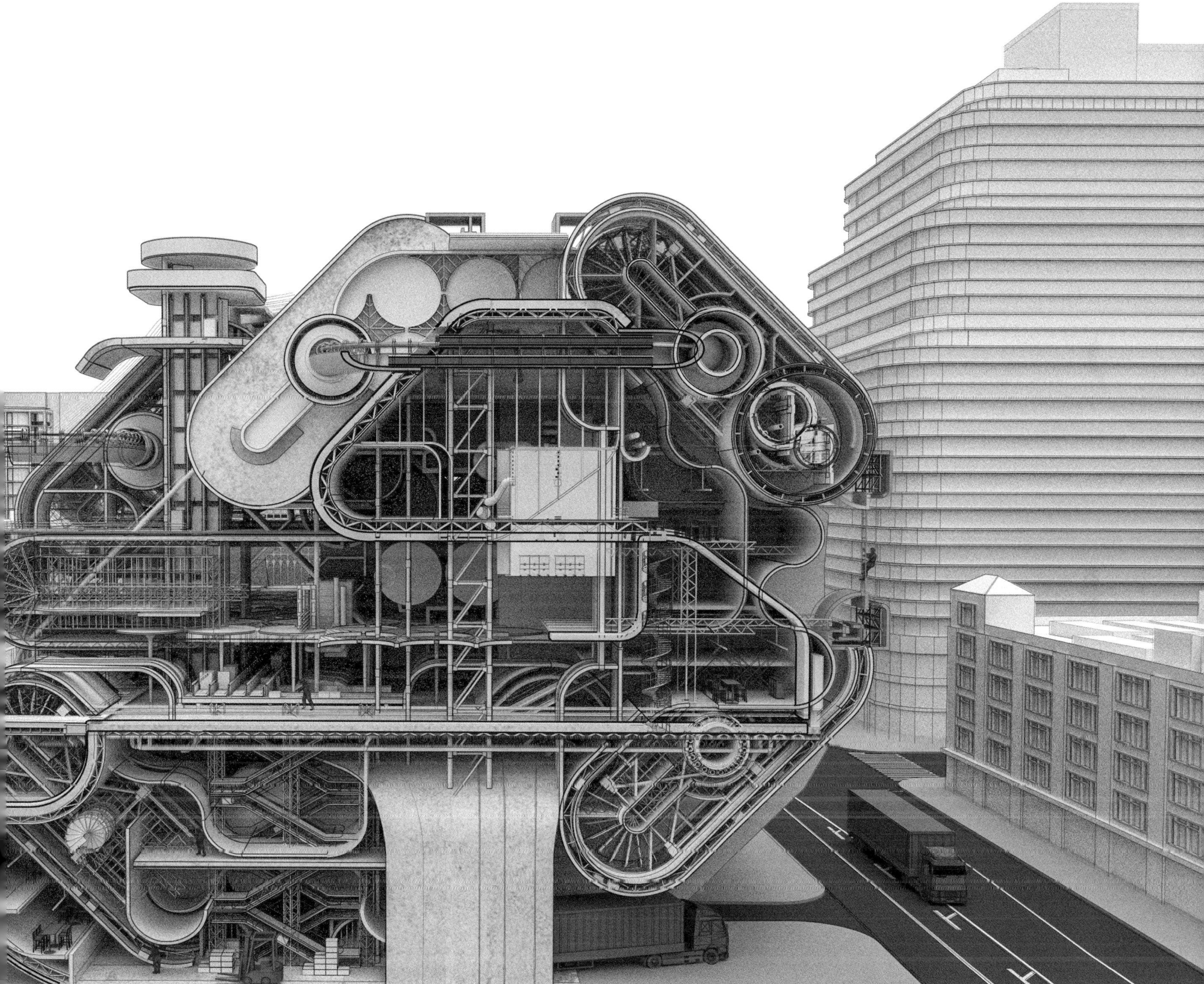

Right: Physical Section Model, 2'x2'x2', 3D Printed PLA

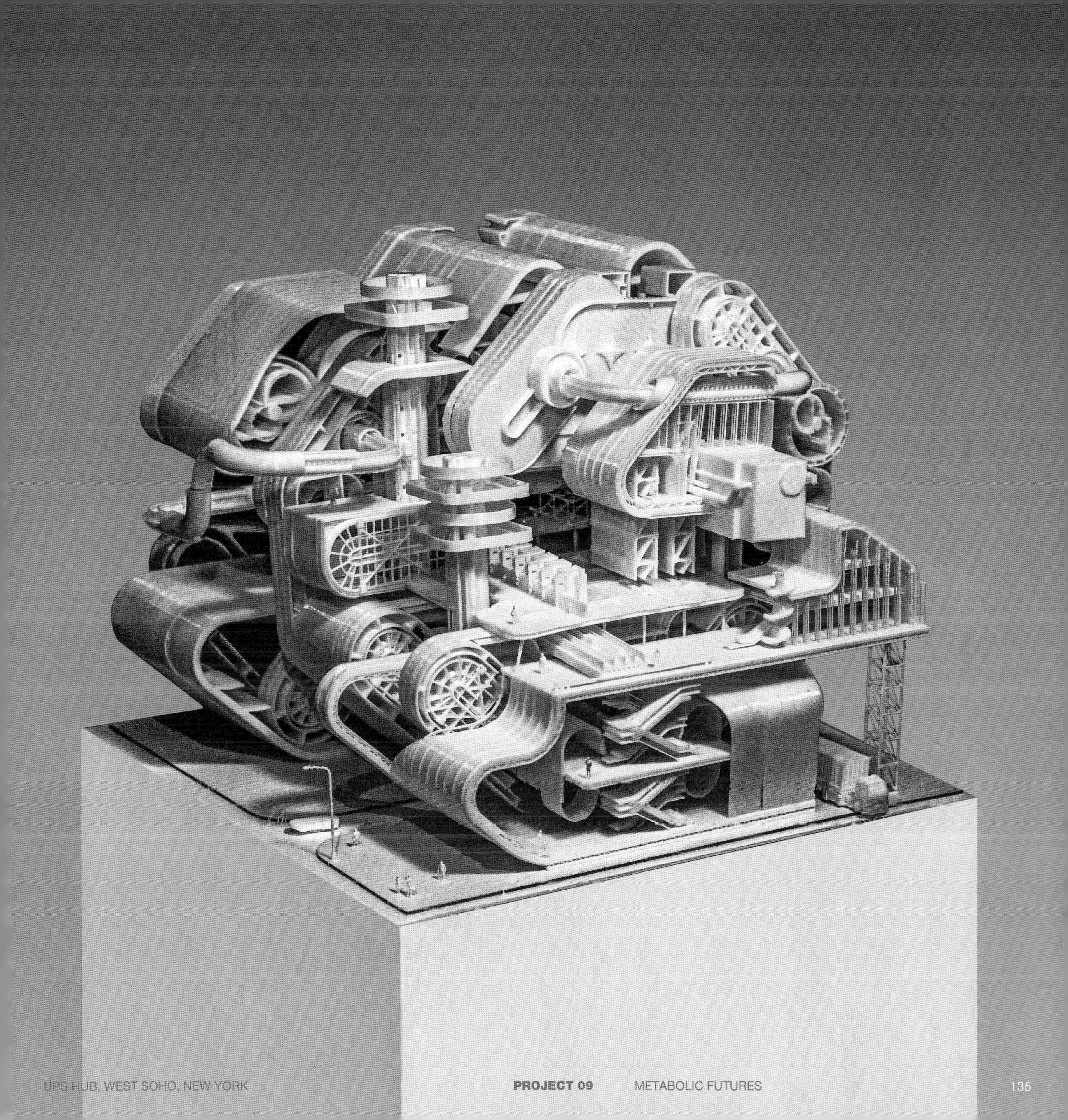

04 STICKY HYBRIDS, A PROPOSITION FOR THE FUTURE OFFICE

Patrick Monte

On March 23rd, 2021, the *Ever Given*, a somehow aptly named 1,300-foot Japanese-owned container ship en route from China to Europe, ran aground in the middle of the Suez Canal, cutting off a major global trade route and prompting a media frenzy over how and when it would be dislodged as well as why it found itself in such a predicament in the first place (Fig. 01). In contrast to the stillness of the massive ship was its instantaneous monitoring. Swarms of experts and naval authorities scrambled to dislodge the grounded vessel. Economists, lawyers, investors, and journalists counted the dollars per second being lost to commerce and damages ($10 billion per day, according to some estimates).[1] Memes, news stories, blog posts, and livestreams proliferated across media. It became the perfect metaphor for the fragility of the liberal global capitalist world order—preceded in 2020 by the onset of the COVID-19 pandemic and followed a year later in 2022 by Russia's invasion of Ukraine. During those slow days, one of the great myths of the digital era, of "open and instantaneous access," was confronted with the multiple constraints of hard infrastructure, logistics, spatial assets, the flow of people and goods, and of time itself. The ship was simply stuck; everybody could see it. After six days, the *Ever Given* was back on track to Europe, the media buzz and chatter died down, and the internet and media moved on to the next thing. But during those six days it was glaringly apparent that space itself can be uncompromisingly stubborn, or, well, sticky, and moreover that there can be tremendous power in that.

Buildings and infrastructure, in complete contrast to the constant change of the virtual—the ebb and flow of apps, games, and metaverses—are by and large meant to last. That permanence often "gets in the way," so to speak, exerts an influence over space and culture for years, decades, centuries, even millennia to come. Every building is in some sense an *Ever Given* run aground but within its own milieu, bound to impact cultural and economic flows and networks. The extent of that impact depends on typical criteria like the size and location of a building, its intended use, etc.; however, its specific contours are tied to design, composition, and aesthetics, which can be normative, disruptive, or transformative. Design creates linkages between built realities and value systems whether public, religious, ecological, or economic in nature, and such linkages are much more malleable than the buildings themselves.

The office tower, for instance, as a figure of urban architecture, has a peculiar stubbornness to it. It is somehow stuck as both a sign of the city, but also as an increasingly outmoded physical way of structuring spaces of work. It is stuck compositionally to past technologies, workplace hierarchies, and office cultures. It is stuck legally to zoning policies that govern use and architectural features. It is stuck ecologically and culturally to an economic model that privileges a 1:1 relationship between space and profit. All of this on top of the fact that large buildings by their nature are difficult and expensive to demolish; they are stuck in place. The proliferation of remote work during the COVID-19 pandemic made this

01 Tugboats trying to free the Ever Given after running aground in the Suez Canal, as viewed from the International Space Station, March 27, 2021. Courtesy of NASA Johnson Space Center, the Earth Science and Remote Sensing Unit

all increasingly palpable—so much so that in July of 2022, New York City Mayor Adams' administration announced the creation of the Office Adaptive Reuse Task Force to study and make citywide recommendations regarding the conversion of underused and unviable commercial office space across New York City (a development discussed further below).[2]

It is difficult to imagine the future of today's cities without skyscrapers. In New York City, for one, nearly a third of Manhattan buildings have some type of landmark status and will prospectively never be purposefully demolished.[3] At the same time, offices, the core programmatic driver of skyscraper design, itself may play a diminishing role in how such buildings are configured and operate in the future. As such, one has to ask and imagine not so much what the future of office buildings will or should be as what will current office buildings become. The reimagining of existing office towers represents a major consideration for architects as these buildings reach critical life cycles, and as the relevance of the programmatic considerations that informed their composition is in increasing tension with current modes of work. As this body of architecture already has an outweighed influence on urban organization and culture, it is pertinent that future renovations consider their role in how cities transform. There are many opportunities for designers to assert new and different forms of public interaction with these buildings, to create new possibilities of public affect toward them, and to benefit societal and ecological imperatives.

How can designers find strategies, opportunities, and leverage within existing architecture in the interest of a robust, diversified, and resilient urban culture? This question is addressed throughout the remainder of this essay in the context of New York City, with special attention to the past and future preservation of office skyscrapers. I first elaborate upon the concept of "stickiness" as it relates to architecture, public space, and urban culture. Then, I use stickiness as a framing device to discuss preservation efforts that have leveraged its power to achieve innovative urban solutions in the context of industrial architecture, using the Domino Sugar Factory Masterplan as a case study. I will follow by providing a brief overview of the history of skyscraper demolition, preservation, and renovation. With these in mind, I propose strategies for office tower redevelopment that use the concept of stickiness to dramatically reframe the potential role of architectural preservation and renovation in articulating urban public culture given expected shifts in the nature of work.

STICKINESS AND STICKY ARCHITECTURE

In her seminal work, *The Cultural Politics of Emotion*, Sara Ahmed describes the "accumulation of affective value" as "stickiness."[4] She argues that "objects become sticky, or saturated with affect, as sites of personal and social tension."[5] Ahmed is primarily concerned with this dynamic as it relates to the body and identity, how such dynamics track politically through forms of disgust, hate, and fear of groups, as well as their binding capacity through shared experience and emotion. To draw a parallel analogy in architecture and urban design, "stickiness" is driven by people's feelings towards the objects and spaces of architecture and results in their desire to linger or to pass by, to feel comfortable and included or uncomfortable, afraid and excluded, the desire to cherish and preserve or, on the contrary, to despise and destroy. This concept has been extrapolated by urban designers and theorists concerned with urban culture and the question of what makes a city appealing, what gives it a sense of place that people want to experience and enjoy.[6]

By and large, these examples highlight the cultural and economic value of streets and urban objects that attract people to gather and linger as well as their capacity for spontaneous happenings. These are set in contrast to Modernist urban planning strategies that prioritize efficiency through maximizing the ease and speed of vehicular and pedestrian flows: "It's often the things that slow pedestrians down that make a street great. Prime examples are the sidewalk cafe or bar patio—both of which are a pain for planners hoping to maximize a street's transportation efficiency, but a major asset to place makers looking to create attractive public space."[7] While "attractive space" may also read simply as "profitable," the gravity of the concept considered across the socio-political spectrum adds greater dimension. Questions emerge like what makes a neighborhood or particular space attractive or repulsive to,

02 The United States Government de-installed Richard Serra's public art on March 15, 1989. Tilted Arc, Richard Serra, Federal Plaza, New York, 1981. Photography by Anthony T. Troncale
03 Enzi Elements, PPAG Architects, MuseumsQuartier, Vienna, 2002. Photography by Lisi Gradnitzer, Courtesy of PPAG Architects

for instance, different racial, socio-economic, and different age groups? To queer people, women, men, or disabled persons? In what ways do spaces become sticky and accumulate affective value for such groups?

The crux of Ahmed's thesis is the idea that emotions, as elusive or ephemeral as they may be, can stick to bodies and objects in the people's psyches, and, in so doing, become sources for actions that range from social norms, rules, and behavior, to forms of speech, to media representations, to policy initiatives and regulations that all feed into, structure, or change aspects of society in concrete and observable ways. To illustrate this concept in an urban and architectural context, Richard Serra's *Tilted Arc* (1981) (Fig. 02) provides a compelling case study. The work consisted of a 120-foot long, 12-foot high, 2.5-inch thick corten steel wall tilted at a slight angle. It was installed in Foley Federal Plaza in Manhattan from 1981-1989 and positioned in an obvious tension with the circulation design of the plaza. Two aspects of the work stand out in delineating the concept of stickiness: its disruptive physicality and its provocation of an emotionally charged public debate.

First, it was sticky in a distinctly spatial sense, that is it disrupts space and flows of people in observable and unmistakable physical ways. Comers and goers from the surrounding buildings had to pool up around it in order to cross the plaza, as it was positioned like a blockage in a drain or the *Ever Given* in the Suez. While this disruption was in keeping with Serra's conceptual intentions to provoke relationships between sculpture, perception, circulation, and environment, many local workers were not intrigued, which raises the second point regarding emotions and public debate. Many workers from the surrounding buildings were outraged by *Tilted Arc*, it was a daily source of displeasure, frustration, even hatred. Its minimalist aesthetics and spatial impracticality became a target of the cultural rage that typified the "culture wars" of the 1980s. A public petition to remove the art work was followed by a public trial in which a jury voted to remove the sculpture.[8] Serra sued the government on contractual and constitutional grounds but lost in a case that rose to the U.S. Court of Appeals for the Second Circuit. Here, the sculpture, because of its stickiness, both physically and emotionally, activates a cultural politics that includes media representations of the episode, legal precedents for speech, ownership, and handling as they relate to public art, and, of course, the sculpture's physical removal from the plaza.

What is curious looking back at *Tilted Arc* is that many of its underlying concepts now inform celebrated strategies for public space surrounding office buildings. The introduction of stylized urban furniture and modular sculptures, often in bright saturated colors that are intended to "activate" streets by offering gathering spaces and respite for passers-by. Works such as J. Mayer H.'s X-shaped lounge chairs in Times Square or PPAG Architects' Enzi furniture in Vienna can be observed in countless urban areas around the world (Fig. 03). These strategies are successful because of their popular aesthetics, non-confrontational positioning, their ability to complement accepted consumer-driven activities, and their easeful figuration in photographs shared on social media. Cultural and aesthetic judgement aside, such examples represent a positive emotive counterpoint to the type of negativity that accumulated around *Tilted Arc*. This polarity is important in analyzing how such dynamics scale up to architecture and urban design.

Since the 1970s, numerous examples of large-scale nineteenth- and twentieth-century industrial architecture—including mills, warehouses, factories, and ports—have undergone major efforts on behalf of municipalities, community organizations, and businesses to ensure their continued presence in the urban landscape. These efforts have figured in importantly to the redevelopment and revitalization of deindustrialized urban areas. Such buildings and industrial areas, because of both their substantial urban footprints and their ability to represent the urban past, exemplify stickiness at the urban scale.

The Domino Sugar Refinery in Brooklyn, NY, is one such example and raises several issues around historic preservation, master planning, the workplace, and urban public culture. Located just north of the Williamsburg Bridge on the East River waterfront, the refinery, built 1881–84, is the largest surviving example of Brooklyn's booming nineteenth-century sugar industry, which at times produced three-quarters of the nation's sugar supply.[9] The refinery's main building, originally known as the Havemeyer & Elders Filter, Pan & Finishing House, consists of a 155-foot tall thick-walled brick structure with a 250- by 150-foot footprint and an oval chimney that rises an additional fifty feet and projects out of the west (Manhattan-facing) façade (Fig. 04). Its monolithic dark red bricks, towering chimney, its approximately 65- by 40-foot iconic yellow neon sign, and its visibility from the Williamsburg Bridge and East Side of Manhattan made it a singular visual urban landmark over and above its symbolism of Brooklyn's industrial past. Throughout the twentieth century it underwent numerous renovations and updates before declining in use during the

Post-World War II period and finally ceasing operations in 2004. At that point the entire 11-acre site was sold to C.P.C. Resources, the for-profit development arm of the Community Preservation Corporation (CPC), a lending consortium of banks and insurance companies known for residential redevelopment projects which have been associated with gentrification in New York City.[10] In 2005, the following year, much of the Williamsburg and Greenpoint waterfront north of the site was rezoned to allow for redevelopment of its industrial sites into up to 40-story luxury apartment buildings as well as retail shops and recreation areas.[11] In 2007, the Pan, Filtering, and Finishing House (the main original brick building on the site) was designated an historic landmark, though the future of the plant's numerous twentieth-century structures, as well as its iconic sign, remained uncertain. Community members and officials split over the future development of the site with one side fed up with overdevelopment and gentrification in the surrounding neighborhoods, and the other side advocating for increased housing supply as well as a variety of public amenities.[12]

A street campaign emerged in the surrounding neighborhoods under the epithet "Save Domino" and included posters and stencils featuring a silhouette of the refinery pasted across walls and spraypainted onto sidewalks, as well as a seven-story red LED sign erected on the façade of a neighboring building.[13] The CPC's 2010 plan, designed by Rafael Viñoly, included 2,200 units across nine buildings, four of which would have been over 300 feet. The plan was passed by the City Council but stalled due to community opposition, and facing financial troubles due to its investment in the plan, the CPC sold the site to Two Trees Development in 2012.

Shop Architects designed a new masterplan for Two Trees, which was approved in 2014 (Fig. 05). The plan achieves the same number of units as the Viñoly plan for the CDC but with four buildings rising up to 50 stories, three of which feature distinctive central voids. This allowed a more generous allocation of public space, including a waterfront park featuring bocce courts, a dog run, volleyball courts, riverside seating, picnic areas, a beer garden, and flex lawn and bench spaces. Running across the park is an "artifact walk" where artifacts

04 The Domino Sugar Refinery as seen from Manhattan in 2010 before the site's redevelopment. Photography by Beyond My Ken
05 Domino Sugar Masterplan bird's eye rendering looking southeast, SHoP Architects, New York, 2014. Rendering by SHoP Architects

from Domino's industrial past such as syrup tanks, a bucket conveyor, lounge screw conveyor, crane platforms and tracks, and gantries are permanently displayed. The Domino sign was moved and prominently re-erected on the historic refinery building. Critics may fluctuate.

On the one hand, some would celebrate uniquely preserving historic structures while creating generous new public spaces, 700 affordable housing units, tax-revenue generating office and mixed-use buildings, and a touristic/consumer destination. On the other hand, some might argue that the plan is a superficial commodification of urban history and architecture that bears little or no meaningful relationship to the history and future of working-class people that contributed to the site's perceived cultural importance and the wealth it generated. What cannot be denied, however, is that the affectual accumulation around this site—its "stickiness," in a word—was the central factor in its development. The refinery's iconicity, Domino's deep branding within American culture, its visibility within the city, its signification of New York City's industrial past, its sheer size and physical imprint, as well as the accumulation of debate and emotions around the site all imbued it with stickiness and augmented its figuration in the development of the Brooklyn waterfront. It was a tool that could be yielded for critics on either side; it impacted the form of the final design in essential ways and sealed a monumental status for the site in contemporary and future urban space and culture.

STICKY SKYSCRAPERS

Unlike the historic industrial spaces typified by Domino, the question of office towers and skyscrapers with regard to preservation, demolition, and adaptive-reuse is relatively new and rare. In New York City, however, many have already entered local, national, and international registries of historic landmarks. As such, their future use, configuration, and role in the city, their relationship to public culture is an imminent concern. Several prominent strategies and practices are already in place. For one, demolition and new construction, though a costly endeavor with high potential for regulatory setbacks, remains an option for many sites. There have been two major phases of skyscraper demolition in New York City.

06 The Singer Building Tower, Ernest Flagg, New York, around 1898-1908. Photography by Irving Underhill

07 Union Carbide Building, 270 Park Avenue, SOM, New York, 1960–2021. Courtesy of Google Satellite

08 Rendering of the new 270 Park Avenue. Slated for completion in 2025, the new structure will be 1388ft (423m) tall, nearly double the height of its predecessor. The JPMorgan Chase Building, Foster+Partners, 2022, New York. Rendering by CrossingLights

First, in the 1960s, many skyscrapers built between 1860-1930 reached critical building cycles and were competing with tremendous innovations in building technology that allowed for higher towers and increased efficiency in spatial organization. Of these, the Singer building (1908-1968) was the tallest to be demolished and still remains the second tallest building in NYC to be demolished (Fig. 06). As was the case with similar though smaller profile buildings, demolition and new construction was a way to capitalize vertically on Manhattan's highly profitable and sought-after land parcels. This phase of demolition coincided with, and also propelled, the preservation of many of the city's iconic late-nineteenth and early-twentieth-century buildings like the Chrysler Building, the Flatiron Building, and the Plaza Hotel, to name a few. Second, in the 2010s, following a critical rezoning that opened up air rights for vertical redevelopment, the Union Carbide Building (1960-2021)—a.k.a. 270 Park Avenue or the JPMorgan Chase Tower—was slated for demolition to make way for construction of the new 270 Park Avenue on an expanded site.[14] At the time, the 707-foot-tall Union Carbide Building was the tallest to ever be peacefully demolished (Figs. 07-08).[15] While new construction always offers opportunities for urban public culture, given the risk and financial stakes of demolition and construction, it seems likely that developers will take as few chances as possible when it comes to creating new types of public space in and around new buildings outside of established precedents.

For landmarked structures, late-nineteenth and early-twentieth-century office towers represent a whole body of prestige historic New York architecture undergoing major renovations and shifts in use since the 2000s. Owners and developers of buildings including the Woolworth Building, 111 W57th Street (Steinway Hall), the Waldorf-Astoria, One Wall Street, and the Crown Building, among others, have all turned to high-end luxury residential renovations. Of these, the Woolworth Building is the most prominent because of its sheer height (at 241 meters in 1913, it was once the tallest building in the world), its gothic style, and its unmistakable patina copper spire in the New York City skyline. The turn to residential conversions is symptomatic of several shifts in both office design and work itself. Architecturally, New York's legacy skyscrapers face several limitations in terms of tenant desire. These include the constrained form of floor plates in upper levels due to footprint setbacks staggered vertically, the relatively small scale of elevators, limited natural lighting, and a general lack of twenty-first-century amenities. Urbanistically, remote work, the appeal of more horizontal workspaces pioneered by the tech industry, as well as workplaces in greater dialogue with street culture all present challenges to the office tower typology in general, and even more so to less-flexible historic towers. In the case of the Woolworth Building, to address the setback issue, plans were announced in 2012 to convert each of its upper 30 floors into luxury single residences. Its five-floor spire was converted into a penthouse dubbed by marketers as a "castle in the sky" and originally listed in 2014 for a record $110-million.[16] It is at least questionable whether the spire of such a landmark should be in the hands of a single individual; if it had attained a cultural and historical significance, should that not be shared through some public utility other than its façade? Given that luxury residential development benefits from exclusivity, it seems that this avenue of redevelopment will be determined to withhold itself from public access and urban culture for the foreseeable future rather than engage with it without tremendous public pressure.

Preservation and upgrades to existing office towers built in the latter half of the 20th century, offer some differing, more inviting attitudes toward public space and urban culture. Union Carbide's Park Avenue twin, the Lever House building, was deemed to be a finer example of the International Style and received landmark status in 1982; it is now being renovated by the firm that originally built it, SOM. Current plans for the Lever House renovation typify one attitude toward office tower preservation: repair and restore elements of the building to maintain the integrity of the original design while making upgrades to materials and performance that meet contemporary standards like LEED certification. The most visible changes are those proposed for its two most public-facing areas—the ground floor, where new pavers will replicate the building's original 1952 design, and the building's signature third floor terrace, where landscaping will be denser and more filled out with birch trees, shrubs, and flowers.[17] In this case, the original design with upgrades are considered adequate and desirable for maintaining the building's intended use as a place of work. By closely honoring the original design, such strategies also invest in the public image of specific buildings, hedging on their iconicity as a future asset and allure.

Other skyscraper renovations capitalize on public aspects of buildings as assets for creating increased desirability and continuity of use that navigate shifts in work. Attention to the ground plane, as in the Lever House renovation, is at the center of numerous office tower renovations. For instance, 100 Pearl Street, a 29-story office tower built in the financial district in 1983, is not landmarked but its proximity to landmarked buildings across the street and location within an historic district ruled out demolition. The renovation represents a host

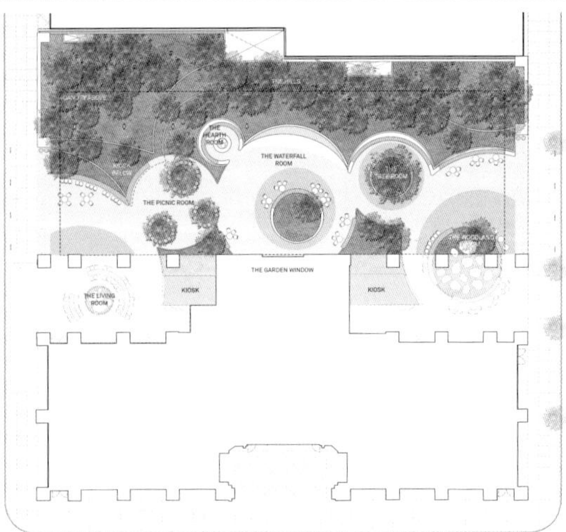

09 The revitalized POPS running along the building's west (rear) face. 550 Madison Avenue Garden, Snøhetta, New York, 2022. Photography by Barrett Doherty, Courtesy of Snøhetta

10 Ground Floor Plan. 550 Madison Avenue Garden, Snøhetta, New York, 2022. Drawing by Snøhetta

of common current strategies in skyscraper redevelopment. These include an increased focus on publicly accessible ground floor amenities, such as a publicly accessible arcade-style market hall that mixes an assortment of casual eateries and bars with flexible seating arrangements, lobbies that emphasize transparency and natural light, roof top terraces that emphasize lush greenery and leisure amenities for tenants, as well as duplex and double-height interior modifications to create spacious open floor plans. Snøhetta's modifications to 550 Madison Avenue's lobby and exterior also leverage public space and visibility (Figs. 09-10). Built in 1984 and landmarked in 2018, renovations to Philip Johnson's postmodern icon include the opening up of the circular portal windows on its North and South façades, increased visibility and access on the ground floor through the removal of infill retail storefronts, and the construction of a publicly-accessible canopied greenspace on the West (back) end of the tower. The public area of the project consists of several informal seating and gathering areas articulated by semi-circular planted terraces in dialogue with Johnson's circular design motifs. The garden is designated as a Privately Owned Public Space (POPS), runs North-South connecting 55th and 56th streets, and features numerous evergreens, perennials, and flowering shrubs. The prominence of the garden on the back end and the elimination of the retail on the front end represent an assertion of aesthetic and public values over a straightforward space to profit logic.

What is changing in renovations like 100 Pearl Street and 550 Madison is a different positivistic valuation of a building's potential for affectual accumulation—its stickiness—in making it desirable as a place to work, its positionality as a social object in a work ecosystem and the urban environment, and how these translate into continued relevance, resilience, and economic viability for the office tower amidst dramatic technological and social change. Ultimately, this revaluation may simply be a more culturally and aesthetically nuanced strategy for balancing the bottom line. It highlights, however, that the cumulative forces of preservation, building aging (physical and programmatic), and shifts in the culture of work are opening up new opportunities for architects, policy makers, and activists to assert new forms of public culture in existing office towers.

STICKY HYBRIDS

It is not hard to see how investment in public space and culture is a win for the public, the city, and surrounding businesses. The Highline seemed risky at the time of its redevelopment—it might have been easier and safer to demolish it, sell off any land rights, and call it a day—yet it is clear that its conversion into an elevated parkscape and greenway was entirely transformative for the whole west side of Manhattan below 59th street. There is no reason that this logic should not be experimented with vertically through the remaking of office towers. It is a way to carve out public spaces while generating new attraction points and diversifying urban space. Who would deny that if the Woolworth building's five-floor penthouse had been converted into a concert hall, museum, or some other fantastical public space that it would not be an instantaneous, celebrated global destination and cultural and economic generator for the city and surrounding area? Probably only for real estate development corporations looking to turn a relatively short-term profit. Cities, on the other hand, have the benefit of time and long-term planning. The future of New York City's office towers is not in newfound heights but in innovative interior transformations that reinvent and reimagine the city.

To this end, in an analysis of public spaces inside and around skyscrapers, Vuk Radović suggests a shift in perspective from viewing skyscrapers as "architectural singularities towards urban multiplicities."[18] Radović's view holds that within an urban morphology moving up in scale from building to village to city to region, large skyscrapers should be treated more akin to villages in terms of design formulation, policy and governance, relationships between public and private space, and their broader cultural functioning. Radović rightly observes through a cross-comparison of skyscrapers in New York and London that the dominant conception of public space, and specifically the location of POPS, is always pushed to segregated peripheral zones such as exterior public plazas, the ground floor plane, and upper-level viewing/leisure decks; they are never integrated throughout the building. The same holds true for Snøhetta's renovation of 550 Madison Avenue mentioned previously. Picking up on Ken Yeang's vertical theory of urban design, Radović suggests vertical reinterpretations of horizontal

11 The Westin Bonaventure Hotel & Suites, John Portman, Los Angeles, 1977. Photography by Alexandre Georges, Courtesy of the Portman Archives

strategies, such as sky courts, plazas, streets-in-the-sky, and green lungs.[19]

Along these lines, alternative precedents for the design of internal public space include the city-within-a-skyscraper and megastructure designs that characterize John Portman's signature high-rise hotels or contemporary proposals like SURE Architecture's *Endless City* (2014) (Fig. 11). Portman's designs integrated central circulation strategies with gathering spaces, city views, plantings, and amenities around full-building-height atria that could be traversed vertically through seemingly infinite systems of elevators, escalators, ramps, and stairs. While such work has been criticized for being anti-urban, for ignoring or outright alienating the exterior public realm in favor of highly controlled, "safe," utopian interior, it still offers strategies and a vision of the public interior for architects to draw from. SURE's *Endless City* offers a more contemporary vision that more closely mirrors the diversity, spontaneity, and navigability of spaces that characterize street- and parkscapes. The project also integrates more with the wider public realm both visually through transparencies, exterior platforms, and building openings as well as through street-level access. These form a stark contrast to Portman and his contemporaries' designs. Such design strategies can form the basis of not a mixed-use skyscraper but a hybridized public/private realm or *sticky hybrid*.

Cities should invest in whole pockets of existing skyscrapers to create new internal networks of public spaces and amenities in dialogue with streets, transportation, parks, and other public spaces. If this seems far-fetched, one need only look to transportation networks themselves that have direct entrances to buildings, industrial architecture integrated with water and rail freight networks, or pedestrian circulation for multi-building complexes. Inversely, airports too, where the city owns and operates a kind of building infrastructure that provides a shared space and circulation network punctuated by interchangeable amenities, serve as a model. To take a different example, in 2020 during the COVID-19 pandemic, Whole Foods Markets suddenly converted large portions of their stores into Amazon fulfillment centers, hybridizing retail and logistics into a singular space and experience. What is important is a vision for such a

1 Peter S. Goodman, "In Suez Canal, Stuck Ship Is a Warning About Excessive Globalization," The New York Times, March 26, 2021. https://www.nytimes.com/2021/03/26/business/ship-suez-canal.html.

2 NYC Office Adaptive Reuse Task Force, "NYC Office Adaptive Reuse Study - January 2023." New York City Planning Department, January 2023, 4, https://www.nyc.gov/assets/planning/download/pdf/plans-studies/office-reuse-task-force/office-adaptive-reuse-study.pdf.

3 Real Estate Board of New York, "An Analysis of Landmarked Properties in Manhattan," REBNY Press, June, 2013, https://www.rebny.com/reports/an-analysis-of-landmarked-properties-in-manhattan/.

4 Sara Ahmed, The Cultural Politics of Emotion, (New York: Routledge, 2004), 11.

5 Ibid.

6 See for instance John Gallagher, "How 'sticky' Detroit locations add up to lively downtown," Detroit Free Press, May 25, 2017, https://www.freep.com/story/money/business/john-gallagher/2017/05/26/detroit-landscape-esplanade-downtown/335981001/. Huê-Tâm Jamme "Sticky Flows' and 'Productive Frictions': Untangling the Mechanisms of Street Urbanism," AESOP 2019 Conference, July 2019. Peter Goffin, "The Case for Sticky Streets," The Torontoist, July 2, 2014, https://torontoist.com/2014/07/the-case-for-sticky-streets/.

7 Brent Toderian quoted in Goffin, "The Case for Sticky Streets."

8 Bresler, Judith. "Serra v. USA and its Aftermath: Mandate for Moral Rights in America?" in The Trials of Art, edited by Daniel McClean, (London: Ridinghouse, 2007), 195-211.

9 Matthew A. Postal, "Havemeyers & Elder Filter, Pan & Finishing House, Designation List 396 LP-2268," New York City Landmarks Preservation Commission, September 25, 2007, https://www.nyc.gov/html/records/pdf/govpub/3311domino.desigrep.pdf

10 Diane Cardwell and Rosalie Radomsky, "Developers Known for Residential Work Buy Domino Sugar Plant on Brooklyn Waterfront," The New York Times, July 1, 2004, https://www.nytimes.com/2004/07/01/nyregion/developers-known-for-residential-work-buy-domino-sugar-plant-brooklyn-waterfront.html

network and a planning methodology for pursuing it. In its assessment of adaptive reuse of offices, the Adams' administration task force made recommendations almost entirely related to easing and incentivizing the conversion of office buildings to residential.[20]

While residential conversion, especially in the interest of developing affordable housing could help alleviate pressures on the city's housing stock, the incentives for developers are low and regulatory hurdles are high. By also pursuing the reinvention of smaller pieces of buildings in addition to wholesale conversions, the city can start incubating existing office buildings with new types of urban space and culture, typologically transforming the office and the city with it. These should include housing but should also vary widely: education and innovation centers offering workshops and professional training; recreational facilities like a public pool or rock-climbing center; special exhibition halls for city museums; public schools and day care centers; experimental vertical farms and green lungs; bird sanctuaries; pollution mitigation and green energy infrastructure; youth sports centers; dog parks; an aquarium and aquaponics center; and more. These could work to form a sticky network within an existing office tower that first utilizes vacant or underutilized space, second serves a public utility, third spatially diversifies the office from the inside out, and fourth opens up the skyscraper to wider public to produce more culturally vibrant and diverse places.

To this last point, most office towers, while they are ubiquitous and deeply entangled with collective images and impressions of the city, are completely inaccessible to virtually everyone. New internal forms of public access and engagement with these buildings will allow people to reidentify their very relationship to the city and accumulate attachments to it that form the basis of urban culture. Where the typical skyscraper shuttles the public to its peripheries or workers to and from highly contained and controlled office environments, the sticky hybrid skyscraper invites all into its gooey interiors. New adjacencies between unexpected programs and building occupants create new encounters that accumulate as forms of urban culture within buildings. The sticky hybrid then becomes not just an architectural and cultural framework for the future office but also for the future urban public.

---

11 Diane Cardwell, "City Is Backing Makeover for Decaying Brooklyn Waterfront," The New York Times, May 3, 2005, https://www.nytimes.com/2005/05/03/nyregion/city-is-backing-makeover-for-decaying-brooklyn-waterfront.html.

12 Charles V. Bagli, "2 Sides Clash at City Hall Over Domino Housing Plan," The New York Times, June 22, 2010, https://www.nytimes.com/2010/06/23/nyregion/23domino.html

13 See Save Domino Facebook Group https://www.facebook.com/SaveDominoNY and Dana Rubenstein "Domino fight lights up hood," Brooklyn Paper, August 4, 2007, https://www.brooklynpaper.com/domino-fight-lights-up-hood/.

14 Charles V. Bagli, "Out With the Old Building, In With the New for JPMorgan Chase," The New York Times, Feb 12, 2018.

15 Ibid

16 Heather Perlberg, "NYC Woolworth Tower Condo Priced at Record $110 Million," Bloomberg, June 2, 2014. https://www.bloomberg.com/news/articles/2014-06-02/nyc-woolworth-tower-condo-priced-at-record-110-million#xj4y7vzkg.

17 Lizzie Crook, "SOM unveils plans for 1950s Lever House renovation in New York" Dezeen, February 17, 2022, https://www.dezeen.com/2022/02/17/som-lever-house-skyscraper-renovation/.

18 Vuk Radović, "The Skyscraper and Public Space: An uneasy history and the capacity for radical reinvention" in Mehta, V. and Palazzo eds., Companion to Public Space (New York: Taylor & Francis, 2020), 316.

19 See Kevin Yeang, Reinventing the Skyscraper: A Vertical Theory of Urban Design (West Sussex: Wiley-Academy, 2002).

20 "NYC Office Adaptive Reuse Study - January 2023."

05 FERAL ENVELOPES FOR THE FUTURE OFFICE

Ariane Lourie Harrison

The office has an uncertain future according to recent press on the New York City office market's "real estate apocalypse."[1] Local Law 43, enacted early in 2022, offers one type of response through program adaptation: its task force seeks to convert unviable office space to other potential uses, such as schools or residential. Another approach, advocated here, would imagine an adaptation of the office as a mixed-use amenity-rich typology, one whose hybrid functions meld office work with the planetary work of creating habitat for other species.[2] If the future office is reconstituted as a vertical campus, it will nevertheless do so on a building footprint of a carbon-conscious city, one that likely avoids demolition for adaption. The future office will likely occupy a building from the past. Its futurity, however, will become manifest in its building envelope. Countermanding the interior-centric vision of LEED standards for building envelopes, the future office may stand out in the cityscape as buildings with feral surfaces: teeming with human, animal, and machinic species that collaborate and blend building maintenance with planetary care.[3]

While the term “feral” refers to animals that are wild or untamed, it derives from the Latin *feralis*, meaning funerary, or belonging to the dead. In today’s Anthropocene period, in which humans’ role as the largest evolutionary force on the planet coincides with the current sixth mass extinction event for non-human species, these two sets of meanings take on a distinctive resonance. In one word, feral, we find these qualities: animal, wildness, funerary, and the dead. The meanings tangle together to invoke the losses caused by the acidifying oceans, warming atmospheres, and planetary urbanization of the Anthropocene.

A feral envelope for a building would manifest an ecological awareness—one tinged with sadness, inevitability, and the confrontation of actual loss—of the consequences of urbanization, an activity that caused the loss. A feral envelope for an office building would transform an increasingly unusable modernist typology that zoned work apart from life—a façade that manifests planetary consciousness becomes a way to distinguish the future office. An argument made by many ecological philosophers and theorists is that aesthetics represents a fundamental communicative value between humans as well as between and among non-humans.[4] A feral aesthetic then brings the relationship between the human and the non-human into greater visibility within an ecological consciousness specific to our Anthropocene period.

What format does a feral envelope take? It is somewhat ironic that historical commemorative architecture for humans—chapels and mausolea—offers a foothold for creatures we consider feral; craggy surfaces and deep niches of gothic architecture are replete with birds and insects. The brownstone entryway of Brooklyn’s Green-Wood Cemetery, for instance, has become a habitat for a raucous fleet of monk parakeets

01 A monk parakeet and a common starling flying around a parakeet nest in the Green-Wood Cemetery gate, 2017. Photography by Rhododendrites

02 Musee Du Quai Branly Greenwall Installation, Patrick Blanc, Paris, 2005. Photography by Jean-Pierre Dalbéra

03 Wrapped Reichstag, Christo and Jeanne-Claude, Berlin, 1995. Photography by Gertrud K.

since the 1980s (Fig. 01). They have modified the brownstone spires by adding new layers of twigs and twine, and, according to Green-Wood's manager of horticultural operations, the birds are self-sufficient: finding food and maintaining their habitat with no intervention from Green-Wood employees.[5]

There are hints of the feral in our cities: coyotes curled up in empty buses, eagles with Instagram accounts following their ledge-lifestyle, and, from time to time, the displaced swarm of honeybees that makes a surprise landing on a piece of infrastructure. The ubiquity of glazing in commercial buildings is promoted on the merits of its "sleek, clean, and modern aesthetic," despite the extensive ecological cost of the materials that constitute the modern aesthetic, as demonstrated in the work of Kiel Moe and Elisa Iturbe, among others.[6] In contrast to the reflective corporate towers or the smooth cladding systems featured in Zaera-Polo and Anderson's *The Ecologies of the Building Envelope*, textured surface of "premodern" structures provides a literal living space for non-humans.[7] The patterning, the texture of the wall, the rooftop or window ledge, is where the feral anchors. The selfsame intricate materiality that houses animals on the building surface can become, on a facade, the locus across which the intentional critical act of architecture registers. Neither smooth nor monolithic, a feral envelope invokes the qualities of wildness, overgrowth, decay, and metabolic cycling of elements that attends organic processes.

EXCHANGE SURFACES

New York City buildings comprise approximately 3,000 square miles of building facades. These surfaces can become, in Paul Mankiewicz's terms, "exchange surfaces" for the city's fluid geometries of atmosphere and water.[8] The exchange promised by blue and green surfaces takes heat, humidity, stormwater, and airborne pollution as inputs. Facades wrapped in absorbent, filtering and capturing materials can process these inputs while tempering urban climates.

Exchange surfaces exist in large cities. Vegetated walls, green facades, and a type of vertical landscape urbanism emerged in Kuala Lumpur and Singapore with Ken Yeang's bioclimactic towers of the 1980s and 1990s. Living walls leapt into European regard with Patrick Blanc's installation for the quai Branly in Paris (2004), while Stefano Boeri's *Easyhomo Huanggang Vertical Forest City Complex* (2021) expands the space of his successful prototypes in Milan (*Bosco Verticale*, 2014) and Eindhoven (*Trudo Vertical Forest*, 2021). In these cases, new residential building, both luxury and social housing, extend deep terraces into the city, leveraging urban forestry's capacity to absorb air pollution. Singapore-based WOHA envelopes buildings in greenery, as the Singapore Pavilion of the Dubai Expo 2020 demonstrates, while Vietnamese architect Vo Trong Nghia has completed many new residential buildings that feature bamboo bedecked terraces and rooftop fruit-tree orchards. New construction seems to increasingly create deep pockets and semi-permeable spaces for plant life (Fig. 02).

But projects that engage the material sensuality and layered nonhuman surface remain speculative. For example, Amid Cero9 proposed *The Magic Mountain* in 2002 as an "ecosystem mask" for the Iowa Ames Power Station, one that drapes the historical building in honeysuckle, roses and lights and beckons insects and avian species to nest within its layers. The flowers propose a sumptuous vestment for the existing building, but it is the techniques of draping, masking, and cloaking with living material that points to the aesthetic potential of the feral. The floral veil approximates the baggy form and shaggy shapes of kudzu-bedecked infrastructure. The act of veiling, as the works of Christo and Jeanne-Claude have long demonstrated, brings new figures and potential out of existing architecture (Fig. 03).

As *The Magic Mountain* indicates, the exchange surface adapts and brings new value to underused buildings. Furthermore, if carbon accounting makes demolition too costly, the exchange surface accommodates by wrapping, extending, densifying, and bio-diversifing what was a monolithic volume of glass, cement, and masonry. This approach makes ecological and economic sense, as it refashions the building envelope into a novel form of climate-conscious branding. The plant curtain—steel mesh and creeping vines—draped over Vo Trong Nghia Architects' *Breathing House* (2019) in Ho Chi Minh City, the pocket jungle flowing into the courtyard of WOHA's own office on 29 HongKong Street, or the scaffolds, trellises, and inserts proposed for New York by Brooklyn-based Leaf Island points to a contemporary shaggy and tangled aesthetic.

The aforementioned projects are plant-centric. And yet, we know that plants exist in an ecosystem of pollinating and decomposing insects, which add mass, debris and accumulation to the feral surface. A more equitable exchange surface would begin to integrate substrates for and maintenance of non-human habitats, taking on the manifold challenges of creating analogous habitats. The exchange surface becomes feral by way of accumulating the diverse and changing materialities, infrastructures, and access points that accommodate the cycles of growth, change, and decay across the building envelope.

ANALOGOUS HABITATS

The parallel vectors of increasing urbanization accommodating human population growth and diminished habitats for nonhumans prompt us to ask whether, on a disciplinary basis, architecture needs to address building for multiple species. Harrison Atelier's position is clear from a programmatic approach: why would we restrict architecture to the design of habitation of one species? We understand that we share the planet with 1.7 million identified species and potentially 10 million others that slip unnoticed into extinction due to the anthropocentric environments we produce and reproduce. If, according to the oft-cited statistic, by 2050, 68% of the human population will be living in cities, then we can project further depletion of habitats for non-humans. But can we build new habitats?

"Analogous habitats" refer to man-made artificial ecosystems that can support native biodiversity, in part due to material, structural, or functional resemblance to natural ecosystems. Urban and industrial ecosystems can integrate man-made habitats that function as analogues to natural ecosystems; these point to a role for design in reconciliation ecology, "the science of inventing, establishing and maintaining new habitats to conserve species diversity in places where people live, work, and play."[9]

Let's consider native pollinators as potential candidates for feral surfaces. Ninety percent of the planet's 25,000 bee species are native bees, responsible for 75% of non-agricultural pollination globally. While these bees are diverse in size, color, and foraging—representing the biodiversity of each continent—the majority are considered "solitary," that is, they do not form hives and social structures. Their inhabitation is for nesting (laying eggs and provisioning the future larvae) and tends to be opportunistic and discreet—in patches of bare earth, abandoned burrows, holes, and reeds—making many solitary bee habitats hard to identify but easy to eradicate.

04 UHPC Ductal panels (front and rear) for Pollinators Pavilion, Harrison Atelier, Hudson, New York, 2019. Photography by Harrison Atelier
05 Mycelium-hempcrete panels for Hempcrete Habitat for Governors Island, Harrison Atelier, New York, 2022. Photography by Harrison Atelier

Despite this critical role, our understanding of some basic aspects of solitary bee biology, including species level distributional and inhabitation patterns, remains incomplete.[10] And adding to the challenges of identification, solitary bees are identified typically in a process called destructive sampling involving trapping, capture, and killing the bee subject. The elusive nature of solitary bee nesting sites makes monitoring a time-consuming and expensive prospect, and destructive sampling further reduces solitary bee populations. Many of these bees inhabit holes and burrows of one centimeter in diameter and ten centimeters in depth. This modest scale nests comfortably into the thickness of building cladding.

Making building surfaces inhabitable brings a new weight—conceptual and literal—to building cladding. COOKFOX/Buro Happold's 2022 *Living Façade* envisions a terra-cotta Voronoi modular system of slip-cast pods with metal fasteners integrating into a curtain wall system.[11] Harrison Atelier's 2017 *Species Wall* for the Clermont Historical Center deployed thin cast concrete panels (50cm x 50cm; 11–15 kilograms) that bulged on one side to create nesting space, while the grooved inside surface shunted water and waste away from the existing wall. We developed a "roomier" panel with Harrison Atelier's 2020 *Pollinators Pavilion*: trapezoidal panels hand cast in UHPC Ductal concrete plied the ductility of this material to create a large protrusion that serves as a rain canopy on one face of the panel, and, on the inside, creates sufficient space for the species monitoring system (Fig. 04).[12] A thorn-like protrusion houses the camera and microprocessor that is powered by a rooftop solar array. The larger of our Ductal panels (100cm x 70 cm), while located at the base of the *Pollinators Pavilion*, nevertheless weighed in at 25kg. Harrison Atelier's recent work using hempcrete brings us a lower-carbon material but thicker panels and more weight for cladding as habitat (Fig. 05). When such surfaces begin to absorb stormwater as vegetated patches, the weight increases.

Designing habitation for non-humans brings architecture to consider different scales and materials, as well as the conflict of human and non-human preferences. We like glass windows, but birds do not. Up to one billion birds die every year in the U.S. due to collisions with windows, which birds do not see as a barrier and fly into it at full speed. We like lights at night, but dozens of migratory species become disoriented by the artificial illumination of the sky. We appreciate the unified aesthetic (and construction economy) of a building clad the same way on all four vertical facades. But many species prefer habitation with specific orientation to the sun, so the overall building-envelop enclosure envisioned by COOKFOX/Happold, while appealing visually to humans, would not achieve its goal of full inhabitation. Yet the gesture of creating habitat across the façade remains significant, literally grafting new life into the underused office building façade.

The Anthropocene period precludes any return to wildness, in the feral sense, yet an analogous habitat embraces both its artificial construction and an open-ended exposure to the elements and weather. Conceived as a framework for growth rather than a manicured wall product, the feral surface offers a space for discovery. That we do not actually know the range of factors in designing analogous habitats is not surprising: it points to a pressing need to integrate a range of disciplines, from landscape architecture to conservation biology and urban geography into the adaptation of building fabric that has some capacity as a maintained exchange surface. This lack of expertise in constructing viable analogous habitats presents new "work" for the future office. Can the office facade become habitats and monitors of other species, deploying robotics, sensors, and AI to collect and sort data at the scale of species too small for human regard?

FAÇADE MAINTENANCE

The hybrid materiality of the feral surface requires maintenance. Lots of it, including consistent monitoring of material flows, of the peregrinations of human, animal, and machinic species, of the quasi-agricultural rhythms of the building envelope. It could be argued (somewhat cynically) that a new and significant dimension of work at the future office is the maintenance and cultivation of its own building façade: an extension of biophilic benefits for worker productivity. The workscape—defined as the work environment in which people perform their tasks—might be enlivened by this conceptual stress on the "scape" of work: feral surfaces extend the "office work" out of the building envelope and into an urban interior exposed to elements and entities.

But maintenance work itself has something of a feral sensibility. It deals with decay and death; it is intensely material and addresses an inevitable accumulation of matter that can transform the familiar into a wilderness of junk. In the work of Mierle Ukeles, who spent 39 years as unpaid artist-in-residence at New York City's Department of Sanitation, maintenance is radical, political, and ecological. Ukeles's "Manifesto for Maintenance Art 1969!" highlights the tension between the "perpetuation and MAINTENANCE of the species"

06 Pollinators Pavilion, Harrison Atelier, Hudson, New York, 2019. Photography by Harrison Atelier

and its practice: "Maintenance is a drag: it takes all the fucking time, the mind boggles and chafes at the boredom."[13] Her manifesto concludes with Earth Maintenance, an ambitious proposal to treat, rehabilitate and recycle the following on a daily basis: "the contents of one sanitation truck," "polluted air," "polluted Hudson River" water, and "ravaged land."[14] Ukeles's 1976 collaboration with 300 maintenance workers at the Whitney Museum, titled "I Make Maintenance Art One Hour Every Day," resulted in a photographic record of unseen labor: it is prescient in registering the need to document the unseen labor that tends our cultural systems. Her Polaroid of maintenance work anticipates our GeoTIFF(COG), one unit of biodiversity-tracking landscape data-both are data collections that reveal the management of space.[15] Maintenance participates in what Nate Millington describes as a relational and everyday practice of repair that promotes a consistent dialogue with the materials and systems of a structure.[16] The critical aspect of the practice involves observation: in Shannon Mattern's terms: "To study maintenance is itself an act of maintenance. To fill in the gaps in this literature, to draw connections among different disciplines, is an act of repair or, simply, of taking care—connecting threads, mending holes, amplifying quiet voices."[17] Maintenance needs designed and dedicated space.

The feral surfaces that we are making at Harrison Atelier integrate such spaces for maintenance. For the *Pollinators Pavilion* in Hudson (Fig. 06), Ductal panels house 30–50 nesting tubes within a mesh-capped PVC pipe with airholes. We placed 152mm long nesting tubes (which can accommodate three to six native bee egg cells) of diameters from 3mm–9mm in cardboard, paper, reed, and bamboo into the PVC container, which affixes to the cement panel. This tedious detail performs the considerations of maintenance: is there airflow? Is it protected? Can you clean it out? A second type of maintenance occurs at the regional scale but contributes to planetary biodiversity-support efforts: cameras, sensors, and microprocessors equip each panel, which is powered to operate 6 hours a day, collecting 1,000 images per day per camera (3 pictures per minute, 6 hours per day). The images feed a database and AI model (supported by Microsoft's AI for Earth Program) trained to automate bee identification (to genus) as a no-kill method of addressing data gaps on native pollinators. Maintenance may be a drag, but machines can become cost-effective collaborators in the long hours of observation. Observation through distributed sensing becomes part of species maintenance, and its architecture helps, in Mattern's terms, connect, mend, and amplify a planetary fabric.

The urban potential of distributed sensing was powerfully developed in Mark Shepard's *Sentient City* (2011), but could be amplified as AI and automated species identification is increasingly present across citizen science apps such as i-Naturalist.[18] Robots represent another labor resource and are prominently represented in speculative architecture and urbanism such as the "automated landscapes" research of the Het Nieuwe Instituut.[19] The spatial configuration of vertical urban surfaces might incorporate fully automated workscapes, given that agricultural and greenhouse technologies accommodate precise responses to ambient (or aeroponic) conditions. Automated labor is controversial in its potential disruption of human labor in the construction industry, but were the set of concerns broadened to monitoring some of the 1.7 million identified species and applied to New York's thousands of miles of building surfaces, we might agree that there is work for all.

Suppose the future office's feral envelope integrates sensors and cameras—not dedicated to surveilling human productivity but instead to scanning bird tags and insect faces, tracking wing veining patterns and exoskeleton segmentation? Automated insect identification represents a small segment of the planetary efforts to document species decline: Microsoft's Planetary Computer assembles the myriad environmental monitoring projects and is an example of Big Data's support of biodiversity through information infrastructure which has generated cautious optimism.[20] The AI engines which produce architectural interfaces that "smile back" in Jenny Sabin Lab's stunning fiber-knit work for the Microsoft Research Center, can become the inspiration for developing AI capacities that recognize the "faces," as it were, of other species. Conceptualized as surfaces dotted with niches and nesting spaces, absorbent mediums and data-gathering interfaces become a living fabric with ecological benefits for many species. The textures of the built environment can harbor biodiversity and with that ground the resilience of the city.

RADICAL REPAIR BY THE FUTURE OFFICE

If we had to think about avoiding the displacement of our multi-species through maintenance and repair, then building surface care becomes part of the work of the future office. A pause from a spreadsheet might include a casual glance at the habitat and its denizens framing your window. The proverbial water cooler might sponsor gossip on the weirdly cute behavior

1 Arpit Gupta Arpit, Vrinda Mittal, and Stijn Van Nieuwerburgh, "Work From Home and the Office Real Estate Apocalypse," Social Scientific Research Network, September 26, 2022, 1, https://ssrn.com/abstract=4124698.

2 New York City Planning Department, "Office Adaptive Reuse Task Force," nyc.gov, https://www1.nyc.gov/site/planning/plans/office-reuse-task-force/office-reuse-task-force.page.

3 NBBJ's "The Helix" building for Amazon's new Arlington, VA, headquarters would not constitute an example of a feral surface: its extensive glazing and docile array of windswept trees would likely not provide the coherent matrix for non-human species to anchor. On the other hand, Terraform's "Monarch Sanctuary," for the Cooper Hewitt Design Triennial (2019) offers a vision of a building envelope that caters to more than one species, in this case promoting habitat for monarch butterflies.

4 Theorists of Object Oriented Ontology (OOO) and speculative realism, Graham Harman, Timothy Morton, Ian Bogost, and Levi Bryant, among others, propose models of a world comprised of objects—many nested within one other—removing the dichotomies of "inside/outside," "society/nature," and even the concept of an exterior "environment." In a series of elegant arguments, Harman and Bryant describe the manner in which objects are fundamentally withdrawn, both from each other and from themselves, see Graham Harman, Immaterialism: Objects and Social Theory (Cambridge: Polity, 2016); Levi Bryant, The Democracy of Objects (London: Open Humanities Press, 2011). Harman describes the role of aesthetics in both bridging and preserving the paradoxical distance among and between objects: "The separation of a thing from its quality is no longer a local phenomenon of human experience, but instead is the root of all relations between real objects, including causal relations. In other words, allure belongs to ontology as a whole, not to the special metaphysics of animal perception. Relations between all real objects, including mindless chunks of dirt, occur only by means of some form of allusion. But insofar as we have identified allure with an aesthetic effect, this means that aesthetics becomes first philosophy..." (Graham Harman, "On Vicarious Causation," Collapse II, Urbanomics, 2007, 187-221, 221). Morton also suggests that given the distance between objects, aesthetics becomes a primary mode of relation among objects: "OOO believes that reality is mysterious and magical, because beings withdraw and because beings influence each other aesthetically, which is to say, at a distance," (Timothy Morton, Dark Ecology: For a Logic of Future Coexistence (New York: Columbia University Press, 2016), 17.

5 Shaye Weaver, "Green-Wood is home to a flock of feral parrots," Timeout, July 1, 2022, https://www.timeout.com/newyork/news/green-wood-cemetery-is-home-to-a-flock-of-feral-parrots-070122.

6 Michael Tobias, "Why is Glass so Common in Commercial Buildings?," Nearby Engineers, July 8, 2019, https://www.ny-engineers.com/blog/why-is-glass-so-common-in-commercial-buildings#:~:text=Glass%20allows%20natural%20lighting%2C%20reducing,synergy%20with%20efficient%20MEP%20systems.; See also Kiel Moe, Convergence: an Architectural Agenda for Energy (New York: Routledge, 2013); Kiel Moe, Unless: The Seagram Building Construction Ecology (New York: Actar, 2021); Elisa Iturbe, "Overcoming Carbon Form," Log 47, Fall 2019.

7 Alejandro Zaera Polo and Jeffrey Anderson, The Ecologies of the Envelope (New York: Actar, 2021). See also David Gissen, Subnature: Architecture's Other Environments (Princeton: Princeton Architectural Press, 2009) for examples of buildings incorporating spaces for animals including some modernist work such as Oscar Niemeyer's Praca dos Tres Poderes dovecote in Brasilia (1961).

8 Paul Mankiewicz, "Trellis Green Wall System," Leafisland.org, https://leafisland.org/green-walls/.

of bugs in addition to that of your colleagues. The coffee break would produce actual grounds for a composting session. And each toilet flush is synced with the filtering capacities of vegetated surfaces. The biophilic benefits of such maintenance work would liven office spaces and potentially forge new formats of collegiality. "Maintenance and repair are correctives to visions of the future and a present that neglects the inevitability of breakdown. Maintenance is work and labor, but it is also about forms of collective presence that fill in the cracks of a world in breakdown."[21]

A feral surface operates on multiple layers, in terms of materials (organic and synthetic), users (human and non-human), and programs (bio-diversifying, energy-producing, pollution-attenuating, community-building) and could adapt a historic building into the lively tangle that is the future office.

The feral envelope manifests a collaborative effort between humans, animals, and machines—an effort that manifests the tenuous existence of all species on a warming planet.

---

9 Jeremy T. Lundholm and Paul J. Richardson, "Habitat analogues for reconciliation ecology in urban and industrial environments," Journal of Applied Ecology 2010, 47, 966–975, 966. See also Adrian Ayres Fisher "Ethics and Ecosystem Interactions: Why Reconciliation Ecology Matters," resilience.org, https://www.resilience.org/stories/2016-04-28/ethics-and-ecosystem-interactions-why-reconciliation-ecology-matters/.

10 While Europe has the best described bee fauna globally (2,000 spe¬cies), even this data is surprisingly poor for solitary bee species (of which 60% were deemed "data-deficient"). The US native bee fauna is far less well described. See Kelsey Kopec "Landmark report: Hundreds of Native Bee Species Sliding Toward Extinction," Center for Biological Diversity, March 1, 2017, https://www.biologicaldiversity.org/news/press_releases/2017/bees 03 01 2017.php

11 COOKFOX and Buro Happold, "COOKFOX and Buro Happold Design Bird and Bee Friendly Façade for Architectural Ceramics Assemblies Workshop," Cookfox.com, June 23, 2022, https://cookfox.com/news/cookfox-and-buro-happold-acaw/.

12 Andrew Pinnecke and Kelly Henry at Lafarge-Holcim's Ductal Workshop in the Brooklyn Navy Yard are gratefully acknowledged as our sponsors and collaborators for the UHPC Ductal concrete.

13 Jillian Steinhauer, "How Mierle Laderman Ukeles Turned Maintenance Work into Art" Hyperallergic, February 20 2017, https://hyperallergic.com/355255/how-mierle-laderman-ukeles-turned-maintenance-work-into-art/.

14 Ibid.

15 "MoBI. Map of Biodiversity Importance," Microsoft.com, https://planetarycomputer.microsoft.com/dataset/mobi.

16 Nate Millington, "Critical Spatial Practices of Repair," Society and Space, August 26, 2019, https://www.societyandspace.org/articles/critical-spatial-practices-of-repair.

17 Shannon Mattern, "Maintenance and Care," Places Journal, November 2018, https://placesjournal.org/article/maintenance-and-care/.

18 Mark Shepard, ed., Sentient City: ubiquitous computing, architecture, and the future of urban space (Cambridge: MIT Press, 2011).

19 "Automated Landscapes," Het Nieu Instituut, https://automated-landscapes.hetnieuweinstituut.nl/en.

20 P.M. Lukacz, "Data Capitalism, Microsoft's Planetary Computer, and the Biodiversity Informatics Community" in Malte Smits ed. Information for a Better World: Shaping the Global Future, Proceedings of the 17th International Conference, iConference 2022. https://doi.org/10.1007/978-3-030-96957-8_31. For Harrison Atelier at AI for Earth see "Microsoft AI for Earth Grantee Gallery," Microsoft.com, https://microsoft.github.io/AIforEarth-Grantees/.

21 Millington, "Critical Spatial Practices of Repair."

06 MIXED-REALITIES AT WORK

Patrik Schumacher

The work spaces of the future should be designed simultaneously as both physical and virtual navigation and communication realms, as cyber-urban spaces, seamlessly integrating physically immediate and digitally mediated communicative interactions, constituting a new mixed reality. The 1990s conception of the web as cyber-space can now be realized via technology transfer from the multi-player video game industry. The design of "cyber-space" or "the metaverse" falls squarely within the remit of the discipline of architecture. The virtual environments in the metaverse we are pursuing at Zaha Hadid Architects (ZHA) are functionally continuous with the physical environments we are designing for our clients. Both are part of a single social interaction process. We are not interested in a "metaverse" that offers a fictitious world to escape social reality. Our metaverse designs do not pursue spectacle, entertainment, or storytelling. Rather, they become part of productive societal life and enhance knowledge exchange and cooperation within society, enabling fulfilling and productive lives, as well as boosting overall societal prosperity.

All organizations—firms, charities, political parties, cultural institutions etc.—will host virtual environments in the metaverse. Most of them will retain their urban premises, too. It therefore makes sense that both physical and virtual premises are congenial extensions of each other and are designed together by architects that operate across this divide. This makes all the more sense as the utilization of the built environment as primary source domain for analogical transfers is the very essence of cyber-space: virtual designed spaces, buildings, and cities. Architecture will take the lead, and the only digitally native architectural style—parametricism—recommends itself here.[1]

A NEW SOCIO-TECHNOLOGICAL CONTEXT

The new computationally empowered post-Fordist network economy implies a shift from routine work to intensely collaborative work patterns. Nearly all work becomes creative work: R&D, media & marketing, and finance together feeding the world of continuous innovation via robotic fabrication and software as service upgrades. This implies a momentous intensification of communication and collaboration.

Agglomeration economies and co-location synergies motivate urban densification, allowing for the roaming exploration of social spaces, affording unplanned and unexpected (but never wholly random) encounters. Start-up culture will further proliferate in this ongoing historical transformation. Recently, the world discovered that this creative knowledge work is uniquely capable of shifting from physical to virtual collaboration spaces. This was demonstrated during the lockdowns implemented around the world to combat the COVID-19 pandemic. While in the UK and elsewhere the COVID-19 lockdowns, and indeed all COVID-19 restrictions, are coming to an end, the remote working that was engendered by the pandemic continues. After two years of experiencing the convenience and productivity of remote working from home, knowledge workers are reluctant to return to the pre-COVID normality, and employers seem happy to grant flexibility in this respect.

01 Renders with OpenAI DALL-E 2 launched in occasion of "Meta-Horizons: The Future Now" at DDP Design Museum. Architecting the Metaverse, Zaha Hadid Architects and Refik Anadol Studio, Seoul, 2022. Courtesy of Zaha Hadid Architects

The fast pervasive spread of video conferencing technology made remote collaborative work possible without any loss of productivity. This lesson cannot be unlearned. The self-directedness and result-orientation of most knowledge work, whether it is individual or teamwork, means that controlling when and where the work gets done is becoming increasingly pointless. So is there any point in gathering in shared office spaces?

As communication and collaboration moves into the digital domain, utilizing tools like "Zoom," communication events must be scheduled and the opportunities for unscheduled, informal encounters and exchanges are lost. These encounters between knowledge workers in an innovative business field, however, are very important. Specialization in our advanced technological age is intense, and nobody knows more than a fragment of what successful innovation requires. The key point is that many information deficits and opportunities are "unknown unknowns," which must, first of all, be discovered in a random exploration within strategically located social search spaces. There are thus still some important aspects of contemporary knowledge work with respect to which spatial co-location can make an important contribution: unscheduled, serendipitous encounters and conversations, and informal group gatherings are important facilitators for knowledge exchange that are impossible to plan.

Coming to work has the nearly automatic but vital side effect of getting continuous updates about what is going on beyond one's own project. That is why there are still many who prefer to go to the office, and that is why many firms do not want to give up on gathering their staff in a single location. The inter-visibility and inter-awareness in a shared space allows all to observe all, and thus allows workers to approach one another in the moment when such an approach is most likely to succeed and be productive. Standard video conferencing tools like Zoom cannot deliver these forms of social functionality that depend on the inter-visible simultaneity of many spontaneous social activities, and the multi-modal recognition of good communication chances.

Some workers are coming in, some are working from home. This implies that today all formal, scheduled meetings must take place on tools like Zoom, with everybody joining from their individual desks, whether they are at home or in the office. Nobody must be left to feel like a second-class participant. Therefore, as long as Zoom meetings are the only form of integrating remote workers, all forgo the advantage of being there physically, at least with respect to scheduled meetings. This is wasteful. Remote workers, however, remain excluded from unscheduled, spontaneous communications. The pressure is thus on to find ways to let remote workers also experience informal exchanges. Work environments will have to be seamlessly connected up with the virtual communication spaces for all those who will participate remotely rather than via physical co-presence. Architects will have to design for mixed meetings where multiple real and multiple virtual participants join a single communication event. This is the agenda of cyber-physical hybridity, or cyber-physical fusion.

ALL WORK BECOMES MIXED REALITY WORK

The metaverse is part of the real world. This is why the appropriate conceptual pair is virtual vs. physical, rather than virtual vs. real. This paper thus distinguishes virtual spaces from physical spaces, both understood to frame social reality. As architects we are striving to create well adapted, high-performance spaces, both physically and virtually (Fig. 01). Each realm has its specific advantages. It makes no sense to ask which realm is more real or more important. To be sure, we cannot escape physical reality as long as we are physically embodied. But it is imaginable that the whole of social life, all communication, goes altogether virtual. New tools for tele-collaboration are being conceived, built, and perfected at a rapid pace. These new VR-based tools allow for an immersive, intuitive, and interactive form of tele-presence, a virtual co-location, that starts to replicate, or at least approximate, the vividness and the affordances of physical co-location. Start-up ventures developing virtual environments for collaborative work, conferencing, socializing, and exhibiting have been proliferating in the last two years. We are witnessing a dramatic technology transfer from the mature video game industry to the nascent metaverse industry. Massively multiplayer online (MMO) video-games have advanced technologies that support "open worlds" where hundreds or even thousands of players can freely roam and interact. In virtual conferencing worlds like Confer-O-Matic—using the technological advances delivered by the video-game industry—informal encounters and spontaneous fringe activities become possible again. In a spatially rather than graphically structured internet navigation and event framing, the events become more layered and dynamic, increasing inter-visibility, and allow for dynamically shifting hierarchies within the scene, in contrast to the static page layouts of websites or the static grid of faces or letters identifying participants in tools like Zoom.

However, even if the whole of societal life could shift into the virtual realm, this is not the thesis and agenda promoted here. The thesis promoted here is that the most productive way forward is the agenda of cyber-physical integration, a mixed social reality that integrates and sometimes fuses these two realms. This paper argues that the virtual co-location will not and should not be conceived as altogether substituting physical co-presence but should be conceived as seamlessly fusing with physical co-presence. This idea implies that the virtual spaces are not only joined and experienced individually from a headset or laptop interface at home. Instead, the shared physical spaces become the interface through which the virtual spaces are entered and navigated, not by isolated individuals, but by the groups gathered here physically. Physical spaces will be featuring panoramic screens that deliver virtual *trompe-l'œil* expansions of the physical space as windows into virtual spaces, as well as holographic projections for the vivid telepresence of remote participants. This is also conceivable with respect to urban spaces.

The question thus arises how these virtual spaces and cities integrate with physical spaces and cities. Some metaverse projects take a digital twin of the surface of planet earth as the backdrop for placement of virtual spaces, buildings, and cities. This strategy sets the scene for the interlacing of physical and virtual environments (Fig. 02). Transmira's "Omniscape" is building a metaverse based on this concept. The virtual buildings placed in this metaverse can be viewed and experienced at the equivalent physical city locations via AR devices. Such a conception hooks up its spatiology to the ready-made physical order on planet Earth, i.e. it foregoes the opportunity to develop an original spatial order. The disadvantage here is the dispersal of virtual venues that might rather want to huddle together in a single location, in a large meta-metropolis configuration that has no physical complement, although some of its parts might have. This tension might be solved by delivering virtual venues simultaneously into several contexts, albeit without giving up on bringing all the visitors that enter the venue from the various contexts into a single interior experience. The further exploration of the opportunities and problems of the various strategies metaverse urbanism and virtual urban co-location goes beyond the scope of this paper. These remain open questions. The focus here is instead on the architectural opportunities and problems connected with cyber-physical hybridity in the realm of knowledge work environments, on the scale of architecture and small urban clusters.

ALL DESIGN IS COMMUNICATIVE FRAMING

The architectural design for cyber-space—while implying a total substitution of the entire engineering stack—follows the same premises that guide architectural design in general. By implication, the same applies to the design of cyber-physical hybrid spaces. This expansion of architecture's remit will further distil the discipline's essence and core competency, namely the spatio-visual ordering of communicative interaction, upgraded via investment into the sub-disciplines of spatiology, phenomenology, and semiology. Matters of communication and communicative framing, dynamic or static, are here—in the context of metaverse design—foregrounded and distilled as the essential function of all design. In recent months, the author has increasingly felt compelled to refer to dramaturgy as another sub-discipline and key ingredient of our discipline's competency. In the context of the design of virtual communication spaces, it makes sense to interpret the architect's task as UI/UX design. This concept of an interface design and interaction/experience design can be generalized across all design disciplines, including architectural design. All architecture and design is UX/UI design, involving organization (spatiology), articulation (phenomenology), signification (semiology), and interaction design (dramaturgy). In the realm of virtual environment design, the desire for adaptive, kinetic, actively self-transforming communicative architectural frames is much easier to realize. On this count, dramaturgy will be much more foregrounded in the metaverse than it ever was in the context of physical architecture.

There are three premises of metaverse design posited by architectural theory:[2]

Premise 1: The Universal Power of Design

Architecture and the design disciplines together bear universal and exclusive responsibility with respect to the phenomenal appearance of the totality of the built environment and the world of artefacts, i.e. with respect to the totality of our phenomenal world. Appearances are important contributors to social functionality; they are indispensable orienting communications. Everything that surrounds us, meets our senses, and, as interface, mediates our communications with the social world has been visualized by a colleague designer. The design disciplines include urban design, landscape design, architecture, interior design, furniture design, fashion design, product design, as well as graphic design and web-design—and in the near future, metaverse design.

Premise 2: Framing as Societal Responsibility of Design

The life process of society is a communication process that is ordered via a rich typology of communicative situations. It is the designed environment, both physical and virtual, that distributes, frames, stabilizes, and coordinates these distinct situations and unfolds them within a designed order that allows us to self-sort as participants of various specific social interactions. The social function of all design—physical or virtual— is the spatio-visual framing of communicative interaction. The designed spaces—physical or virtual—are themselves communications: they are communications that define, premise, and prime the communicative interactions that are expected to take place within the respectively framed territory. These framing communications are a crucial aspect in ordering society by differentiating, defining, and structuring specific social situations with specific purposes, social protocols, and conditions of success.

Premise 3: The Task posed by the Contemporary Condition

With respect to our complex and dynamic post-Fordist network society, the design task of framing implies that complex, dynamic, dense, and diverse (but legible) information-rich environments are to facilitate orientation, navigation, and recognition (the identification of specific social situations) for an interaction-rich, productive, communicative, and collaborative social life process. This applies equally to the design of physical and virtual environments or frames.

All the design disciplines together form a single discourse and function system of society with the shared societal function of

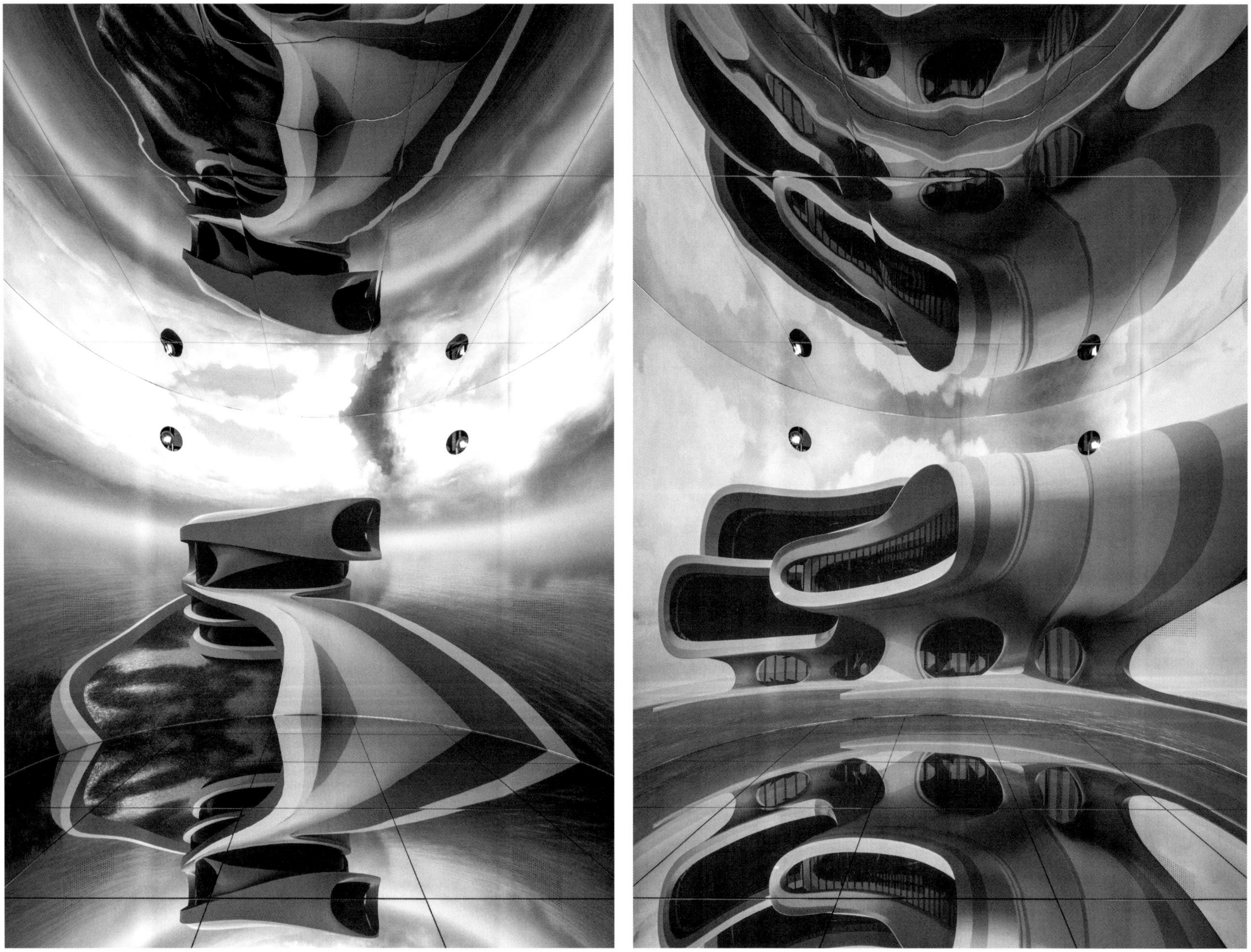

02 Architecting the Metaverse, Zaha Hadid Architects and Refik Anadol Studio, Seoul, 2022. Photography by Kyungsub Shin, Courtesy of Zaha Hadid Architects

the spatio-visual framing of all communicative interactions. This discourse revolves around the lead distinction of form (internal reference) versus function (external reference) and is structured by the persistent binary code of (formally and functionally) "resolved" versus "unresolved." The criteria for the concrete application of these code values is being programmed and re-programmed by the design disciplines' historically evolving, adapting style. To the extent that all designers respond to the global design discourse, this discourse is omnipotent with respect to the spatio-visual and tactile shaping of the phenomenal world, within the economic constraints and social functionality expectations set by (private or public) clients.

Designing is communicative framing. This insight is made the explicit premise and agenda for a systematic design research project that bridges physical architecture and virtual interaction design. The design task of the communicative spatio-visual framing of the societal life process must draw on four distinct but interrelated domains of expertise with their respective subtasks as follows:

- spatiology: organisation
- phenomenology: articulation
- semiology: signification
- dramaturgy: interaction

'Spatiology' is concerned with spatial organization and plots out the geometric premises, seting the scene as it were, for the other three agendas of phenomenology, semiology, and dramaturgy. Spatiology guides the distribution of places in space with respect to distancing, adjacencies, and connections. This task dimension involves the selection of strategies of spatial organization like axial ordering, grids, stacking, nesting, overlapping, etc. An expanded spatiological expertise might draw on conceptual and computational resources provided by the mathematics of network theory.

'Phenomenology', as understood in this essay (and in the author's theory of architecture in general), is concerned with morphological articulation and addresses the problem of the perceptual tractability of complex spatial/social scenes, i.e. the task of maintaining legibility in the face of complexity.

03 Trompe-l'œil space expansions. Project "Cybertecture"
by Stefan Tzon Manousof, Qi Yang, Amin Yassin, and Yang Yu

The psychology of perception in general, and the subfield of spatial cognition in particular, provides a key resource with respect to this task dimension.

'Semiology' is concerned with communication via signification. The meaning of spaces and designs coincides with the social interactions they frame, i.e. meaning is or anticipates social use. The semiological project sets out the task of increasing the information-richness of the built environment by means of crafting a spatio-visual language or system of signification that is empowered by the combinatorial potency of grammar. Here linguistics serves as a fertile source domain for conceptual inspiration.

'Dramaturgy' is concerned with patterns and potentials of interaction. In the context of architecture, and in the context of designing for the metaverse, understood as a spatial immersive world wide web, dramaturgy is closely related to what in web-design is pursued under the heading of interaction design. Dramaturgy implies environmental action in the time dimension, i.e. the design of a built environment, physical or virtual, that is both kinetically responsive to user interaction as well as spontaneously engaging users.

Spatiology, phenomenology, semiology and dramaturgy identify and define central aspects of architecture's task domain. These aspects of architectural learning respond to key challenges contemporary architecture faces with respect to its need to adapt its intelligence and design resources to the density, complexity, and dynamism of 21st century social life.

It is especially in this context of cyberspace and metaverse design that the task dimensions of spatiology, phenomenology, semiology, and dramaturgy as key dimensions of a spatial UI/UX design effort are foregrounded and distilled as indispensable competencies. Here too architecture must cope with increasing levels of social communicative density, complexity, and dynamism. As physical construction constraints disappear, spatial cognition, information density and interaction richness come to the fore as the critical performance criteria of all design.

THE CYBER-URBAN INCUBATOR

Co-working and incubator spaces will make up an increasing part of the urban fabric, interlaced with education venues and spaces for a more freewheeling networking and socializing. The idea of a Cyber-Urban Incubator is proposing to double up these urban realms with corresponding virtual realms, not as digital twin replicas but as congenial extensions with their own laws of navigation, encounter, and modes of interaction. However, these two realms are connected via spatial interfaces and via a unified spatio-visual language as integrated system of signification. Physical spaces will afford windows into virtual spaces where the semiology is the same and the logic of gathering and communicating is similar enough to allow for the transfer of competencies from the physical to the virtual realm. These competencies are the complementary competencies of both designers and end users.

Inspiration is drawn from metaverses like "Decentraland" and "Somnium Space," playful social VR environments like VRChat. The metaverse is inhabited via avatars and allows for virtual land ownership, virtual construction, and (mostly crypto-mediated) economic transactions. However, the Cyber-Urban Incubator is not a free-for-all playing field but a designed high-performance work environment for curated clusters of creative start-up companies.

The project presented below to illustrate the idea of cyber-physical hybridity is a post-graduate design research thesis developed in the context of the Design Research Lab at the Architectural Association (AADRL) in London. The project, developed by a team of four graduate students, was part of a cluster of four such projects forming a creative industry start-up urban district at the Queens waterfront in New York. The project started by conceptualizing and sketching a series of hybrid interaction scenarios. There are a number of technologies that allow for the telepresence of remote participants, for instance holographic projections, or more advanced options like VROOM, Microsoft's telepresence option via remote controlled robots. Low tech options for tele-presence include the possibility of mixing physical presence with remote participation by interweaving physical chairs with virtual chairs (screens) around a table. Another intriguing option is to work with large panoramic screens that function as a virtual expansion of the physical space, similar to a *trompe-l'œil*, but inhabited by avatars representing the remote participants (Fig. 03).

These projected space expansions function like windows into virtual spaces. These virtual spaces continue the geometry of the physical space and simulate its materiality via photorealistic real time rendering as is now possible, for instance, with the

04 Architecting the Metaverse, Zaha Hadid Architects and Refik Anadol Studio, Seoul, 2022. Photography by Kyungsub Shin, Courtesy of Zaha Hadid Architects

latest version of Epic's "Unreal Engine." However, geometric and stylistic continuity at the edges might be enough to establish a sense of immersive connection with the physical space, allowing then also for inventive transformations of the virtual space expansion, like various degrees of abstraction, or an enhanced kinetic malleability. A further obvious possibility that is being explored in the AADRL studio is the opportunity to work with info-graphic overlays that deliver further information about the space and its participants. These overlays can also be overlaid onto the physical space via augmented reality (AR) technology. The design inspiration flows in both directions of the physical–virtual divide.

The spatiological strategy for the project assumes that the intensity with which physical spaces are laced with connections into virtual realms is a matter of degree. There are areas where physical presence dominates, like in the current office environment where only the desk tops, laptops and mobile phone screens connect with the virtual world, without giving a sense of spatial integration. On the other end of this spectrum we find spaces, like VR caves, where the immersion into virtual interaction scenarios dominates, even when several individuals are also physically co-located while joining a virtual space. The spatiology here distributes a series of blob-shaped voids that cut across the building's slabs to establish the places with a high degree of virtuality as multi-storey mega-caves that are also visible on the exterior of the building as glowing, animated domes. These mega-blobs occasionally also form meta-ball formations. Between these high virtuality center's and the low virtuality periphery, users can follow a gradient of variously calibrated mixed reality spaces that are ordered in a trajectory of increasing mediation towards the virtuality nodes.

In terms of phenomenology and semiology, the gradient is reinforced in the following way: Those local space expansions that are closer to the periphery and where physical co-location is foregrounded and dominates the mixed reality scenario, the virtual spaces are rendered in photo-realistic fashion, mimicking closely the form and materiality of the physical space. As the mixed reality spaces approach the voids, and the balance between physical and virtual presence shifts, the way the virtual spaces are rendered also shifts towards

1 See ed. Patrik Schumacher *AD: Parametricism 2.0: Rethinking Architecture's Agenda for the 21st Century, Architectural Design*, March/April 2016.

2 See Patrik Schumacher *The Autopoiesis of Architecture, Volume 1, A New Framework for Architecture*, (London: John Wiley & Sons, 2010) and *The Autopoiesis of Architecture, Volume 2, A New Agenda for Architecture*, (London: John Wiley & Sons, 2012).

abstraction, increased kinetic malleability, and generally towards greater and greater emancipation from the presuppositions of the physical design. The degree of rendering abstraction and design emancipation displayed in the virtual space expansions is thus signifying the degree to which the respective communication events are locally or globally focused. The opportunity and intensity of dramaturgical design ideas also increases with the increasing shift of balance towards the virtual realm. However, dramaturgy is never altogether absent even from physically focused spaces.

It is one of the ambitions of the author to use the increased dramaturgical design opportunities delivered by the emergence of metaverse architecture to also advance the dramaturgical project in the realm of physical architecture (Fig. 04). This has been a longstanding theme within the author's design research agenda, previously pursuit under labels like "responsive environments" and "spontaneous environments."[3] Here is also an important role for AI to enter and empower architectural spaces, both virtual and physical. The ambition is to design an environment where many (if not all) architectural elements become self-directed, learning architectural agents that form a productive collaborative ecology together with the human participants, eschewing remote control for the free unfolding of artificial architectural intelligence. In both the physical and virtual spaces, AI-empowered creatures will, more and more, become our valued collaborators. The life-process of the future will thus become a man-machine ecology, another form of hybridity at work.

3 Patrik Schumacher, "The Future of Architecture - Spontaneous and Virtual," *Economic Times*, 2020.

PROJECTS: DECENTERED FUTURES

The aesthetics of workplace design is inundated with workplace hierarchies that oscillate between pragmatic and problematic. In the typical 20th century office tower, top floor executive suites, corner administrative offices, open floor plans that accommodate a range of mid-level workers, and lower level and basement spaces for the purely functional aspects of maintenance and service, all illustrate such spatial social hierarchies well. Emphasis on "flat hierarchies" and amenity-laden horizontal work campuses pioneered by the tech industry has resulted in a return to "open office" concepts; innovation in architectural composition has stagnated and underlying hierarchies persist. The successes of remote work and increased labor automation indicate that new configurations of the office and its relationship to other systems are necessary and even vital to its future relevance. This section's projects push the aesthetic boundaries and implications of hybridized work environments with decentralized operational logics for architecture and urbanism. They contemplate new urban figures and form, performance criteria, new building systems, compositional logics, and circulatory possibilities. They shift between cohesively choreographed surface articulations that suggest complex inner workings and assemblages of materials and systems with astounding phenomenological effects.

PROJECT 10

EDIFICE

UPS Hub, West SOHO, New York

Xiaotong Ni, Mingda Guo

Edifice draws inspiration from a range of sources, including Brutalism, Cubism, and the architecture of logistics (e.g. data centers). The result is a stunning and imposing urban monument that reimagines the traditional office typology in a dynamic and forward-thinking way. At the heart of Edifice's design is its striking façade, which is composed of a series of monolithic large interlocking three-dimensionally asymmetric parts. The use of such an asymmetrical design provides the building with a sense of movement and dynamism. Internally, these parts work together to choreograph logistical operations and workflows. The building is designed with areas allocated to different functions, such as collaborative spaces, private offices, and shared workspaces. This allows for a high degree of flexibility and adaptability, ensuring that the building can meet the changing needs of its occupants.

Top Right: Elevation Rendering

Bottom: Typcial Floor Plan

01 Package Distribution System
02 Package Storage
03 Pedestrian Bridge
04 Offices
05 Lounge Space
06 Atrium
07 Lobby

03
03
05
06
04
04
01
06
A

Long Building Section

01 Package Distribution System
02 Package Storage
03 Pedestrian Bridge
04 Offices
05 Lounge Space
06 Atrium
07 Lobby

A

Physical Section Model, 2'x2'x2', 3D Printed PLA

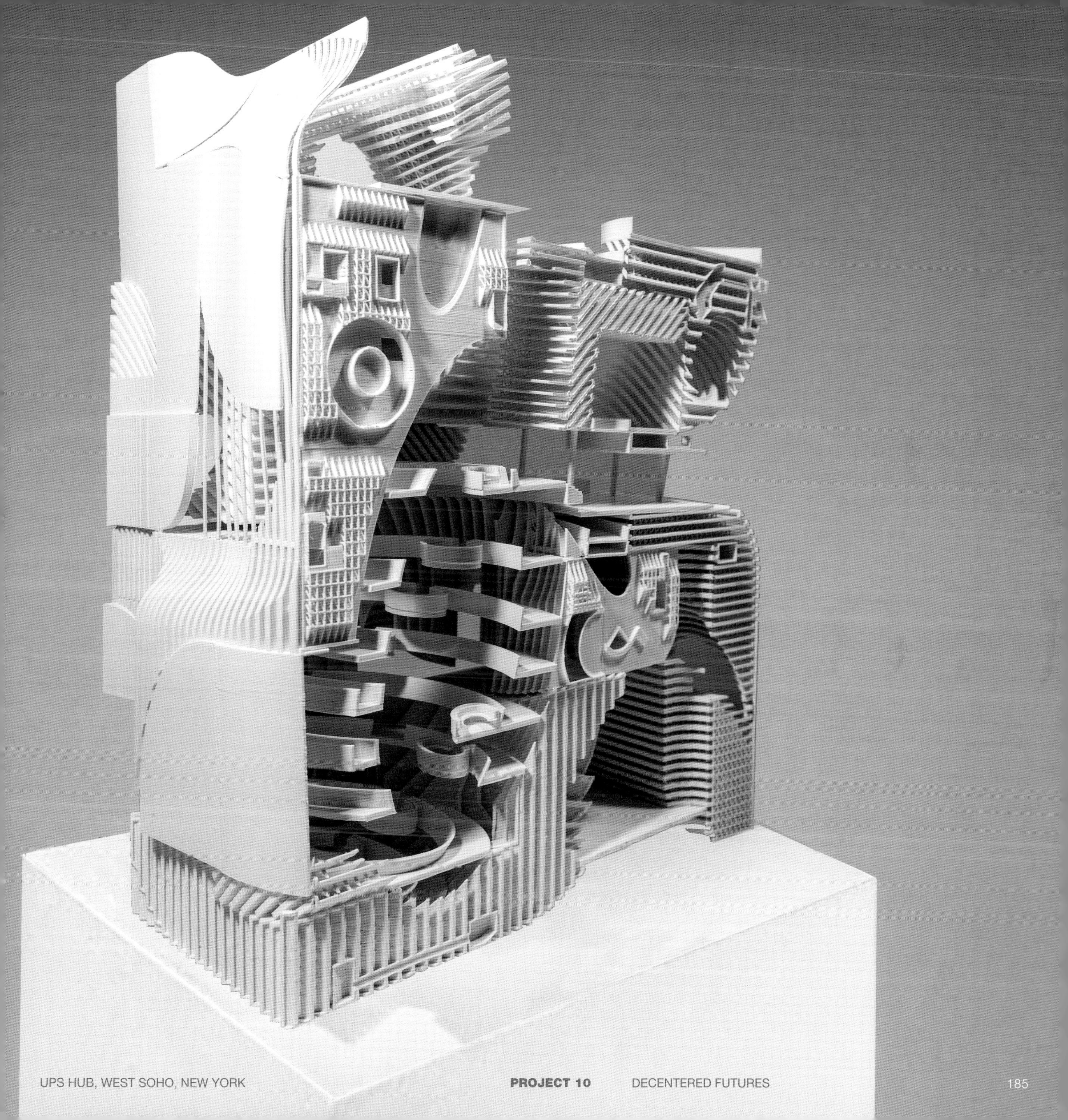

PROJECT 11

SHIFT

UPS Hub, West SOHO, New York

Zheyuan Fu, Yiqi You

Shift reflects current and future changes in work and the workplace through scalar shifts in building program and organization. Typology-defying internal spatial networks are created laterally and vertically through the project's signature curving partition structures. Modular office design is left behind in favor of large collaborative spaces with impressive unique architectural features and light qualities. Logistical operations are embedded in the building's sleek design, a composition of smooth curvilinear surfaces punctuated with grooves and apertures.

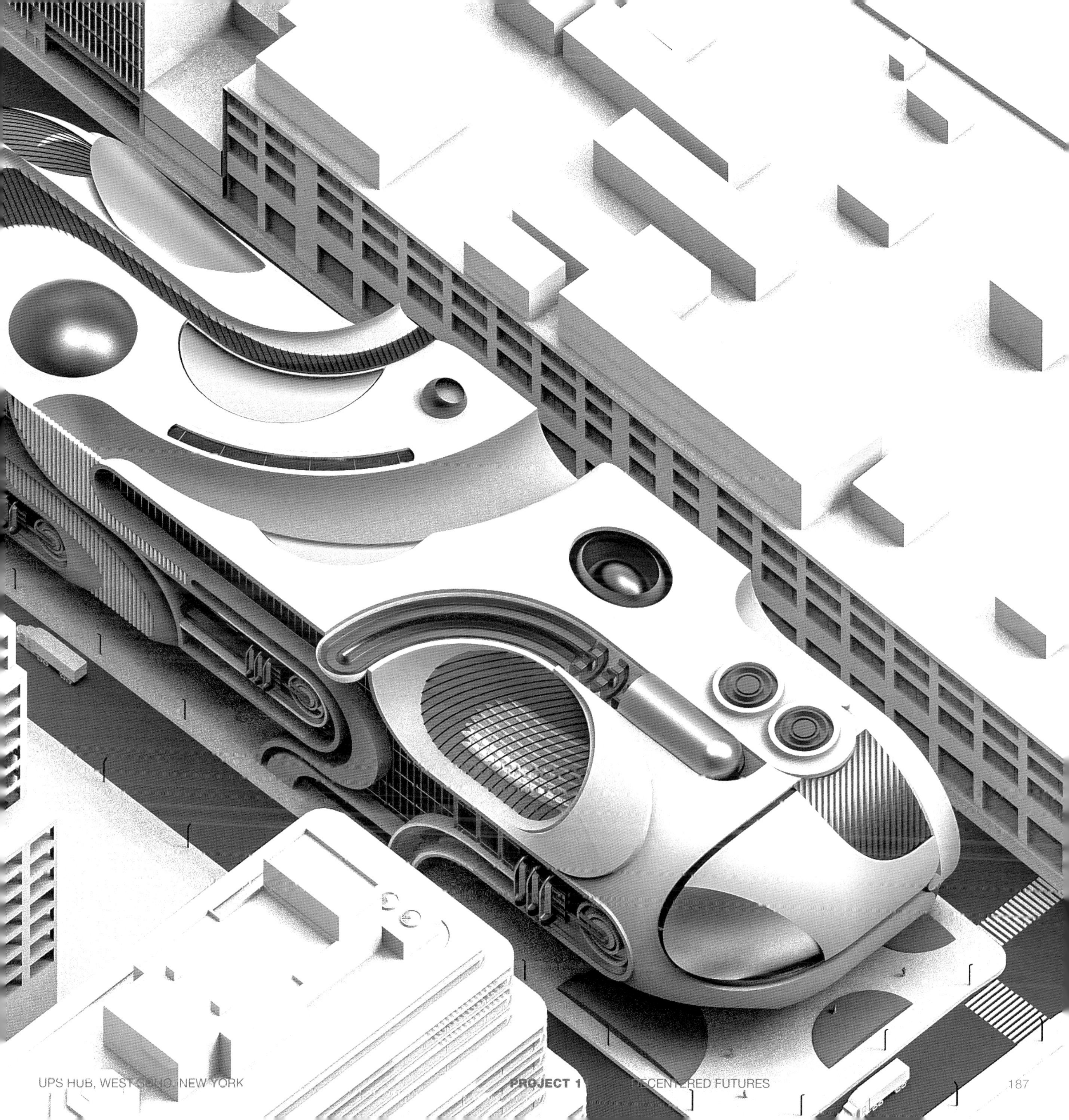

Right: Section Model Rendering

Left: Perspective Rendering

01 Package Distribution System
02 Package Storage
03 Auditorium
04 Offices
05 Meeting Area
06 Atrium
07 Lobby

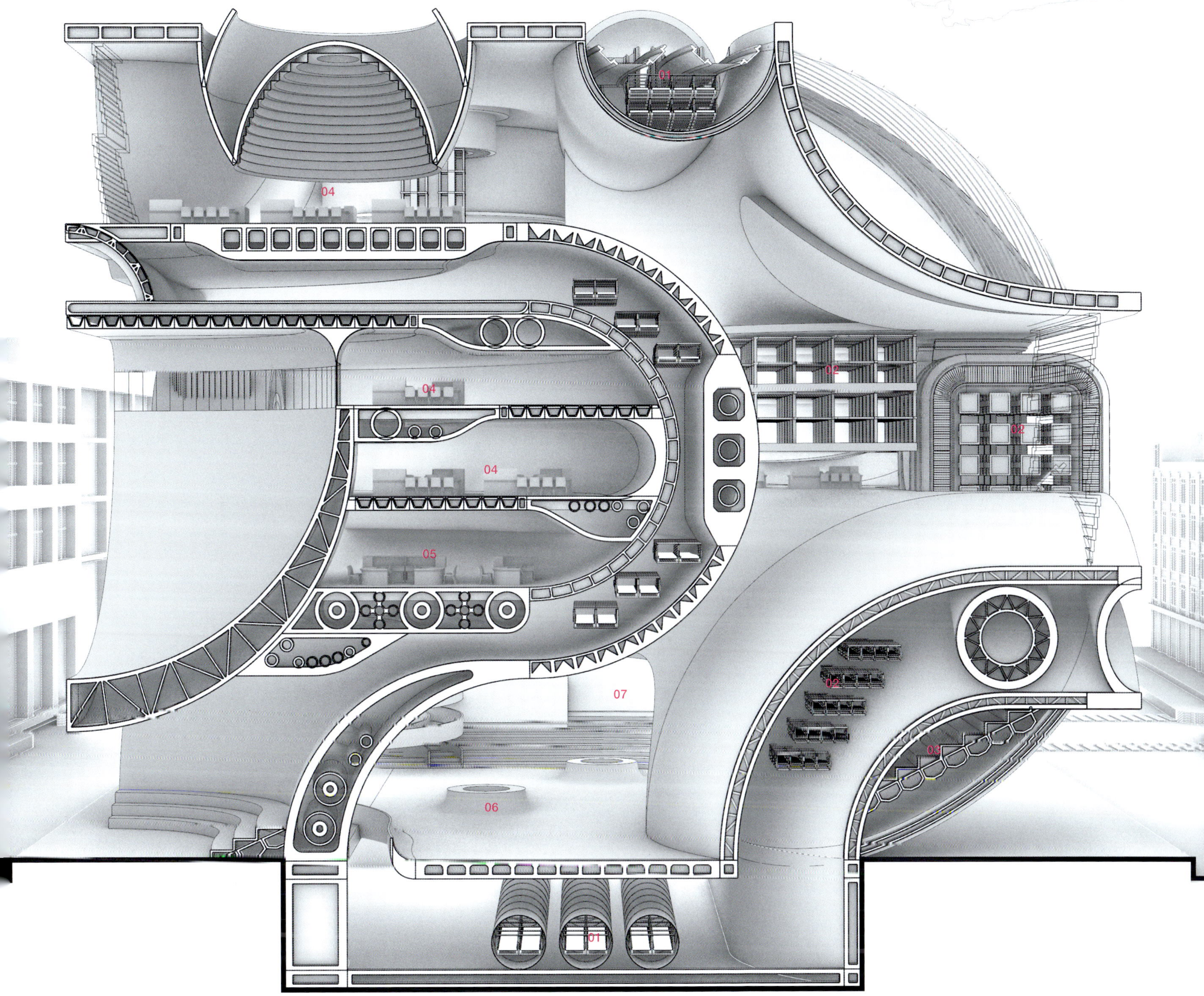
01
04
04
02
02
04
05
07
02
03
06
01

Elevation Rendering

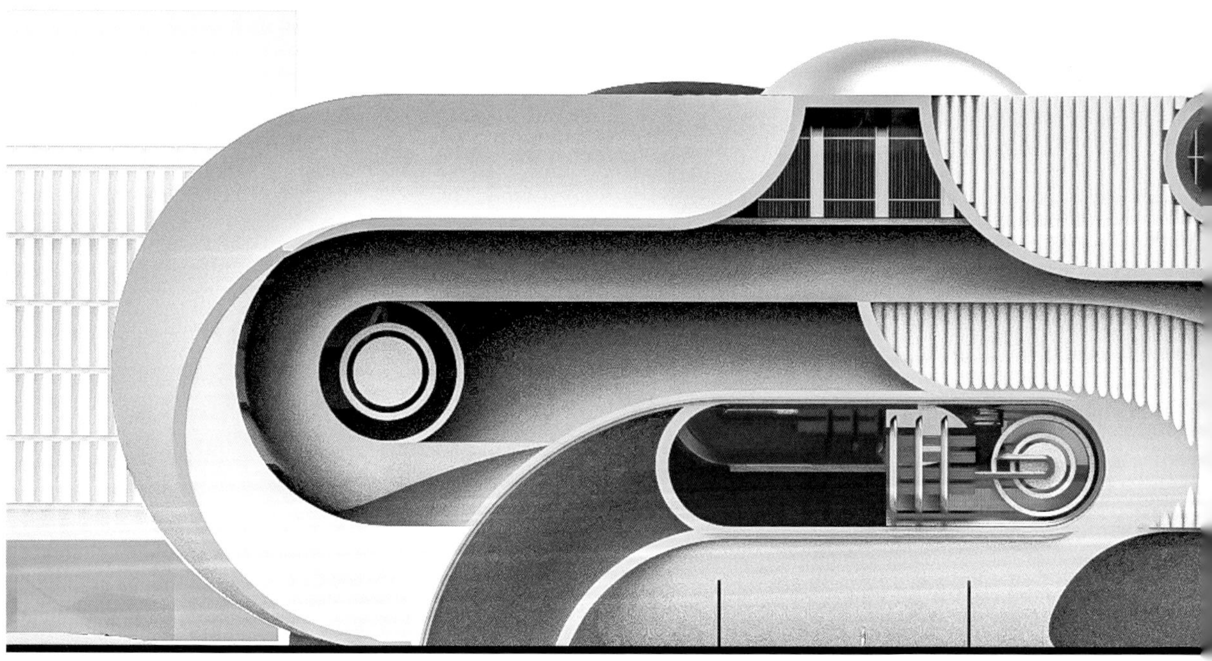

Section Model Rendering

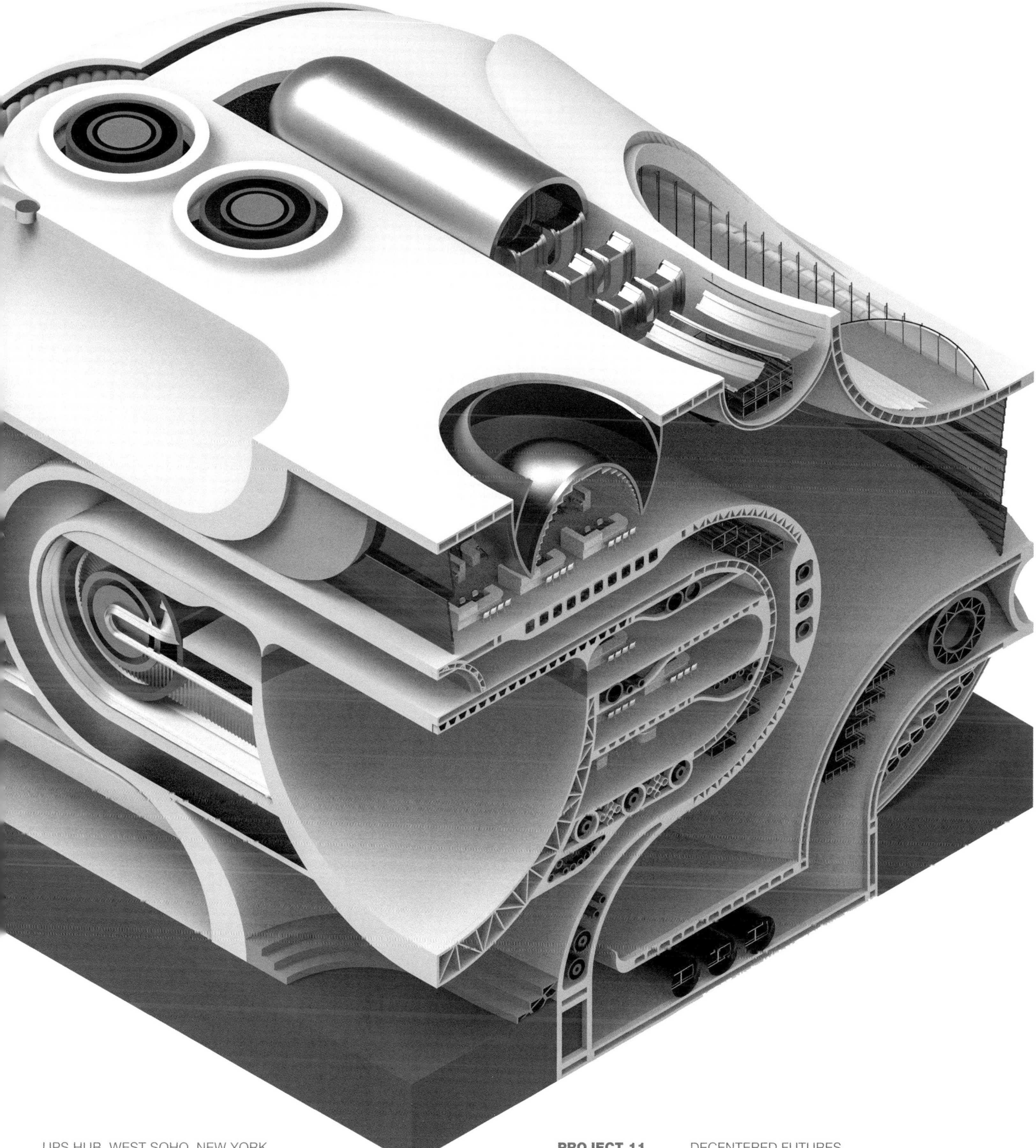

PROJECT 12

CIRCUIT

UPS Hub, West SOHO, New York

Maoqiang Li, Bohao Sun, Youyu Zhang

The project refashions a deconstructivist attitude toward building composition in a design that is at once functionalist and aesthetic. The project is inspired by circuit board and electronics engineering that seek to assemble discrete components in a constrained space. When explored at the architectural scale, this approach produces new and unanticipated spatial qualities. Manufacturing and logistics mechanisms cut through open workspaces in unexpected ways, creating productive frictions and adjacencies between programs as well as a unique and dynamic environment that stimulates collaboration and creativity.

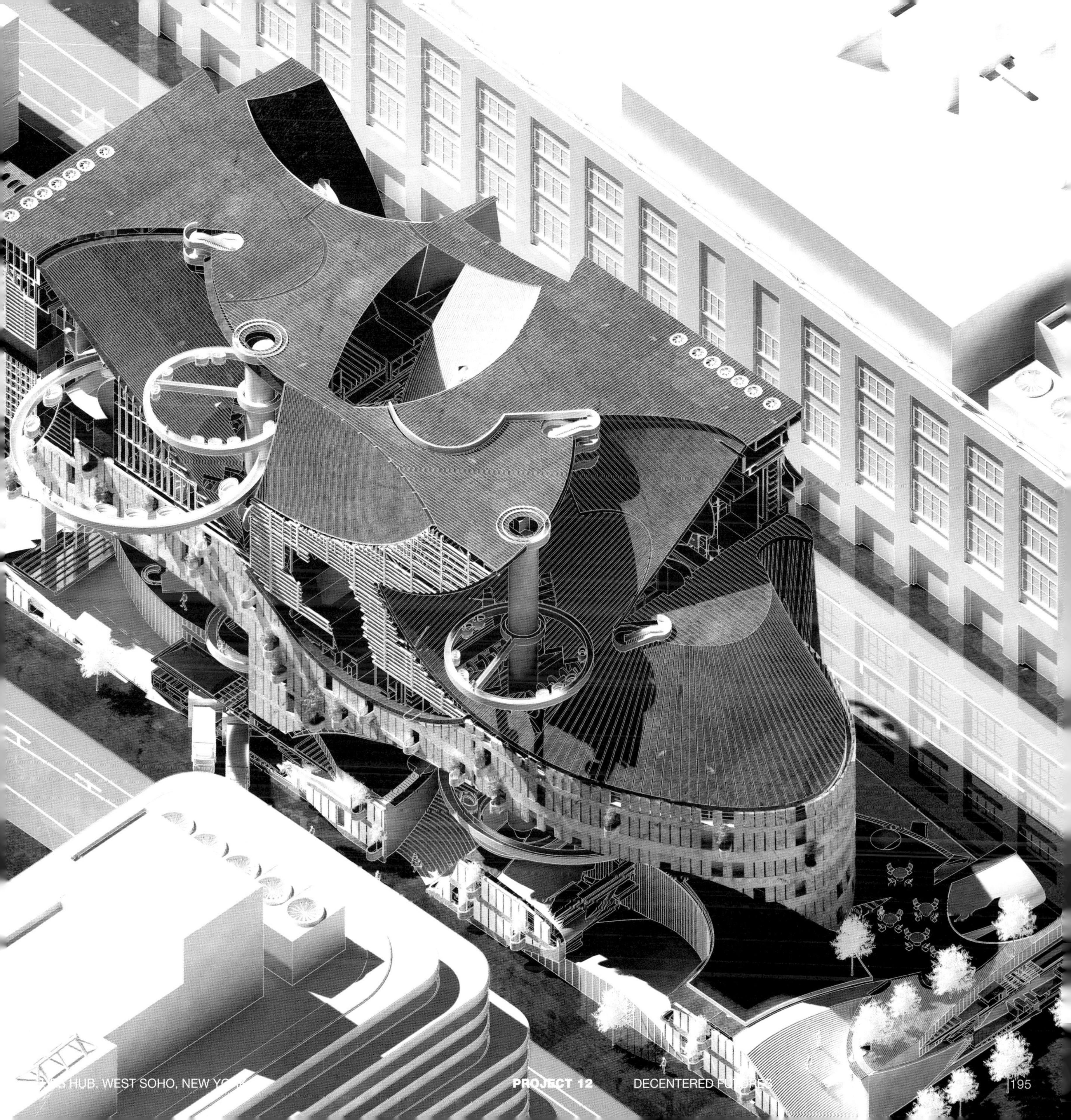

Elevation Rendering

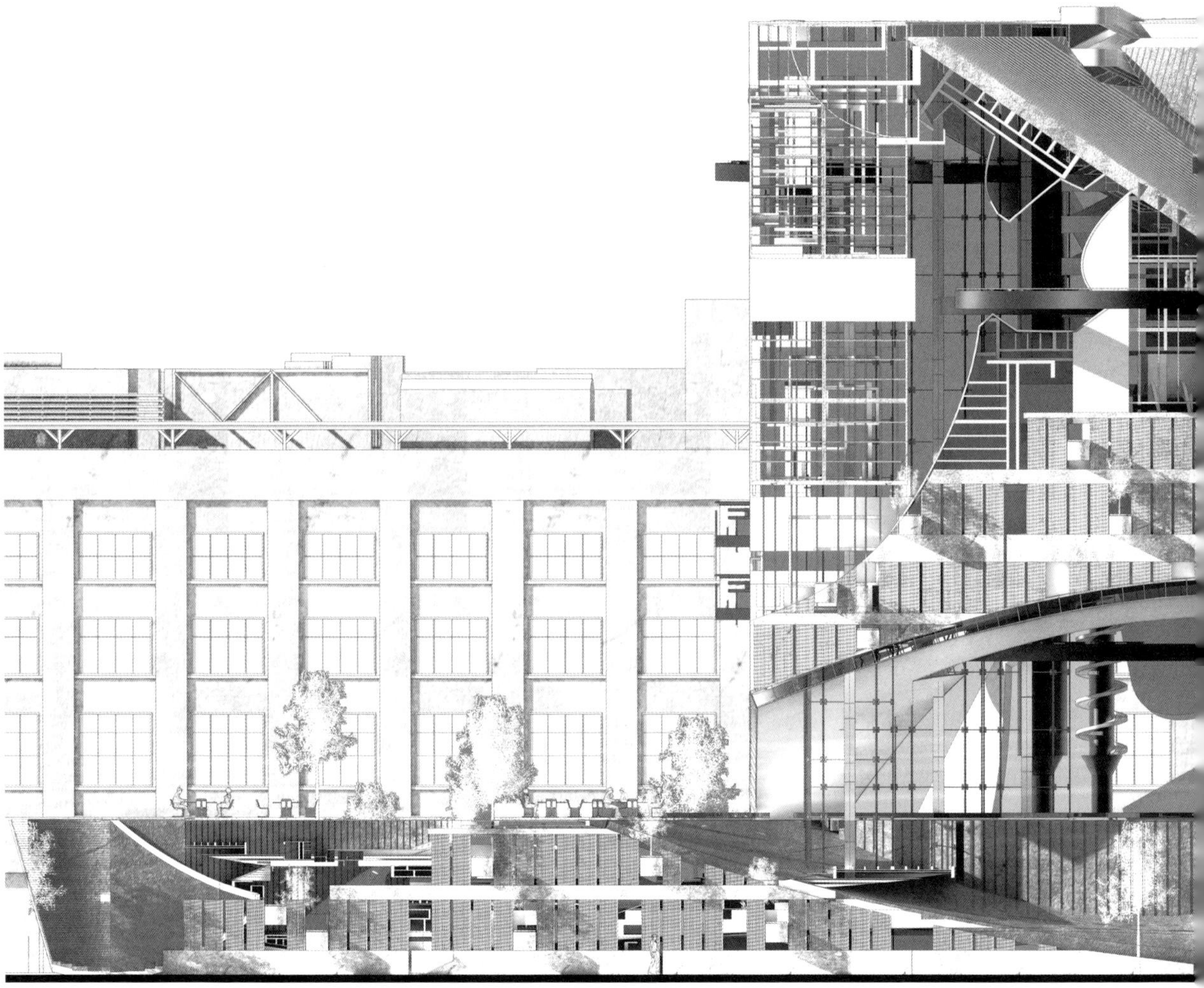

Right: Physical Section Model, 2'x2'x2', 3D Printed PLA

Left: Short Building Section

01 Package Distribution System
02 Package Drop-off Area
03 Visitor Drop-off Area
04 Meeting Room
05 Offices
06 Package Storage
07 Pacakge Sorting System
08 Atrium
09 Lounge
10 Stair

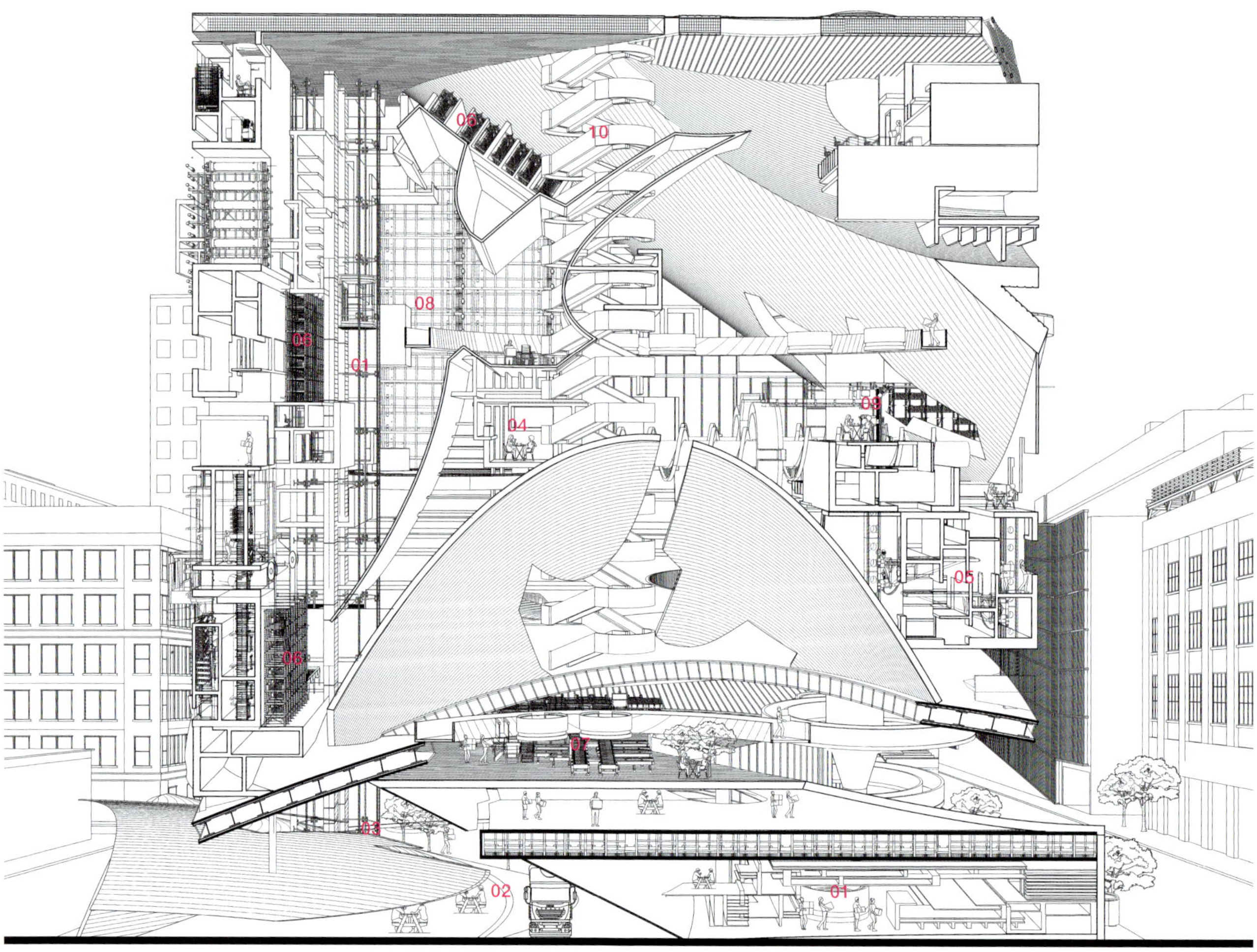

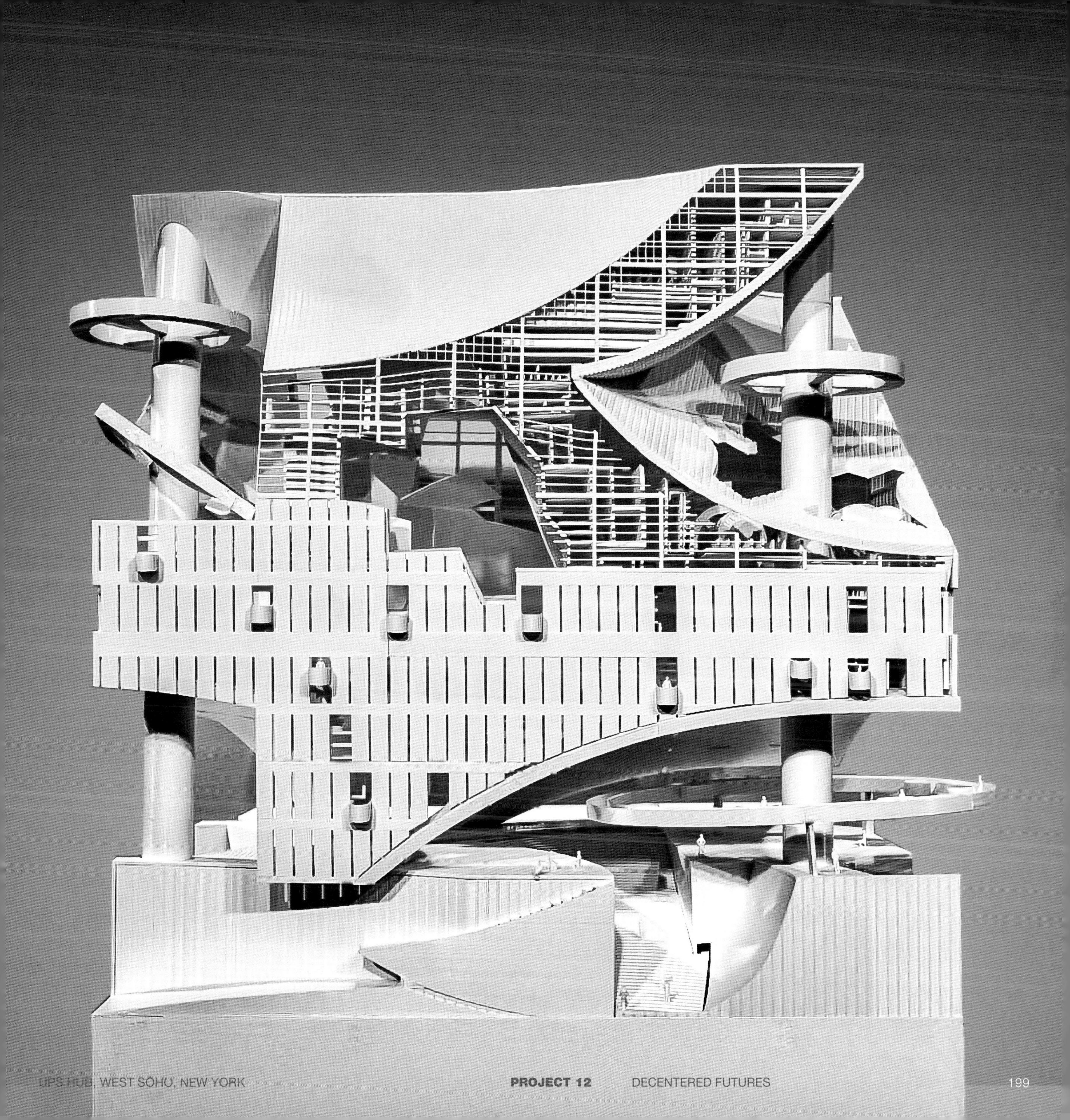

PROJECT 13

RUIN

UPS Hub, West SOHO, New York

Xing Guo, Xianlong Deng, In Pun

The project takes the concept of the office as architectural ruin as a starting point for speculating upon its possible futures. Mangled and condensed scaffold-like structures vary in size and take on logistical functions while large building cavities and structural disjunctions serve a variety of workplace and public functions at multiple scales. The irregularly shaped spaces can be used as break areas, meeting rooms, or even performance spaces. The building's unique layout also encourages interaction and collaboration between workers, as the unusual spatial qualities create opportunities for chance encounters and unexpected connections.

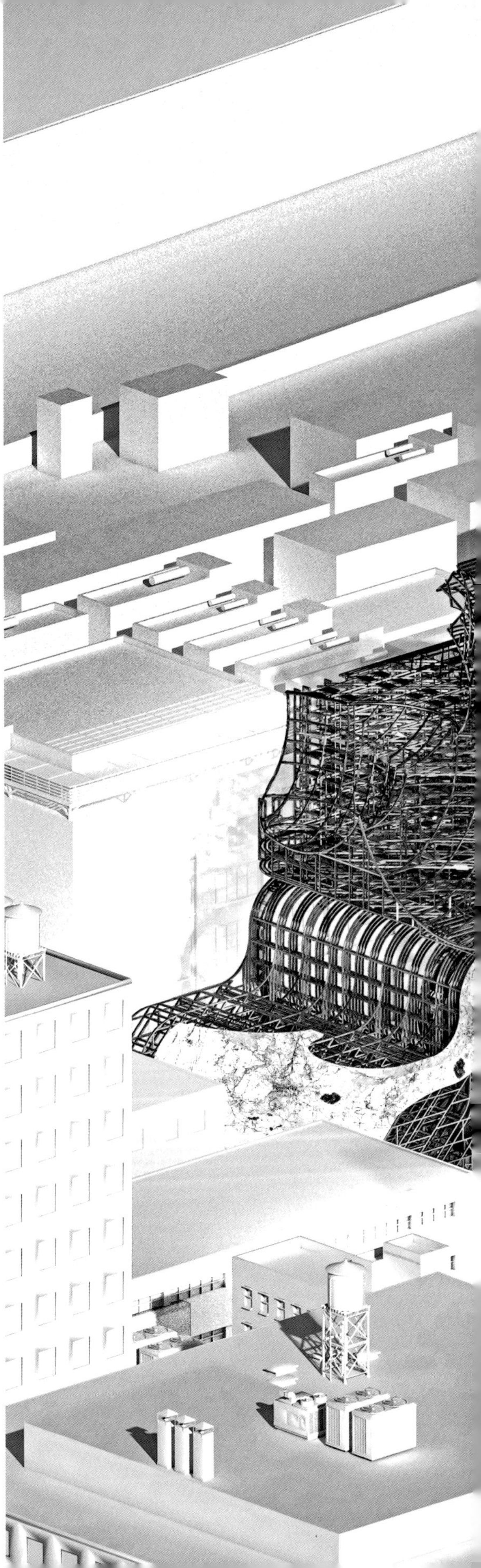

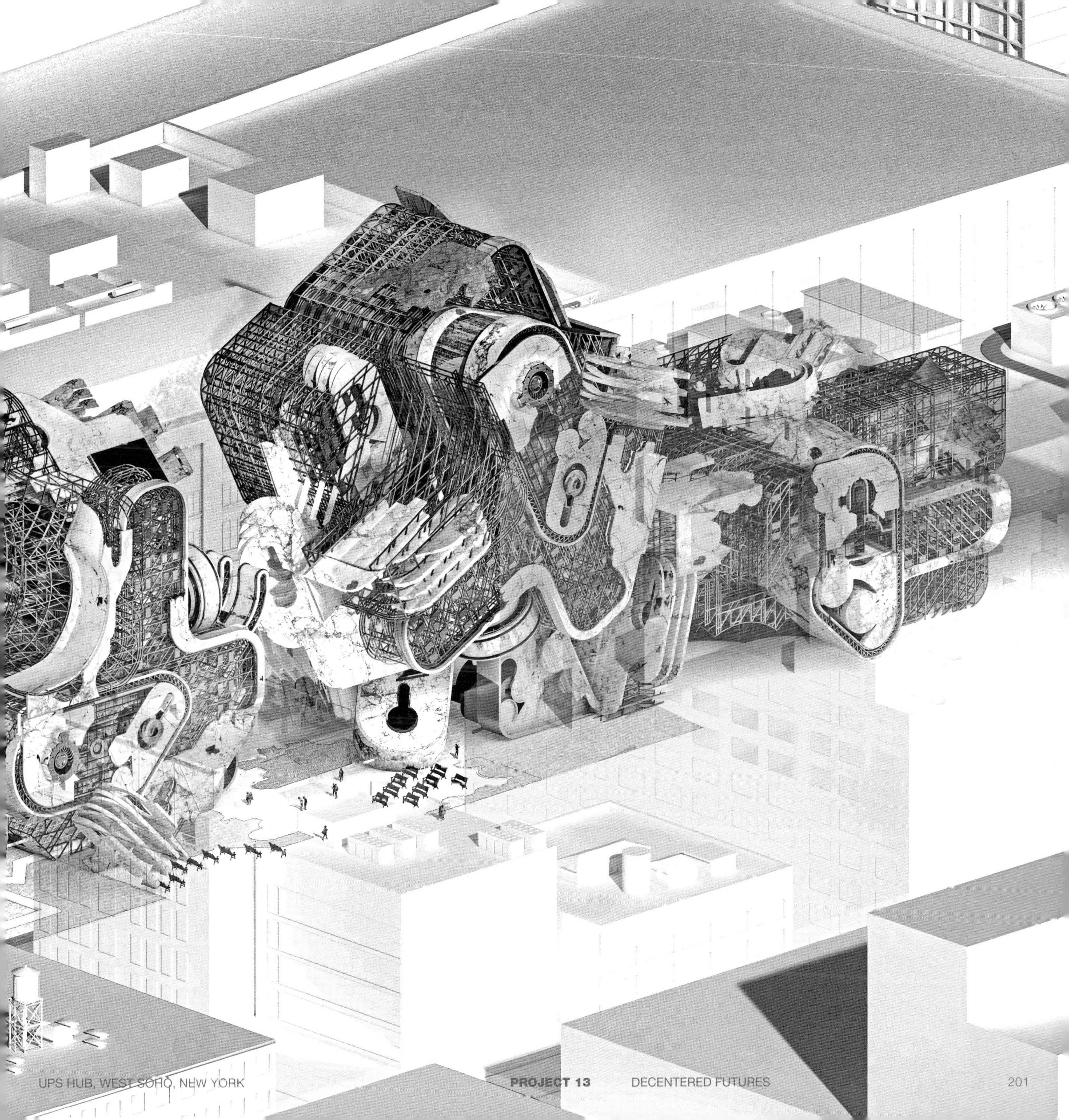

Top Right: Long Building Section

Bottom: Typical Floor Plan

01 Lobby
02 Package Distribution System
03 Auditorium
04 Package Drop-off Area
05 Mechanical Room
06 Package Storage
07 Board Room
08 Offices
09 Lounge Space
10 Meeting Room
11 Package Sort Area

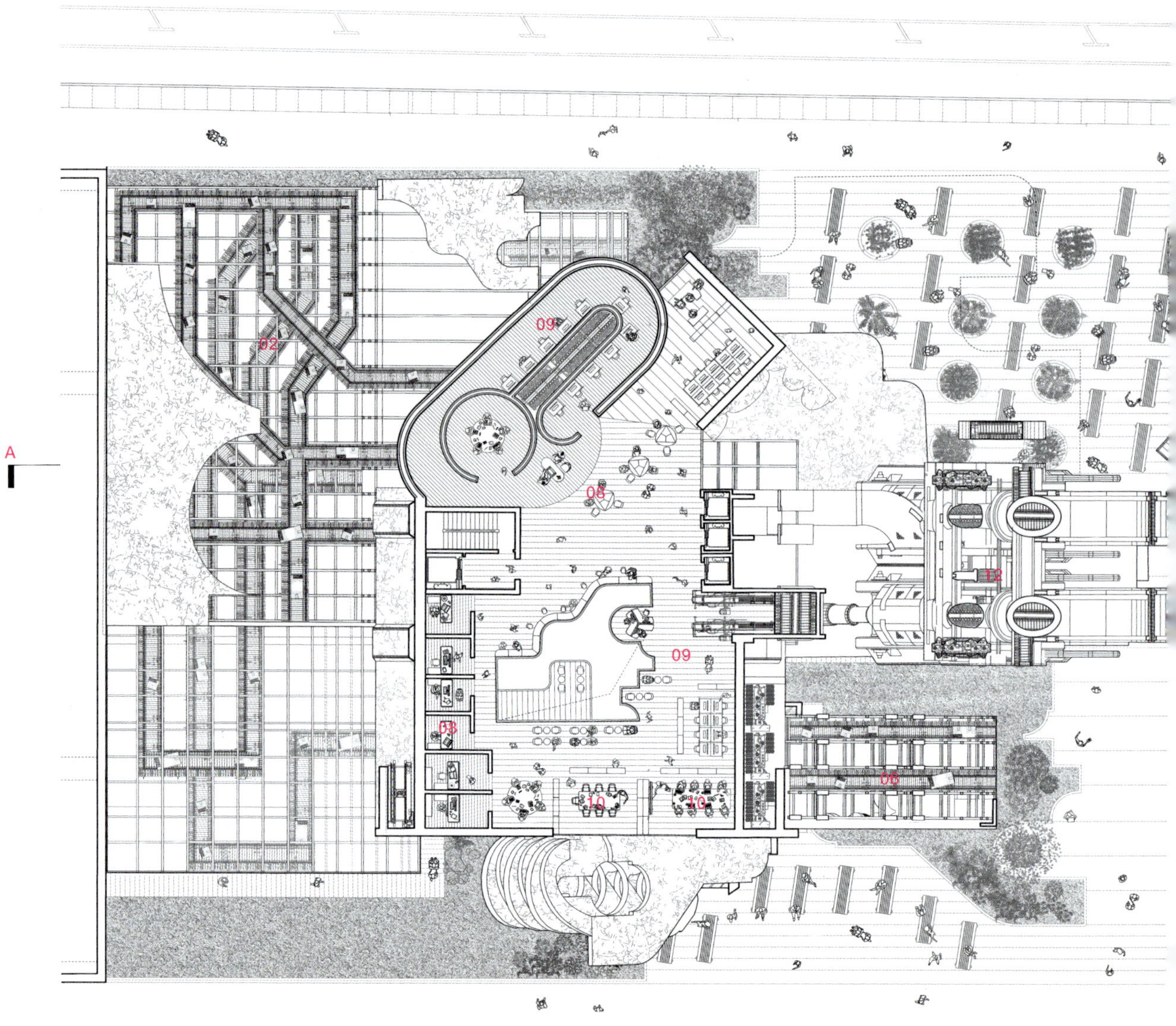

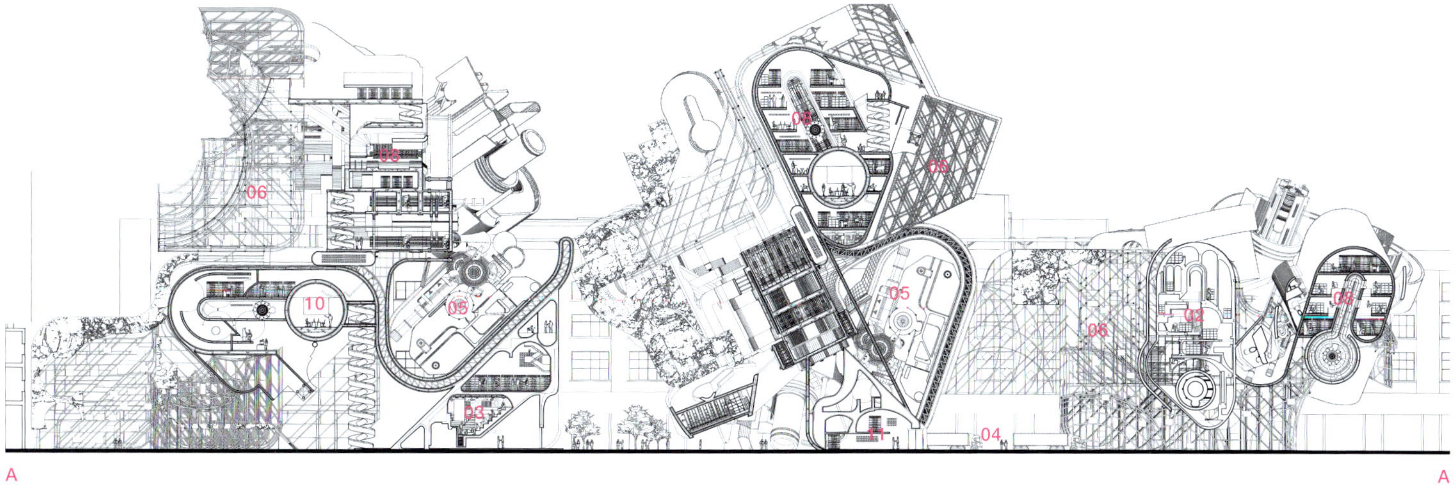

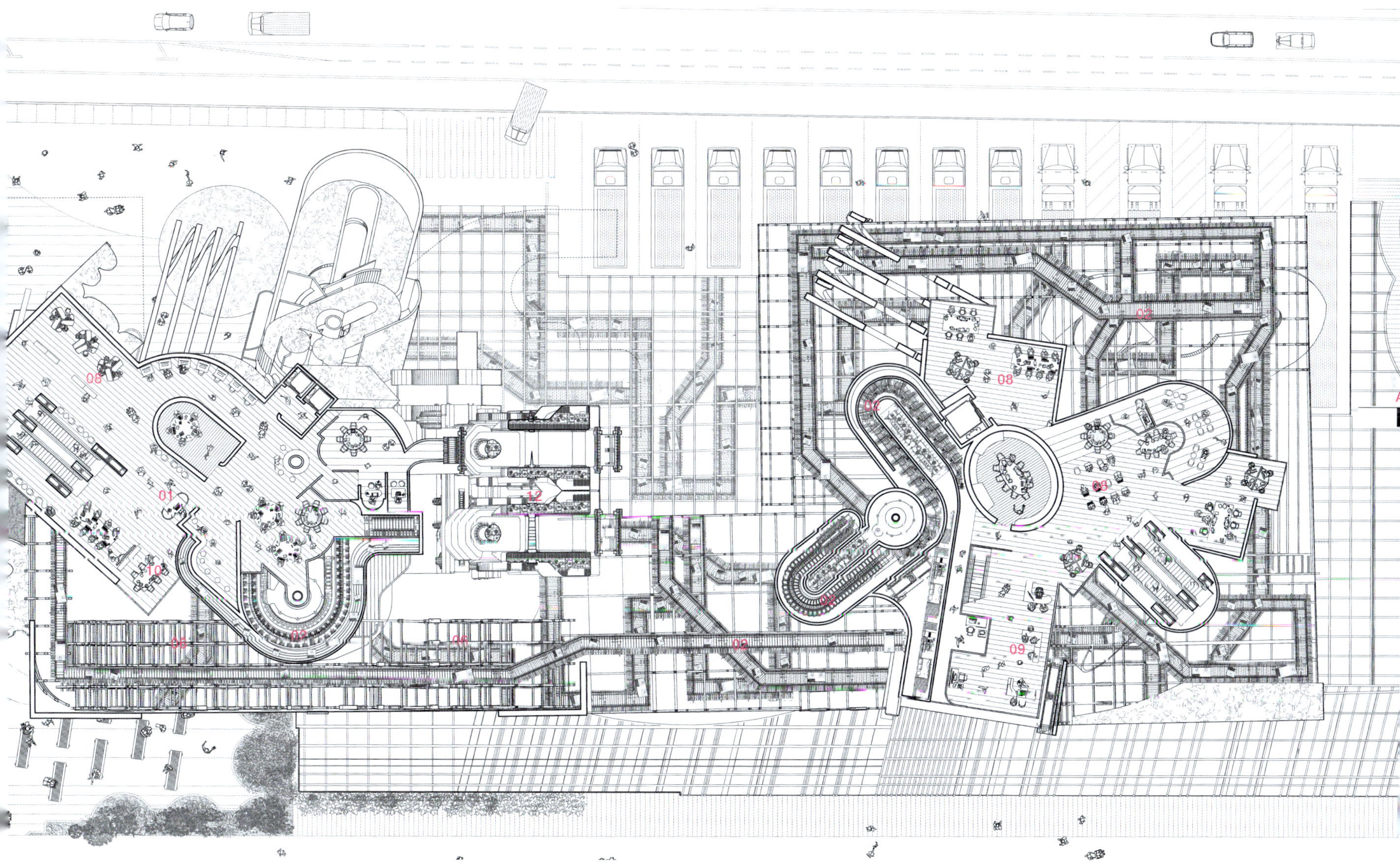

Elevation Rendering

Physical Section Model, 2'x2'x2', 3D Printed PLA

CONTRIBUTORS' BIOGRAPHIES

Ali Rahim

Director MSD-AAD, Author

Ali Rahim is Professor of Architecture at the University of Pennsylvania Stuart Weitzman School of Design, where he directs the Master of Science in Design with a concentration in Advanced Architectural Design program (MSD-AAD). He has served as the Studio Zaha Hadid Visiting Professor at the University of Applied Arts in Vienna, the Louis I. Kahn Visiting Professor at Yale University, and as a Visiting Architecture Professor at Harvard University and Southern California Institute of Architecture (SCI-Arc).

He is the Founder and Co-director of Contemporary Architecture Practice with Hina Jamelle with offices in New York City and Shanghai. The firm is renowned for its award-winning and futuristic work utilizing digital techniques for the design and manufacture of architecture. His projects have been exhibited extensively, at locations including the Museum of Modern Art (New York), the Venice Biennale (Venice), Serpentine Gallery (London), and the Tel Aviv Museum of Art (Tel Aviv). He has received numerous awards, including being named one of "Fifty Under Fifty Innovators of the 21st Century and receiving Architectural Record's Design Vanguard.

His work has been published in over 200 domestic and international magazines, journals, and newspapers. He is the author of *Catalytic Formations: Architecture and Digital Design* (Routledge, 2006), and he has edited and co-edited numerous volumes on architecture including *Turbulence* (Norten and Company, 2011), four issues of *Architectural Design—AD Impact* (2021), *AD Elegance* (2007), *AD Contemporary Techniques in Architecture* (2002), and *AD Contemporary Processes in Architecture* (2000)—*Future Airports* (ORO Editions, 2020), and *Asset Architecture 1, 2, and 3* (ORO Editions, 2016, 2017, and 2018). He holds a Master of Architecture degree from Columbia University, where he won the Award in Design Excellence, and a Bachelor of Science degree in Architecture from the University of Michigan.

Brian DeLuna

Critic MSD-AAD

Brian DeLuna is a Lecturer at the University of Pennsylvania Stuart Weitzman School of Design. He was a Visiting Assistant Professor at Pratt Institute and has also taught at Rensseleaer Polytechnic Institute, the New Jersey Institute of Technology, and at Princeton University as an assistant to Hani Rashid. He has conducted several workshops throughout the United States focusing on digital design and visualization. He is the Principal of Parabol, an interdisciplinary design firm operating in New York and Los Angeles. His prior work experience includes collaborating with international architecture firms including Xefirotarch, Los Angeles, and Asymptote Architecture, New York, where he supervised a wide range of high-profile projects as a senior designer. He holds a Master of Science in Advanced Architecture Design degree from Columbia University and a Bachelor of Architecture degree from the Southern California Institute of Architecture.

Na Wei

Critic MSD-AAD

Na Wei is the Founding Principal of WEI architects, a design firm initially established in New York and currently based in Beijing since 2009. She is an Associate Professor of architecture at Tianjin University and a Visiting Associate Professor at the University of Pennsylvania Weitzman School of Design. She has taught and lectured at numerous universities, including Tsinghua University, Central Academy of Fine Arts, Yale School of Architecture, Syracuse University, and the University of Cincinnati. Na Wei is the author of *Suffused Space* (China Architecture & Building Press, 2019). Her work has been featured in various publications and exhibitions worldwide, including *New Chinese Architecture: Twenty Women Building the Future* (Thames & Hudson, 2019), *Beyond the West: New Global Architecture* (Gestalten, 2020), *A Retrospective on Ten Years of Practice in Eastern Contexts* (2018) at Yale School of Architecture, and the 17th Venice Architecture Biennale (2021). Na Wei holds a Bachelor of Architecture degree from the Tsinghua University School of Architecture and a Master of Architecture degree from the Yale School of Architecture.

Nathan Hume

Critic MSD-AAD

Nathan Hume is a Lecturer at the University of Pennsylvania Stuart Weitzman School of Design. He is a licensed architect and partner at Hume Coover Studio with Abigail Hume in Brookyn, New York. Nathan and Abigail's work and writings have been published in *The New York Times*, *Wired*, *Metropolis*, *Tarp*, and *Project* and exhibited at the Yale University School of Architecture, the New York Center for Architecture and the Museum of Modern Art. Abigail and Nathan are also co-creators and editors of succkerPUNCHdaily.com, a website that reviews the work of contemporary artists, architects, and designers. Through succkerPUNCH, they created the exhibition *Fresh Punches* at the Land of Tomorrow gallery and published an accompanying book of the same title. He holds a Master of Architecture degree from the Yale University School of Architecture, and a Bachelor of Architecture degree from The Ohio State University.

Mo Zheng

Critic MSD-AAD

Mo Zheng is a co-founding Partner of the international architecture firm Antistatics based in Beijing and New York. Her work spans architecture, installation, city planning, and interior design. Known for refined dexterity in complex form and systemic logics, Antistatics innovative methodology, inspired by biomimicry, sustainability and emerging tech, has brought solutions to dozens of projects across the globe from the MaoHaus to the New Capital City for Indonesia. Before founding Antistatics, she was a project architect for Asymptote Architecture, overseeing several projects at various scales. Zheng studied at the Central Academy of Fine Arts in Beijing, holds a Bachelor of Architecture degree from the University of Buffalo and a Master of Architecture degree from the University of Pennsylvania Weitzman School of Design.

Verda Alexander

Author

Verda Alexander is a co-founder of Studio O+A, a design firm based in San Francisco. Studio O+A is responsible for numerous high-profile contemporary office designs including work for Facebook, Microsoft, Slack, and McDonalds, among others. Named by *Contract Magazine* "Designer of the Year" with Primo Orpilla in 2012, Alexander is also a member of *Interior Design Magazine*'s Hall of Fame. In 2016 Studio O+A received the Cooper Hewitt National Design Award for interior design. She is co-author of *Studio O+A: Twelve True Tales of Workplace Design* (Frame Publishers 2017) and the self-published *Eco Playbook* (2021). She holds an Master of Fine Arts degree from the San Francisco Art Institute, a Master of Landscape Architecture degree from the University of California Berkeley, and a Bachelor of Arts degree from San Jose State University.

Ariane Harrison

Author

Ariane Lourie Harrison is a Visiting Associate Professor of Architecture at Pratt Institute, where she also serves as the coordinator of the Master of Science in Architecture and Urban Design programs at the Graduate School of Architecture. She is a registered architect in New York State and Principal and co-founder of Harrison Atelier. She was a critic and lecturer at the Yale School of Architecture and Yale College from 2006-2017. Her projects and writing explore concepts of multi-species architecture, which have garnered awards including the NYCML 2018 and Microsoft's AI for the Earth 2019-20 Grant. Her publications include editing *Architectural Theories of the Environment: Posthuman Territory* (Routledge, 2013), *"Feral Architecture" in Aesthetics Equals Politics* (MIT Press, 2019), among others. She holds a Bachelor of Arts degree from Princeton University, a Master of Architecture degree from Columbia University GSAPP, and a PhD from the Institute of Fine Arts at New York University.

Peter Cappelli

Author

Peter Cappelli is the George W. Taylor Professor of Management at the University of Pennsylvania Wharton School and the Director of Wharton's Center for Human Resources. He is also a Research Associate at the National Bureau of Economic Research in Cambridge, Massachusetts. He served as Senior Advisor to the Kingdom of Bahrain for Employment Policy from 2003-2005, was a Distinguished Scholar of the Ministry of Manpower for Singapore, and was Co-Director of the U.S. Department of Education's National Center on the Educational Quality of the Workforce from 1990-1998. He is the author of multiple books on the workplace including *The Future of the Office* (Wharton Press, 2021), a regular contributor to *The Wall Street Journal*, and writes a monthly column for *HR Executive magazine*. He holds a PhD in Labor Economic from Nuffield College, Oxford University and a Bachelor of Science degree in Industrial Relations from Cornell University.

Colin Koop

Author

Colin Koop is a Partner and Senior Designer at Skidmore, Owings & Merrill (SOM). He is a New York State registered architect and member of the American Institute of Architects. His work for SOM includes numerous high profile national and international projects including the Walt Disney Company Headquarters 4 Hudson Square in New York City, The New School University Center, and the Milano Olympic Village in Milan, Italy among others. He received a Master of Architecture degree from the Harvard University Graduate School of Design and a Bachelor of Arts in Architecture from Washington University.

Qiyao Li
Author

Qiyao Li is an Associate Principal and Urban Designer at Skidmore, Owings & Merrill (SOM). She is a member of the New York American Institute of Architects. Her work for SOM includes numerous high profile national and international projects including the Walt Disney Company Headquarters 4 Hudson Square in New York City, the Milano Olympic Village in Milan Italy, and the Hytera Houhai Headquarters in Shenzhen, China among others. She received a Master of Architecture from the University of Pennsylvania and a Bachelor of Science from Peking University.

Ranya Nehmeh
Author

Ranya Nehmeh is an HR Professional who leads HR policies and development for the OPEC Fund for International Development in Vienna, Austria. She is the author of *The Chameleon Leader* (Independently Published, 2019), a book focused on leadership skills and perspectives for the contemporary workplace. She has guest lectured at numerous institutions internationally. She holds a PhD in Business Administration from the Swiss Management University, a Master in Human Resources degree from the London School of Economics and Political Science, and a Bachelor of Arts degree from the Westminster Business School.

Patrick Monte
Author

Patrick Monte is an artist, architectural designer, and writer based in Berlin. His art works have been exhibited internationally at public venues, museums, and galleries including the San Francisco Ferry Building in (San Francisco, California), the Asia Art Center (Gwangju, South Korea), Centro de Cultura Digital (Mexico City, Mexico), Aufbauhaus (Berlin, Germany), and Daegu Station (Daegu, South Korea). His work has been published by *inForma*, the Academy of Fine Arts Prague Press, and the ICMA journal *ARRAY*, among others. He has served as a guest lecturer at the Vienna Academy of Arts and a critic on architectural juries at the Vienna Academy of Arts, the Weitzman School of Design, and California College of the Arts. Patrick holds a Master of Architecture degree from California College of the Arts and a Bachelor of Arts degree in Studio Art from the City College of New York.

Patrik Schumacher
Author

Patrik Schumacher is Principal of Zaha Hadid Architects and has led the firm since Zaha Hadid's passing in 2016. In 1996, he co-founded the Design Research Laboratory at the Architectural Association in London, where he continues to teach. He also leads PhD research groups at the University of Applied Arts in Vienna and Tongji University in Shanghai. He is a member of the Berlin Academy of Arts, the Royal Institute of British Architects, and the Architectural Society of China. He has lectured worldwide and contributed over 120 articles to architectural journals and anthologies. His books include *Digital Hadid – Landscapes in Motion* (2013), and the two-volume work *The Autopoiesis of Architecture* (2010, 2012). He holds a PhD from the Institute for Cultural Science, Klagenfurt University, an honorary Doctor of Social Science from La Universidad Francisco Marroquin, and a Diploma in Architecture from Stuttgart University.

ACKNOWLEDGMENTS

Ali Rahim
Professor of Architecture and Director, MSD-Advanced Architectural Design, University of Pennsylvania, Weitzman School of Design

This book was made possible by funding from the University of Pennsylvania Weitzman School of Design and the Weitzman School's Department of Architecture. I would like to personally thank Dean Frederick Steiner for his support.

I would also like to thank the Master of Science in Design Advanced Architectural Design students and faculty at the University of Pennsylvania. The students worked diligently to conceptualize and develop their work within the studio setting. My colleagues Brian Deluna and Nathan Hume in 2019-2020 and Na Wei and Mo Zheng in 2020-2021 contributed greatly through our many discussions and their teaching the students during desk critiques and reviews of student work. Our teaching assistants Caleb White, Angela Huang, Gary Polk, Yuting He and Wenjia Guo contributed in their roles as teaching various software, drawings, and physical model building.

Finally, I would like to thank all of the participants who contributed to discussions during organized mid-term and final reviews: Kutan Ayata, Richard Blythe, Evan Douglis, Rodolphe El-Khoury, Hina Jamelle, Ferda Kolatan, Elena Manferdini, Andrew Saunders, Patrik Schumacher, and Craig Scott. A special thanks to ARUP New York, Goldman Sachs New York, Zaha Hadid Architects, Kohn Pederson Fox, and Skidmore Owens Merrill New York for contributing towards the intellectual framing and discussion of the future office.

I would also like to thank the authors who contributed their time and effort to write articles for this book including Verda Alexander, Peter Cappelli, Colin Koop, Qiaoyi Li, Ariane Lourie-Harrison Patrick Monte, Ranya Nehmeh, and Patrik Schumacher. Without their support the book would not exist. Lastly, Leon Yi-Liang Ko and Yang Yang, architecture graduates of the MSD-AAD program at the Weitzman School of Design, have been heroic in their work on *Future Offices*. I would also like to thank Caleb White for his assistance in advising on parts of the book, Patrick Monte for his brilliant editing, and Kirby Anderson at ORO Editions for her relentless work on copy editing the texts.

CR BOOK

COVER DESIGN

Caleb White
Leon Yi-Liang Ko

COVER IMAGE

Bingkun Deng
Ming Jiang
Yang Yang

BOOK DESIGN

Leon Yi-Liang Ko
Yang Yang

ORIGINAL TEMPLATE

Dean Di Simone

CR ARTICLES

AUTHORS

Verda Alexander
Peter Cappelli
Ariane Harrison
Colin Koop
Qiyao Li
Patrick Monte
Ranya Nehmeh
Ali Rahim
Patrik Schumacher

CR PROJECTS

CRITICS

Ali Rahim (Program Director)
Brian DeLuna
Nathan Hume
Na Wei
Mo Zhong

TEACHING ASSISTANTS

Wenjia Guo
Grace Yuting He
Zachary Kile
Gary Polk
Caleb White

2019 MSD-AAD STUDENTS

Qi Che
Fang Cheng
Gordern Cheng
Xuechen Chen
Bingkun Deng
Xianlong Deng
Sijie Gao
Chaoqiong Guo
Xing Guo
Ming Jiang
Yichao Jin
Flori Kryethi
Maoqiang Li
Zhihui Li
Yuxuan Liang
Huajie Ma
Sharvari Mhatre
Jingrong Ning
Yue Pan
In Pun
Qian Qiu
Nengjie Qu
Atharva Ranade
Nahye Shin
Bohao Sun
Yu Sun
Tianxiao Wang
Yiding Wang
Yuanguang Wang
Yufei Wang
Donghan Yan
Shuanglin Yang
Xifan Yang
Yang Yang
Jing Yuan
Youyu Zhang
Dianqiu Zheng
Yuan Zheng
Zhe Zhong
Chengzhe Zhu
Yifan Zhuang

2020 MSD-AAD STUDENTS

Jingyi Chen
Pinjie Chen
Yuze Deng
Zheyuan Fu
Ruochen Gao
Yuanben Gao
Zheng Gong
Mingda Guo
Weihang Huang
Yuyuan Huang
Zihao Jin
Jaeung Kim
Sina Lee
Lyuxin Liu
Monica Louis
Xiaotong Ni
Yiliang Shao
Diyang Shen
Wen Tian
Qiao Wang
Ruiwan Wang
Xiaohan Wang
Yanpeng Wang
Yixin Wang
Yujue Wang
Zihang Wang
Linxuan Xie
Yifan Xie
Tao Xu
Zechuan Yang
Yiqi You
Siwei Yu
Han Zhang
Jiayun Zhang
Yichi Zhang
Yuyu Zhang
Chenhe Zhao
Yiming Zhao
Xinyi Zhao

TABLE OF CONTENTS

INTRODUCTION

PROJECTS: HYBRID FUTURES

01 THE RELEVANT OFFICE

02 WORKING FROM HOME

03 DISNEY HEADQUARTERS

© 2023 Skidmore, Owings & Merrill LLC
The Walt Disney Studios Burbank
p. 78 Fig. 8

© 2023 Skidmore, Owings & Merrill LLC
Pixar Animation Studios
p. 78 Fig. 9

© 2023 Skidmore, Owings & Merrill LLC
ABC Studios, 77W 66th Street, New York
p. 78 Fig. 10

© 2023 Skidmore, Owings & Merrill LLC
Disney Headquarters in Hudson Square
p. 78 Fig. 11

© 2023 Skidmore, Owings & Merrill LLC
Typical backlot production studio module
p. 78 Fig. 12

© 2023 Skidmore, Owings & Merrill LLC
Disney Headquarters is under construction.
Disney Headquarters, SOM, New York, 2022
Photography by SOM
p. 80 Fig. 13

© 2023 Skidmore, Owings & Merrill LLC
Building facade close-up. Disney Headquarters, SOM, New York, 2022
Photography by SOM
p. 82 Fig. 14

PROJECTS: METABOLIC FUTURES

Yuxuan Liang, Xuechen Chen, Yue Pan
UPS Hub, West SOHO, New York
pp. 86-95

Bingkun Deng, Ming Jiang, Yang Yang
UPS Hub, West SOHO, New York
pp. 96-105

© Ali Rahim Studio with Caleb White
University of Pennsylvania
Weitzman School of Design
MSD-AAD, 2010

Yanpeng Wang, Jiayun Zhang
UPS Hub, West SOHO, New York
pp. 106-115

Weihang Huang, Sina Lee
UPS Hub, West SOHO, New York
pp. 116-125

© Ali Rahim Studio with Caleb White
University of Pennsylvania
Weitzman School of Design
MSD-AAD, 2020

Yichi Zhang, Ruiwan Wang
UPS Hub, West SOHO, New York
pp. 126-135

© Mo Zheng Studio with Wenjia Guo
University of Pennsylvania
Weitzman School of Design
MSD-AAD, 2020

04 STICKY HYBRIDS, A PROPOSITION FOR THE FUTURE OFFICE

NASA Johnson Space Center, Earth Science and Remote Sensing Unit
ISS064-E-48480
Cataloged by the University of Texas at El Paso
p. 138 Fig. 1

© 2023 Anthony T. Troncale
Tilted Arc, Richard Serra, Federal Plaza, New York, 1981
Photography by Anthony T. Troncale, 1988
p. 140 Fig. 2

© Lisi Gradnitzer, Courtesy of PPAG Architects
Enzi Elements, PPAG Architects, MuseumsQuartier, Vienna, 2002
Photography by Lisi Gradnitzer, Project Design by PPAG Architects
p. 140 Fig. 3

Wikimedia, CC BY-SA 4.0
Domino Sugar refinery
Photography by Beyond My Ken
p. 142 Fig. 4

© SHoP Architects
Domino Sugar Masterplan, SHoP Architects, New York, 2014
Rendering by SHoP Architects
p. 142 Fig. 5

The New York Public Library, The Miriam and Ira D. Wallach Division of Art, Prints and Photographs: Photography Collection
The Singer Building Tower, New York
Photography by Irving Underhill
p. 144 Fig. 6

Google Satellite, CC0
Union Carbide Building, 270 Park Avenue, SOM, New York, 1960–2021
p. 144 Fig. 7

Wikimedia, CC BY 4.0
Artist's impression of the planned JPMorgan Chase Building at 270 Park Avenue
Rendering by CrossingLights
p. 144 Fig. 8

© Snøhetta
The revitalized POPS running along the building's west (rear) face. 550 Madison Avenue Garden, Snøhetta, New York, 2022
Photography by Barrett Doherty
p. 146 Fig. 9

© Snøhetta
Ground Floor Plan. 550 Madison Avenue Garden, Snøhetta, New York, 2022
Rendering by Snøhetta
p. 146 Fig. 10

© 1977 Alexandre Georges, Courtesy of the Portman Archives
Westin Bonaventure atrium, ground view to southwest, looking along northwest lobby seating bench
Photography by Alexandre Georges
p. 148 Fig. 11

05 FERAL ENVELOPES FOR THE FUTURE OFFICE

Wikimedia, CC BY-SA 4.0
A monk parakeet (Myiopsitta monachus) and a common starling (Sturnus vulgaris) flying around a parakeet nest in the Green-Wood Cemetery gate
Photography by Rhododendrites
p.154 Fig. 1

Wikimedia, CC BY 2.0
Mur végétal (Musée du quai Branly) (2684115825)
Photography by Jean-Pierre Dalbéra
p.154 Fig. 2

Flickr, CC BY-NC-SA 2.0
Wrapped Reichstag
Photography by Gertrud K.
p.154 Fig. 3

© Harrison Atelier
UHPC Ductal panels (front and rear) for Pollinators Pavilion, Harrison Atelier, Hudson, New York, 2019
Photography by Harrison Atelier
p. 156 Fig. 4

© Harrison Atelier
Mycelium-hempcrete panels for Hempcrete Habitat for Governors Island, Harrison Atelier, New York, 2022
Photography by Harrison Atelier
p. 156 Fig. 5

© Harrison Atelier
Pollinators Pavilion, Harrison Atelier, Hudson, New York, 2019
Photography by Harrison Atelier
p. 158 Fig. 6

06 MIXED-REALITIES AT WORK

© Zaha Hadid Architects
Renders with OpenAI DALL-E 2 launched in occasion of "Meta-Horizons: The Future Now" at DDP Design Museum. Architecting the Metaverse, Zaha Hadid Architects and Refik Anadol Studio, Seoul, 2022
Collaboration by Zaha Hadid Architects and Refik Anadol Studio
p. 164 Fig. 1

© Kyungsub Shin, Courtesy of Zaha Hadid Architects
Architecting the Metaverse, Zaha Hadid Architects and Refik Anadol Studio, Seoul, 2022
Photography by Kyungsub Shin
p. 168 Fig. 2

Stefan Tzon Manousof, Qi Yang, Amin Yassin, Yang Yu
Cybertecture
Tutored by Patrik Schumacher and Pierandrea Angius, AADRL Studio "Cyber-urban Incubator"
p. 170 Fig. 3

© Kyungsub Shin, Courtesy of Zaha Hadid Architects
Architecting the Metaverse, Zaha Hadid Architects and Refik Anadol Studio, Seoul, 2022
Photography by Kyungsub Shin
p. 172 Fig. 4

PROJECTS: DECENTERED FUTURES

Xiaotong Ni, Mingda Guo
UPS Hub, West SOHO, New York
pp. 178-185

© Ali Rahim Studio with Caleb White
University of Pennsylvania
Weitzman School of Design
MSD-AAD, 2020

Zheyuan Fu, Yiqi You
UPS Hub, West SOHO, New York
pp. 186-193

© Na Wei Studio with Grace Yuting He
University of Pennsylvania
Weitzman School of Design
MSD-AAD, 2020

Maoqiang Li, Bohao Sun, Youyu Zhang
UPS Hub, West SOHO, New York
pp. 194-199

© Brian Deluna Studio with Zachary Kile
University of Pennsylvania
Weitzman School of Design
MSD-AAD, 2019

Xing Guo, Xianlong Deng, In Pun
UPS Hub, West SOHO, New York
pp. 200-207

© Nate Hume Studio with Gary Polk
University of Pennsylvania
Weitzman School of Design
MSD-AAD, 2019